George Burnett Barton

Poets and Prose Writers of New South Wales

George Burnett Barton

Poets and Prose Writers of New South Wales

ISBN/EAN: 9783744696456

Printed in Europe, USA, Canada, Australia, Japan

Cover: Foto ©Thomas Meinert / pixelio.de

More available books at **www.hansebooks.com**

THE
POETS
AND
PROSE WRITERS
OF
NEW SOUTH WALES.

EDITED BY

G. B. BARTON,

OF THE MIDDLE TEMPLE, BARRISTER AT LAW,
READER IN THE ENGLISH LANGUAGE AND LITERATURE TO THE
UNIVERSITY OF SYDNEY.

CONTENTS.

	Page.
INTRODUCTION	1
W. C. WENTWORTH	17
J. D. LANG	33
CHARLES HARPUR	38
W. FORSTER	49
JAMES MARTIN	64
HENRY PARKES	83
D. H. DENIEHY	94
ROBERT SEALY	149
W. B. DALLEY	164
HENRY KENDALL	192
HENRY HALLORAN	207
SIR T. L. MITCHELL	215
J. L. MICHAEL	218
G. R. MORTON	221

ERRATA.

OWING to the extreme haste with which this book has been printed, a few errors of the press have escaped notice. They are as follows:—

Page 111, line 20, for "A vein this which Robert Browning," read *A vein this which cannot, and never dreams of typifying, like Robert Browning.*

,, 114, line 4 from bottom, for "want of specific matter" read *want of consideration of this specific matter.*

,, 117, line 10, for "the first thing," read *the finest thing.*

,, 120, line 11, for "lonely," read *lovely.*

,, 134, line 22, for "regain," read *repair.*

,, 148, line 23, for "thirty-five," read *thirty-seven.*

,, 149, line 10, for "1861," read 1862.

,, 153, line 26, for "love," read *lore.*

,, 205, line 12, for "too," read *to.*

,, 207, line 2, for "of," read *on.*

,, 217, line 29, dele *wild.*

INTRODUCTION.

THIS volume is intended to supplement one already published, under the title of 'Literature in New South Wales;' the object of both being, to illustrate the progress of literature in this colony. In the work mentioned, an attempt has been made to give some account of every publication of importance that has issued from the local press, including those which, having been published elsewhere, have been written either by natives of the colony or by old colonists. These publications have been classified, arranged in chronological order, and accompanied by a critical estimate of each. In this way the Editor endeavoured to compile a work which might not only serve to give distant readers an exact idea of our progress in literature, but might also prove an historical record of some value to ourselves. The task was undertaken at the request of the Executive Commissioner for the Paris Exhibition.

In the present volume, the Editor has endeavoured to carry out the design attempted in the other, by collecting those contributions to our literature which seem of most worth. With few exceptions, every local writer who has gained a reputation among us is represented here. Writings which would otherwise have remained buried in obscure prints are reproduced. In some cases, as for instance in that of Mr. Wentworth's College Poem, the writing is reproduced, not so much on account of its intrinsic merit, as on account of the interest felt in the author. In other cases, as for instance in Mr. Deniehy's, the writing possesses a value of its own sufficient to warrant its republication. Without this republication, no evidence could be furnished to substantiate the eulogies pronounced elsewhere. In the remarks which he has thought fit to make, the Editor has endeavoured to be as concise as possible—desiring to say nothing which was not requisite to illustrate his subject. He regrets that he has been unable to do as much justice to his task as he could have wished to do. Being under the necessity of producing both these volumes within a certain time, in order to serve the purpose of the Exhibition Commissioners, he has been compelled to hurry them through the Press, while the facilities he has had in their compilation have been extremely slight. However, he trusts that, imperfect as they may be, they will yet effect the object for which they were produced.

There is a matter connected with the first of these publications to which the Editor would particularly call the attention of foreign reviewers. Soon after its appearance, a "Review" of it was published in the leading journal of the colony, the *Sydney Morning Herald*. This "Review" was simply a personal attack upon the Editor. The writer made no attempt to criticise the book impartially. His remarks from beginning to end were directed at the Editor, with the view of disparaging him, and by that means of depriving his book of all weight with its readers. Almost every sentence contained either a wilful misstatement or a wilful misrepresentation. The Editor, whose personal history was dragged before the public, was at one moment represented as depreciating the literature of the colony, and at another as exaggerating it: while the book was in one sentence pronounced a valuable one, and in another declared to be not worth the expense of its publication. The *malice prepense* of the article was obvious: but the writer used his weapons so clumsily that, as ROGERS said of CROKER when he 'reviewed' MACAULAY—"he attempted murder, but only committed suicide." His falsehoods and his contradictions were so apparent, that they scarcely required exposure: and his attempts to justify himself exhibited only a worse degree of illogical argument and spiteful insinuation. The Editor, however, would not trouble himself to refer to this matter on the present occasion, were it not for the fact that it affords him an opportunity of still further illustrating the literature of the colony.

The "Review" mentioned was provoked by the critical account of the *Herald* given by the Editor in his work. He stated that

> As a rule, the leading articles of the *Herald* are not distinguished by their brilliancy. Curiously enough, although this journal has been, and is, far more successful than any other in the colony, it has never possessed any reputation for literary ability.

Offence was also taken at his statement with respect to the causes of the *Herald's* prosperity. One of these causes he alleged to be the policy adopted by the proprietors in advocating Tory politics. His argument on this matter will be found at page 28 of the book. In preparing that book, the Editor wished to represent the literature of the colony in as favourable a light as he conscientiously could; and he also wished to avoid giving offence to those whose publications he was called upon to notice. In his account of the leading journal, he stated its merits, and proclaimed its great success, without reserve. He felt that if the leading journal of a wealthy community were represented as a worthless one, nothing more damaging to our literary character could be said. But he would have been false to his functions as a critical historian had he not alluded to the literary deficiencies of the *Herald*. They are so notorious that it is impossible to pass them over. It is 'curiously true' that throughout the whole of its existence—and it has now reached its thirty-fifth year—this journal has never possessed the slightest reputation for literary ability. So far from possessing any such reputation, it has been a public laughing-stock on the score of its imbecility. The evidence on this point, as regards the past, is both written and traditional; as regards the present, it may be found in the journal itself. For the last thirty-five years every contemporary journal in Sydney has ridiculed the intellectual weakness of the *Herald;* and the ridicule has been echoed by the public. Every term that could express or typify mental weakness has been fastened on it. It has generally been spoken of as the Grandmother of the Press, by the popular abbreviation of 'Grannie.' Except in commercial matters, its editorial management has never exercised the slightest influence over the community. Politically, it goes for nothing; but that may be accounted for by the fact that it has always advocated principles antagonistic to those of the people.

It may be asked, How could such a journal as this outstrip its many rivals, and achieve so much success? To answer that question, it is necessary to review the history of our journalism. It cannot be answered by considering the paper as it is now: we must go back, and examine its career from the commencement. When the *Herald* was started in 1831, its appearance was insignificant in the last degree. A badly printed sheet of bad paper, it was destitute of everything that could attract a reader. In its appearance, as well as in its contents, it was inferior to its contemporaries. It did not improve in either respect for some time. The journals it had to compete with were (1) the *Gazette*, established in 1803 as a Government organ — (2) the *Australian*, established in 1824 as an Opposition organ — and (3) the *Monitor*, established in 1826 as a second Opposition organ. The two last-mentioned papers were conducted with much ability, the *Australian* especially. But the *Gazette*—which ought to have retained the lead of all our journals—lost its character through a variety of causes, and never succeeded in recovering it. No journal ever did. The Opposition papers, on the other hand, went too far in their advocacy of liberal politics; they devoted themselves with too much zeal to politics altogether, forgetting that politics alone will never pay the expenses of a newspaper. The *Herald* was brought into existence by men who knew nothing of literature, and cared nothing for politics except as they affected 'business.' It adopted a policy which could not possibly give offence to men of property—a policy which advocated the claims of rank and wealth with unflagging ardour. It was edited for many years by a reverend gentleman who had previously edited the *Gazette*, and whose contributions to our infant literature were rather solid than splendid. By this means, although the paper was little more than a sheetful of advertisements and news—although it was a mere dead letter so far as literature and politics were concerned—it gradually increased its circulation and rendered itself indispensable to a business community. The leading features of its character have been faithfully preserved up to the present day. No one expects to find the graces of literary composition in its leading articles, just as no one expects to find roses or daffydowndillies on a sheep-walk. But it contains all the advertisements and all the news of the passing day—it is the first to publish the European telegrams on the arrival of the mail—it has abundance of foreign correspondence—and it maintains the cause of good old English Toryism in all its glory.

The politics advocated by this journal throughout its career are not Conservative politics merely. There would certainly be nothing in that to render its success a matter of surprise. Its politics are Tory politics, and of the most inveterate stamp : politics not only repulsive to the bulk of the people, but such as few educated men can agree with. The principal feature in the system appears to be a blind adoration of wealth and position. It seemed to the Editor 'a striking fact' that a journal so conducted should, in times like these, in a community overrun by radicalism, not only maintain its ground unshaken, but daily increase in prosperity. The really 'popular' journal—that which advocates radical politics, and advocates them with some degree of ability—is, to use a turf phrase, actually 'nowhere' in the race. Its influence in political matters is infinitely greater than that of its rival. But it seems to be following in the steps of the old liberal journals already mentioned. It devotes its energies to politics with the fiery zeal of a martyr; and thus cuts off from itself the sympathies of an important section of society. This section happens to be a peculiarly important one, so far as the success of our newspapers is concerned. Radical politics will never recommend themselves to merchants and tradesmen. In England, the radical journals are penny journals, and exist on their circulation. Here, the population is not large enough to support a penny journal—at least the experiment has not been tried—and newspapers must consequently depend upon the 'favours' of the mercantile classes. If these are withheld, the newspaper is crippled in its resources, and suffers accordingly.

It will be seen that the Editor's opinion with regard to the *Herald* was mildly and inoffensively expressed in the work referred to. He indulged in no ridicule; he confined himself to a simple statement of notorious facts. The reviewer, however, in the 'cutting up' which he was instructed to administer, replied to this statement by a series of sneers and bad arguments. He insinuated that the Editor depreciated the literary ability of the *Herald* because he was not a contributor to it; and he then argued that literary ability had nothing to do with journalism. The sneer and the argument were of course contradictory, but the reviewer did not see it. He then proceeded to beg the question in the following style:

> To judge of newspaper writing from the point of view of *belles lettres* is to mistake the functions of a journal. Good newspaper writing is good writing for the purposes of a newspaper, just as a good speech at the bar is one that is good for the purposes of the trial, &c.

Here the reviewer insinuates that 'good newspaper writing' is to be found in the leading columns of the *Herald*, and attempts to show that writing which would be bad anywhere else is perfectly good in a newspaper. That is to say, that writing which would elsewhere be execrated as twaddle, is 'good writing for the purposes of a newspaper.' If this is the case, then the editorial columns of the *Herald* contain the very best newspaper writing that journalism can boast of. The reviewer then sailed on another tack. He alluded to the many talented writers whose contributions have appeared in the *Herald*, and claimed a reputation for literary ability on the strength of it. This was simply a misrepresentation of the Editor's statement. It is perfectly true that some of the ablest writers we have had in the colony have contributed to the *Herald*. But what did they contribute? The Editor was speaking of leading articles—they never contributed one. They wrote pieces of poetry, critiques on books, graphic sketches, and so on. In this way, Rowe, Deniehy, Fowler, Evelyn, Harpur, Kendall, and others, have from time to time contributed to the *Herald*. But casual articles of this kind are not enough to give a literary reputation to a newspaper, when its editorial columns display nothing but intellectual barrenness.

The Editor feels it necessary to be precise on these points—for the arguments of the reviewer are calculated to convey a false impression to distant readers as to the actual state of things. From these arguments it might be gathered that literature here is a very flourishing profession, and that any man of letters who might settle in Sydney would make a handsome income. The graphic author of *Southern Lights and Shadows* told the world some years ago, that a thousand a year could be picked up very readily in Australia. This delusion was dispelled by R. H. Horne in his *Australian Facts and Prospects*: but it was none the less incumbent on the Editor to speak the truth a second time. In the introductory part of his 'Literature in New South Wales,' he has shown that literature, as a profession, does not exist here yet, and he has explained the cause. But he was not speaking of political literature, or—as the reviewer expressed himself—'journalistic occupation.' Where there are newspapers, there of course will be occupation for the journalist: though the amount of occupation is another question. The arguments of the Editor were addressed to the question of a 'national literature.' He endeavoured to show that, at present, there is no such literature here; that its growth is impeded by the indifference of the public to local publications and their preference for English periodicals; that so long as this feeling existed, an independent literature could not be expected, because men of letters could not live by their profession; that men of letters in this colony had always suffered, and still do suffer, by devotion to their profession; and that the result was, so far, prejudicial to our character as a community. That these statements are true, no one will deny who is competent to discuss the question. But the reviewer in the *Herald*, while he did not exactly dispute their truth, indulged in a broadside of sneers and bad arguments. He proclaimed that 'the introduction was written in a querulous tone,' proceeded to account for it by 'the personal experiences of the Editor,' and justified his gross personalities by saying that it was 'necessary to explain the querulous tone of the introduction to distant readers.' Now the 'tone' of a book can be judged of only by reading it; and the Editor feels confident that no one who reads his will consider it 'querulous.' If it is 'querulous,' then every man who makes statements which are unpleasantly true, is 'querulous' when he does so. Goldsmith, from whose 'Inquiry into the State of Polite Learning in Europe' the Editor quoted a pathetic passage with reference to men of letters, was 'querulous' to the last degree. After exhausting his personalities, the reviewer proceeded to set matters right with his characteristic logic. The Editor' had shown that the quantity of books and periodicals imported into this colony was extremely large—was much larger than might have been expected—and formed a conclusive proof as to our appreciation of literature. The reviewer replied by asserting precisely the same thing, and implying that the Editor had said the reverse.

The statements made by the same authority with respect to the prospects of men of letters here, require to be read with caution. In the first place, he represents the *Herald*, in his own phase, as 'a convenient outlet' for men of literary ability. It might be inferred that this journal endeavours to combine the functions of a magazine and a newspaper, and is consequently eager to attract talented writers to its columns. Now, although it is undoubtedly creditable to its proprietors that they should have assisted men of genius, when reduced to destitution, by accepting articles from them,—a species of charity which blesseth him that gives quite as much as him that takes,—it would not be correct to infer any such thing. The real state of the matter will be found in page 14 of 'Literature in New South Wales.' The Editor has there quoted a passage from Mr. Horne's work which bears expressly upon the subject. In the second place, it is stated by the reviewer that, 'few, if any, men of talent have vainly sought for journalistic occupation in Australia,' &c. It will be seen that the Editor was not speaking of Australia, but of New South Wales; and not of journalistic occupation, but of literature generally. What is true of New South Wales is undoubtedly not true of Victoria, in the matter of journalism at least. The Melbourne journals are far superior to those published in Sydney. If the *Melbourne Argus* be compared with the *Sydney Morning Herald*, the difference will be seen at once. The former is what a successful newspaper ought to be—the latter is quite the reverse. There is as much difference between the two as there is between the *Australasian* and the *Sydney Mail*.

The Editor declines to follow the example set by the *Herald* in the matter of personalities, as he is quite aware of the distinction between criticism and blackguardism. It would no doubt greatly aid him in 'explaining to distant readers' the miserable character of that journal, if his remarks were illustrated by the biographies of its proprietors and editors. A running comment of that kind could be written with ease, and would be read with amusement: while no complaint could be justly made of one who merely imitated the scrupulous delicacy of our leading journal. He contents himself however with criticising the paper alone. While a sense of duty compels him to touch upon its obvious deficiencies, he is quite ready to admit all that can be said in its favour. He admires its practical usefulness as a commercial organ and a register of passing facts: he admires the good taste with which it is usually conducted, and the skill with which it occasionally handles an enemy: but, above all, he admires the marvellous consistency which it has invariably displayed. It has never altered a single feature in its character. It has never deviated by a single inch from the strict line of its original policy. From first to last, it has possessed the reputation of a twaddling, narrow-minded, illiterate publication; bitterly opposing every man who has raised himself from obscurity, at the same time that it chaunts the praises of wealth; defending every abuse until it is exposed, and then claiming the merit of its exposure; possessing no influence over the political destinies, and retarding, rather than advancing, the intellectual development of the country.

*THE POETS AND PROSE WRITERS
OF NEW SOUTH WALES.*

W. C. WENTWORTH.

WILLIAM CHARLES WENTWORTH was born at Norfolk Island in 1791. His father, D'Arcy Wentworth, went there in the previous year, and a certain authority tells us that he was "particularly noticed by Major Ross (the Commandant), who, on account of his abilities and reputation, immediately appointed him as a Superintending Surgeon of the Island." How long he remained there is not known, but, as the settlement was broken up in 1805, he probably left it then. In 1819 his name occurs rather frequently in the Civil List of the Colony. He was a Magistrate of the Territory and its Dependencies—Principal Surgeon on the Medical Staff—Trustee and Commissioner for Roads—Treasurer of the Police Establishment—Superintendent of Police,—and a Director of the Bank of New South Wales.

His son left the colony in 1817, and went to England. There he read for the Bar and entered himself as a student at Cambridge. In 1819 he published a work on the Colony, in which he aimed at two great objects—the promotion of emigration and the removal of political abuses. It was a 'hasty production, originating in the suggestion of an acquaintance;' and as it was largely occupied with matters of a practical kind, little in the way of literary excellence could be expected from it. It contains passages, however, marked with very great power. Perhaps the

best is the following, in which he denounces the conduct of the
'Exclusives :'—

The covert aim of these men is to convert the ignominy of the great body of the people into an hereditary deformity. They would hand it down from father to son, and raise an eternal barrier of separation between their offspring and the offspring of the unfortunate convict. They would establish distinctions which may serve hereafter to divide the colonists into *castes;* and although none among them dares publicly avow that future generations should be punished for the crimes of their progenitors, yet such are their private sentiments, and they would have the present race branded with disqualifications, not more for the sake of pampering their own vanity, than with a view to reflect disgrace on the offspring of the disfranchised parent, and thus cast on their own children and descendents that future splendour and importance, which they consider to be their present peculiar and distinguishing characteristics. Short sighted fools! they foresee not the consequences of their narrow machinations! They know not that they would be sowing the seeds of discords and commotions, and that by their exalting their own immediate descendants, they would occasion the eventual degradation and overthrow of their posterity. Such would be the result of their ambition; for it is the curse of injustice that it brings with it, sooner or later, its own punishment. Happily for the colony the realization of their projects depends not upon themselves; and his Majesty's ministers will not lend their sanction to schemes of private aggrandizement, which can only be accomplished by the sacrifice of the public good. If these men have not themselves the sagacity to dive into futurity, and to foresee the dangers and contests to which unjust privileges and distinctions must eventually give birth, shall the government be equally blind and improvident? Shall they, in the short space of thirty years, forget the benevolent designs with which this colony was founded, and convert what was intended as an asylum for repentant vice, not into a house merely of salutary correction, which may moderate with reviving morality and cease entirely with complete restoration, but into a prison of endless torture, where though the sufferings of the body may terminate, the worst species of torture, the endurements and mortifications of the soul, are to end only with existence? Shall a vile faction be allowed to inflict on the unfortunate convict a punishment infinitely greater than that to which he has been sentenced by the violated majesty of the law? Has not a jury of impartial freemen solemnly investigated the case of every individual who has been transported to this colony? And have not the measure and duration of their punishments been apportioned to their respective offences? Is it then for any body of men to assert that the law has been too lenient, and that it is necessary to inflict an ulterior punishment which shall have no termination but in the grave? Shall the unhappy culprit, exiled from his native shore, and severed perhaps for ever from the friends of his youth, the objects of his first and best affections, after years of suffering and atonement, still find no resting place, no spot where he may hide his shame and endeavour to forget his errors? Shall the finger of scorn and derision be pointed at him wherever he betakes himself? And must he for ever wander a recreant and outcast on the face of the earth, seeking in vain some friendly shore, where he may at length be freed from ignominious disabilities, and restored to the long lost enjoyment of equal rights and equal protection with his fellows?

In 1823, he competed for the Chancellor's medal for the best English poem on "Australasia." The prize was carried off by W. M. Praed, one of the most brilliant versifiers of the day; the second place in the list being awarded to Mr. Wentworth. A comparison of the two productions will suggest doubts to some readers as to the justice of the award. In local colouring, at least, Wentworth's is altogether superior, as might be expected. Nothing can be more absurd than some passages in Praed's, in which he attempts to describe the character and customs of the aboriginals. He seems to have been hardly aware of the distinction between New Zealand and New Holland; for he first takes the reader to the one, and then hurries him off to the other,— mixing up convicts and Maoris as if they were members of the same community. In one point, however, Praed has a decided superiority; his poem is two hundred lines shorter than Wentworth's. This is certainly no slight merit in a Prize Poem.

AUSTRALASIA.

    Land of my birth! tho' now alas! no more
    Musing I wander on thy sea-girt shore,
    Or climb with eager haste thy barrier cliff,
    To catch a glimmer of the distant skiff,
    That ever and anon breaks into light,
    And then again eludes the aching sight,
    Till, nearer seen, she bends her foaming way
    Majestic onward to yon placid bay,
    Where Sydney's infant turrets proudly rise,
    The new-born glory of the southern skies:—
    Dear Australasia, can I e'er forget
    Thee, Mother Earth? Ah no, my heart e'en yet

With filial fondness loves to call to view
Scenes which, though oft remember'd, still are new ;
Scenes where my playful childhood's thoughtless years
Flew swift away, despite of childhood's tears :
Where later, too, in manhood's op'ning bloom,
The tangled brake, th' eternal forest's gloom,
The wonted brook, where with some truant mate
I lov'd to plunge, or ply the treach'rous bait ;
The spacious harbour with its hundred coves,
And fairy islets—seats of savage loves,
Again beheld—restampt with deeper dye
The fading image of my infancy :
And shall I now, by Cam's old classic stream,
Forbear to sing, and thou propos'd the theme ?
Thy native bard, though on a foreign strand,
Shall I be mute, and see a stranger's hand
Attune the lyre, and, prescient of thy fame,
Foretell the glories that shall grace thy name ?
Forbid it, all ye Nine ! 'twere shame to thee,
My Austral parent : greater shame to me.

Proud Queen of isles ! Thou sittest vast, alone,
A host of vassals bending round thy throne :
Like some fair swan that skims the silver tide,
Her silken cygnets strew'd on every side,
So floatest thou, thy Polynesian brood
Dispers'd around thee on thy Ocean flood,
While ev'ry surge that doth thy bosom lave,
Salutes thee " Empress of the Southern Wave."

Say, Muse, when first of Europe's roving train
Burst on De Quiros' sight this island main,
What golden visions rose to fancy's view,
The towns he plunder'd, and the hosts he slew ;
How on all sides the argent tripods shone,
And temples richer than Peruvia's sun ;
Till av'rice glow'd, while busy thoughts unfurl'd
The imag'd treasures of the new-found world :
'Twas then, triumphant Hope, thy power confess'd,
Hush'd the rude tongue, and calm'd the mourning breast :
Then still'd sedition's buzz, each contrite soul
With awe and gladness hail'd a chief's control,
And ev'ry peril, ev'ry hardship past,
Seem'd to have found full recompence at last.
Say, too, what terror fix'd the natives' eye,

When first they saw, emerging from the sky,
That stranger bark in sullen silence sweep,
A wrathful spirit o'er the troubled deep,
Treading with giant stride the subject wave,
The wind his herald, and the tide his slave ;—
While onward stalking in terrific state
He loom'd portentful of impending fate,
Yet vain the dream of those, the dread of these ;—
For lo ! at length arriv'd with fav'ring breeze,
De Quiros' self directs the straining oar,
And leaps the foremost on the untrod shore—
Follows his band ; but dark on ev'ry side
Repulsive forests frown with path untried ;
While from the hidden foe the frequent spear
Sweeps through their ranks, and wakes unwonted fear ;
Till struck with awe, they cease the hopeless chase,
And to the ship their sullen course retrace.
Ye primal tribes, lords of this old domain,
Swift-footed hunters of the pathless plain,
Unshackled wanderers, enthusiasts free,
Pure native sons of savage liberty,
Who hold all things in common,—earth, sea, air,—
Or only occupy the nightly lair
Whereon each sleeps ; who own no chieftain's pow'r
Save his, that's mightiest at the passing hour ;
Say—whence your ancient lineage, what your name,
And from what shores your rough forefathers came?
Untutor'd children, fresh from Nature's mould,
No songs have ye to trace the times of old :—
No hidden themes like these employ your care,
For you enough the knowledge that ye are :—
Let Learning's sons, who would this secret scan,
Unlock its mystic casket if they can,—
To your unletter'd tastes are sweeter far
The dance of battle, and the song of war,
'Mid hostile ranks the deadly spear to throw,
Or see the foeman stagg'ring 'neath your blow :—
To you, ye sable hunters, sweeter, too,
To spy the track of bounding kangaroo,
Or long-neck'd emu :—quick with eager gaze
His path you follow thro' the tangled maze,
O'er boundless wilds your panting game pursue,
And come, like trusty hounds, at last in view ;
Then creeping round her, soon the forest's pride

Is hemm'd with bristly spears that pierce her side;
And now, the labours of the chase being o'er,
And Nature's keen suggestions heard no more,
In uncouth numbers, seated in a ring,
Your ancient fathers' warlike feats ye sing,
Or striking each his shield, with clatt'ring lance,
The early night exhaust in Pyrrhic dance.

Such, mountain sons of freedom, your delight,
Such your rude sport by day, your mirth by night;
Nor would you these few savage joys forego,
For all the comforts all the arts bestow.
What, if at times the barren chase deny
The scanty fare your niggard wilds supply?
What, if to-day ye miss your sylvan feast?
To-morrow's meal shall then derive a zest,
Unknown to those who live in slothful ease,—
Child of the heath, the mountain, and the breeze.
What, if the wint'ry blast and pelting rain
Howl through the woods and inundate the plain?
To some near cave ye fly, which, jutting o'er,
Wards from your naked limbs the drenching show'r:
While kindled faggots soon with crackling sound
Dispel the gloom and scatter warmth around,
And, nestling close each to his sable love,
Ye sleep, regardless of the storm above.
Had'st thou, old cynic, seen this unclad crew,
Stretch their bare bodies in the nightly dew,
Like hairy Satyrs, 'midst their sylvan seats,
Endure both winter's frosts, and summer's heats;
Thy cloak and tub away thou would'st have cast,
And tried, like them, to brave the piercing blast.

Illustrious Cook! Columbus of our shore,
To whom was left this unknown world t' explore!
Its untrac'd bounds on faithful chart to mark,
And leave a light where all before was dark:—
And thou, the foremost in fair learning's ranks,
Patron of every art, departed Banks!
Who, wealth disdaining and inglorious ease,
The rocks and quicksands dar'd of unknown seas;
Immortal pair! when in yon spacious bay
Ye moor'd awhile its wonders to survey,
How little thought ye, that the name from you
Its graceful shrubs and beauteous wild flowers drew,

Would serve, in after times, with lasting brand
To stamp the soil and designate the land,
And to ungenial climes reluctant scare
Full many a hive that else had settled there!

   Ah why, Britannia's pride, Britannia's boast,
Searcher of ev'ry sea and ev'ry coast,
Lamented Cook! thou bravest, gentlest heart,
Why didst thou fall beneath a savage dart?
Why were thy mangled reliques doom'd to grace
The midnight orgies of a barb'rous race?
Why could'st thou not, thy weary wand'rings past,
At home in honour'd ease recline at last,
And, like the happier partner of thy way,
In cloudless glory close life's setting day?

   And thou, fam'd Gallic Captain, La Perouse!
When from this Bay thou led'st thy fated crews,
Did thy twin vessels sink beneath the shock
Of furious hurricane, or hidden rock?
Fell ye, o'erpower'd on some barbarian strand,
As fell before De Langle's butcher'd band?
Linger'd the remnants of thy shipwreck'd host
On some parch'd coral isle, some torrid coast,—
Where no green tree, no cooling brook is seen,
Nought living is, or e'er before has been,
Save some lone mew, blown from the rocky nest,
Had lit, perchance, her homeward wing to rest;—
Till gnaw'd by want, with joy a comrade dead
They saw, and rav'nous on his body fed,
And soon, his bones pick'd bare, with famish'd eye
Each glar'd around, then drew who first should die;
Till of thy ghastly band the most unblest
Surviv'd,—sad sepulchre of all the rest;
And now his last meal gorg'd, with frenzy fir'd,
And raging thirst, the last lorn wretch expir'd!
Whate'er thy fate, thou saw'st the floating arks
That peopled this new world, the teeming barks
That ardent Phillip led to this far shore,
And seeing them, alas! wert seen no more.

   Ah! could'st thou now behold what man has done,
Tho' sev'n revolving lustres scarce have run,
How would'st thou joy to see the savage earth
The smiling parent of so fair a birth!
Lo! thickly planted o'er the glassy bay,
Where Sydney loves her beauties to survey,

And ev'ry morn, delighted, sees the gleam
Of some fresh pennant dancing in her stream,
A masty forest, stranger vessels moor,
Charg'd with the fruits of ev'ry foreign shore;
While, landward,—the throng'd quay, the creaking crane,
The noisy workman, and the loaded wain,
The lengthen'd street, wide square, and column'd front,
Of stately mansions, and the gushing font,
The solemn church, the busy market throng,
And idle loungers saunt'ring slow among,—
The lofty windmills that with outspread sail
Thick line the hills, and court the rising gale,
Shew that the mournful genius of the plain,
Driv'n from his primal solitary reign,
Has backward fled, and fix'd his drowsy throne
In untrod wilds, to muse and brood alone.
And thou, fair Port! whose triad sister coves
Peninsulate these walls; whose ancient groves
High tow'ring southward, rear their giant form,
And break the fury of the polar storm;—
Fairest of Ocean's daughters! who dost bend
Thy mournful steps to seek thy absent friend,
Whence she,—coy wild-rose, on her virgin couch
Fled loath from Parramatta's am'rous touch;
Skirting thy wat'ry path, lo! frequent stand
The cheerful villas 'midst their well-cropp'd land;
Here lowing kine, there bounding coursers graze,
Here waves the corn, and there the woody maize,
Here the tall peach puts forth its pinky bloom,
And there the orange scatters its perfume,
While, as the merry boatmen row along,
The woods are quicken'd with their lusty song.—
Nor here alone hath labour's victor band
Subdued the glebe, and fertiliz'd the land;
For lo! from where at rocky Portland's head,
Reluctant Hawkesbury quits his sluggard bed,
Merging in Ocean,—to young Windsor's tow'rs,
And Richmond's high green hills, and native bow'rs,—
Thence far along Nepean's pebbled way,
To those rich pastures where the wild herds stray,—
The crowded farm-house lines the winding stream
On either side, and many a plodding team
With shining ploughshare turns the neighb'ring soil,
Which crowns with double crop the lab'rer's toil.

Hail, mighty ridge ! that from thy azure brow
Survey'st these fertile plains, that stretch below,
And look'st with careless, unobservant eye,
As round thy waist the forkëd lightnings ply,
And the loud thunders spring with hoarse rebound
From peak to peak, and fill the welkin round
With deaf'ning voice, till with their boist'rous play
Fatigued, in mutt'ring peals they stalk away ;—
Parent of this deep stream, this awful flood,
That at thy feet its tributary mud,
Like the fam'd Indian, or Egyptian tide,
Doth pay, but direful scatters woe beside ;—
Vast Austral Giant of these rugged steeps,
Within whose secret cells rich glitt'ring heaps
Thick piled are doom'd to sleep, till some one spy
The hidden key that opes thy treasury ;
How mute, how desolate thy stunted woods,
How dread thy chasms, where many an eagle broods,
How dark thy caves, how lone thy torrents' roar,
As down thy cliffs precipitous they pour,
Broke on our hearts, when first with venturous tread
We dar'd to rouse thee from thy mountain bed !
Till, gain'd with toilsome step thy rocky heath,
We spied the cheering smokes ascend beneath,
And, as a meteor shoots athwart the night,
The boundless champaign burst upon our sight,
Till, nearer seen, the beauteous landscape grew,
Op'ning like Canaan on rapt Israel's view.

Ye tranquil scenes ! too long to man unknown,
Your hills remained uncropp'd, your dales unsown :
Yet lo ! at last upon yon distant stream,
Increasing Bathurst's straggling honours beam,
While thick o'erspreading the fresh-cultur'd glade
The ripen'd harvest bends its heavy blade,
And flocks and herds, in thousands strewed around,
Awake the woodlands with their joyous sound.
Soon, Australasia, may thy inmost plains,
A new Arcadia, teem with simple swains ;
Soon a Lycoris' scorn again inspire
A Gallus' song to moan his hopeless fire,
And, while he murmurs forth his plaintive tale,
The list'ning breezes waft it down the dale.

What, though no am'rous shepherd midst thy dells
E'er charm'd responsive Echo from her cells ;

What, though no liquid flute, nor shriller reed
E'er shot their wild notes o'er thy silent mead ;
Thy blue-eyed daughters, with the flaxen hair
And taper ankle, do they bloom less fair
Than those of Europe? do thy primal groves
Ne'er warble forth their feather'd inmates' loves?
Or, say, doth Ceres', or Pomona's reign
With scantier gifts repay thy lab'ring train?
Ah! no, 'tis slavery's badge, the felon's shame
That stills thy voice, and clouds thy op'ning fame ;
'Tis this that makes thy sorrowing Judah weep,
Restrains her song, and hangs her harp to sleep.

Land of my hope! soon may this early blot,
Amid thy growing honours, be forgot :
Soon may a freeman's soul, a freeman's blade,
Nerve ev'ry arm, and gleam thro' ev'ry glade—
No more the outcast convict's clanking chains
Deform thy wilds, and stigmatize thy plains :—
And tho' the fathers—these—of thy new race,
From whom each glorious feat, each deathless grace,
Must yet proceed,—by whom each radiant gem
Be won—to deck thy future diadem :—
Did not of old th' Imperial Eagle rise,
Unfurl his pinions, and astound the skies?
Hatch'd in an aery fouler far than thine,
Did he not dart from Tiber to the Rhine?
From Dacia's Forests to fair Calpe's height,
Fear'd not each cow'ring brood his circling flight?
From Libya's sands to quiver'd Parthia's shore
Mark'd not the scatter'd fowl his victor soar?
From swift Euphrates to bleak Thule's rock,
Did not opposing myriads feel the shock
Of his dread talons, and glad tribute pay,
To 'scape the havoc of his murd'rous way?

Yet ne'er, my country, roll thy battle-car
With deadly axle thro' the ranks of war ;
Of foreign rule ne'er may the ceaseless thirst
Pol'ute thy sons, and render thee accurst
Amid the nations ; ne'er may crouch before
Invading legions sallying from thy shore,
A distant people, that shall not on thee
Have first disgorg'd his hostile chivalry.
In other climes, Bellona's temples shine,

Ceres', Pomona's, Bacchus', Pan's, be thine,
And chaste Minerva's: from thy peaceful plains
May glory's star ne'er charm thy restless swains;
Ne'er may the hope of plunder lure to roam
One Australasian from his happy home;
But rustic arts their tranquil hours employ—
Arts crown'd with plenty, and replete with joy:
Be theirs the task to lay with lusty blow
The ancient giants of the forest low,
With frequent fires the cumber'd plain to clear,
To tame the steed, and yoke the stubborn steer,
With cautious plough to rip the virgin earth,
And watch her first born harvest from its birth,
Till, tinged with summer suns the golden glade
Delight the hind and claim the reaper's blade;—
Theirs too the task, with skilful hand to rear
The varied fruits that gild the ripen'd year;
Whether the melting peach, or juicy pear,
Or golden orange, most engage their care:—
Theirs too round stakes or trellised bow'rs to twine
The pliant tendrils of the shooting vine;
And, when beneath their blushing burdens grow
The yielding stems,—the generous juice to stow
In copious jar, which drain'd on festive day
May warm each heart, and chase its glooms away:—
Theirs too on flow'ry mead or thymy steep
To tend with watchful dog the timid sheep;
And, as their fleecy charge are lying round,
To wake the woodlands with their pipe's soft sound,
While the charm'd Fauns and Dryads skulking near,
Leave their lone haunts, and list with raptur'd ear.

Such be the labours of thy peaceful swains,
Thus may they till, and thus enrich thy plains;
Thus the full flow of population's tide
Its swelling waters pour on every side:—
As, on the topmost boughs of some old wood,
When outcast rooks first hatch their infant brood,
The tufted nests, as buds each vernal year,
In growing groups, and thicker ranks appear,
Till soon the spacious grove, with clam'rous strife,
Resounds throughout, and teems with callow life;—
So, Australasia, may thy exil'd band
Spread their young myriads o'er thy lonely land,
Till village spires, and crowded cities rise

In thick succession to the trav'llers' eyes,
And the grim wolf, chas'd from his secret hold,
No more with hungry howl alarm the fold.
Nor be the rustic arts alone thy pride :—
The ambient ocean half thy care divide ;
Whether thy roving sons on Tropic seas
Spread ev'ry sail to woo the sportive breeze ;—
Or with bare poles and dauntless bosoms brave
The icy horrors of the Antarctic wave ;
Till fruitful commerce in thy lap shall pour
The gifts of ev'ry sea and ev'ry shore.

And thou, fair Science ! pure ethereal light,
Beam on her hills, and chase her mental night ;
Direct her sons to seek the perfect day,
Where Bacon traced, and Newton led the way ;
Till bright Philosophy's full orb arise,
To gild her noon, and cheer her ev'ning skies.
But, 'mid the future treasures of their lore,
Still foremost rank the Greek and Latin ore :
Still in the classic search the midnight oil
Be spent, nor deem'd that pleasing labour toil,
Till to their sight reveal'd all glorious shine
The hidden riches of this ancient mine !
Whether they follow with admiring view
The fam'd retreat of Xenophon's bold few ;
Or in Calypso's Isle, or Ida's grove,
And by Scamander's boiling eddies rove ;
Or see the pilferer of the empyrean fire
Chain'd to his rock, endure the Thund'rer's ire ;
Or hear the caverns of the Lemnian shore
Ring with the raving hero's anguish'd roar ;
Or on Trozene's sands see Phædra's hate
Draw on Hippolytus a guiltless fate !
Or with the glory of th' Augustan reign,
Enraptur'd drink the sweets of Maro's strain !
Or borne along by Tully's whelming flood
Feel all his anger kindling in their blood,
When to wide infamy and deathless shame,
He dooms the plund'rer's, or the traitor's name.

Celestial poesy ! whose genial sway
Earth's furthest habitable shores obey ;
Whose inspirations shed their sacred light,
Far as the regions of the Arctic night,

And to the Laplander his Boreal gleam
Endear not less than Phœbus' brighter beam,—
Descend thou also on my native land,
And on some mountain-summit take thy stand ;
Thence issuing soon a purer font be seen
Than charm'd Castalia or fam'd Hippocrene;
And there a richer, nobler fame arise,
Than on Parnassus met the adoring eyes.
And tho', bright Goddess, on those far blue hills,
That pour their thousand swift pellucid rills,
Where Warragumba's rage has rent in twain
Opposing mountains, thund'ring to the plain,
No child of song has yet invok'd thy aid,
'Neath their primeval solitary shade,—
Still, gracious Pow'r, some kindling soul inspire,
To wake to life my country's unknown lyre,
That from creation's date has slumb'ring lain,
Or only breath'd some savage uncouth strain ;—
And grant that yet an Austral Milton's song
Pactolus-like flow deep and rich along :—
An Austral Shakespeare rise, whose living page
To Nature true may charm in ev'ry age ;—
And that an Austral Pindar daring soar,
Where not the Theban Eagle reach'd before.
   And, oh Britannia ! should'st thou cease to ride
Despotic Empress of old Ocean's tide ;—
Should thy tam'd Lion—spent his former might—
No longer roar, the terror of the fight :—
Should e'er arrive that dark, disastrous hour,
When, bow'd by luxury, thou yield'st to pow'r ;
When thou, no longer freest of the free,
To some proud victor bend'st the vanquish'd knee ;—
May all thy glories in another sphere
Relume, and shine more brightly still than here ;
May this—thy last-born INFANT—then arise,
To glad thy heart, and greet thy PARENT eyes ;
And AUSTRALASIA float, with flag unfurl'd,
A new BRITANNIA in another world !

His Account of the Colony passed through three editions in the course of five years. We may infer from this that it was a successful work ; but it seems to have attracted little notice from the English press. On the appearance of the first edition, the "Edinburgh Review" noticed it as 'a work of merit' in an article on the Colony. When the third edition was brought out, the "Westminster" merely said that its execution was slovenly. But it seems to have made its way with the public, successfully if silently, and to have influenced the course of legislation with respect to the colony. The two last editions were greatly enlarged. In these, the author entered upon an elaborate vindication of Governor Macquarie, who had been severely censured in the Report of Mr. Commissioner Bigge, and who was recalled in consequence. The following passage from this portion of the work is a fine specimen of vigorous eloquence :—

> But the distinguishing characteristic in the state of society is to be traced to the causes which led to the origin of the colony itself. For some considerable time after its foundation, there were of course only two classes,—free persons, consisting almost exclusively of the civil and military officers who were attached to the establishment, and convicts sentenced to various terms of transportation. The distinction between these classes was so broadly drawn, that it soon produced a marked influence on the conduct of each. The former became consequential and overbearing; the latter equally humble and submissive. After a few years, however, a third class slowly sprang up, composed of persons who had been convicts, and had gradually become free, either by the expiration of their respective sentences, or by pardon. This intermediate class soon acquired the distinctive appellation of "emancipists;"—a name by which they are still known, and which serves to contra-distinguish them from those whose emigration has been voluntary. The emancipists soon made considerable strides in number, character, and wealth, but for a long period they possessed no visible influence in society; for the upper class, which had also gained some accession of strength, though by no means a proportionate accession, as well by voluntary emigration, as by the gradual augmentation which occurred from time to time in the civil and military establishments, kept as much aloof from the emancipists as from the convicts themselves, enduring no association with them except for purposes of mere interest or convenience. And, strange as it may appear, such was the arrogance of one party, and such the servility of the other, that the former class did not heap degradation on the latter with more indifference than these seemed to endure it, as if—pending the period of servitude—they had acquired a habit and predilection for slavery, too inveterate for any subsequent enjoyment of freedom to remove. Thus an aristocratic junta gradually arose, who monopolized all situations of power, dignity, and emolument, and at last gained such an ascendancy that they were able for a long

while to domineer alike over the Government and the people. And to such a pitch of insolence did they at last carry their pretentions, that they considered themselves possessed of equal right to the Governor's confidence as if they stood in the same relation to him which the nobility of this country bear to the King, and were *de jure* his hereditary counsellors. Until the accession of Governor Macquarie, the great body of the people, I mean of such as had become free, scarcely possessed any civil privilege, but that of suing and being sued in the courts of justice, and even this privilege they were very cautious of exercising out of their own circle. The whole power and nearly the whole property and commerce of the Colony were in the hands of the few who had risen to this ascendancy at the expense, and to the evident detriment and oppression of the community at large; and even in those instances where the emancipists had been allowed to acquire some little affluence, their success was to be traced to the patronage and protection afforded them by some member or other of the aristocratic party, to whom they either acted as agents in the disposal of merchandise (for it was considered by these gentlemen derogatory from their dignity to keep shops and sell openly), or else resorted for the purchase of goods on their own account. At the prosperity and importance, however, of this faction (for such is their proper appellation), Governor Macquarie, seeing that the power which they had attained was subversive of the very end for which the Colony itself had been instituted, levelled many a deadly blow during his long and judicious administration; and, although he, unhappily, did not succeed in extinguishing them altogether, he at least shore them of all but the inclination to re-establish the domination which they so long exercised. Like the Indian juggler's bag of serpents, their nature is not altered, but they have happily lost their poisonous fangs. Of the measures which this excellent, though most calumniated gentleman adopted, with this view, the most prominent were, first, Prohibiting the military from holdings lands or being concerned in commerce; secondly, Raising to situations of trust and dignity some of the most deserving of the class of emancipists; and thirdly, Throwing open the ports of the Colony to an unlimited importation of all sorts of merchandize. But it was not to be expected that he could effect these great and salutary changes in the policy which had been so long acted upon by his predecessors in the Government, without encountering the most obstinate and rancorous opposition from the party whose monopoly was thus overthrown. He, in fact, instantly drew on himself their unrelenting and systematic hostility. Numberless were the attempts made on all hands to vilify his motives and misrepresent his actions; but, as the leading maxim of his administration—"that it was good policy to restore the deserving emancipist to that rank in society which he had occupied previously to his conviction"—attracted the marked and cordial concurrence both of the Committee of the House of Commons, that reported on transportation in 1812, and of the present Secretary of State for the Colony; they judiciously desisted from cavilling any further with a policy thus sanctioned, although it was still as repugnant as ever to their feelings. With a pliant dexterity they immediately shifted their ground, and, feigning to concede the soundness of the principle itself, they resolved to seize every occasion to condemn its application. Accordingly every emancipist, who was fortunate enough to become the object of the Governor's countenance and protection, was instantly beset by this pack in full cry. Not content with hunting up and giving a false colouring to every little blemish which they could discover in the individual's history, they scrupled not to circulate as facts every species of calumny to which an unbridled and vituperate ingenuity could give birth. In the teeth, however, of all the discouragements and obloquy which the rancorous malignity of this faction contrived to throw in his way, this humane and upright Governor continued his course with the undeviating flexibility of a man who knew that he was pursuing the path of honour and duty. In vain did they assail him with open censure, in vain did they seek to undermine him by secret misrepresentations. To every charge of his enemies his unshaken integrity and unwearied zeal in the performance of all his duties, whether public or private, proved a sufficient refutation ; and in spite of an opposition thus organized and inveterate, he stood, like some frowning solitary rock of the ocean, on its own eternal basis, heedless of the din, and unaffected by the assaults of the boisterous elements around him.

THE REV. DR. LANG.

JOHN DUNMORE LANG was born in Scotland, in 1799, and arrived in this Colony in 1823. Few men, perhaps, of the present day have employed their pens more actively than he has done. The catalogue of his publications is a lengthy one. It stands thus :—

1826. Aurora Australis : a collection of sacred verse.
1833. Emigration.
1834. History of New South Wales, 2 vols.
  „   Origin and Migrations of the Polynesian Nations.
1837. Transportation and Colonization.
  „   Second Edition of his History of New South Wales.
1839. New Zealand.
1840. Religion and Education in America.
1847. Phillipsland.
  „   Cooksland.
1848. Eine Deutsche Colonie in Stillen Ocean. The original was written in English.
1852. Freedom and Independence for Australia.
  „   Third Edition of his History of New South Wales.
1861. Queensland.

In addition to these labours as an author, Dr. Lang has contributed extensively to the Press. In 1835, he established the *Colonist*, one of the best of our old newspapers ; in 1841, the *Colonial Observer;* and in 1851, the *Press*. To each of these journals he contributed numerous editorial writings.

As an author, Dr. Lang is distinguished rather by fertility of thought than by elegance of style. The latter, indeed, he seems to have systematically neglected. Most of his works have been produced under circumstances which, perhaps, did not admit of careful elaboration. It has been his habit to write at sea, during the many voyages he has made to the old world. It is consequently difficult to select any passage from his works at all remarkable for style. Diffuseness and verbiage are found everywhere. Where we are pleased, it is solely by the thought expressed; not at all by the manner of expression.

His work on the Polynesian Nations is by far the most valuable of his writings, in a critical point of view. No other composition from his pen displays such depth of research, such readiness in argument, such capacity for profound philosophical investigation. In this work he has demonstrated, not only the manner in which the Polynesian Islands were peopled, and the origin of the cannibal habits prevailing in them, but also the first settlement of America. In opposition to Dr. Robertson's theory, that the aborgines of that continent reached it by way of the Aleutian Archipelago, he maintains that they came from the islands of the South Sea, by the same succession of accidents which drove them from one island to another. Whether we adopt his theory or not, we cannot but respect the great ingenuity and learning he displays.

The following passages are taken from this work. They describe the peopling of the islands by the adventurers of the Indian Archipelago.

> It would thus appear that on the first opening of the East to Europeans, there were extensive, powerful, and flourishing maritime states of ancient standing established in the Indian Archipelago, the enterprising and warlike populations of which had made no inconsiderable progress in the arts of civilization. The conquests of the Arabs, and the voyages of their seafaring converts in the East to the sepulchre of the Arabian Prophet, may doubtless account for the prevalence of the Malayan language in the Island of Madagascar, although it is much more probable that the settlement of that island had been effected long anterior to the era of Mahomet or the rise of the Saracen power; but the early discovery and the successive settlement of all the islands of the Indian Archi-

pelago, were the natural and the necessary result of the existence of an ancient maritime power in that galaxy of isles. Some of these discoveries were doubtless the result of accident, others the reward of enterprise. With the islands more favourably situated, a precarious communication would doubtless be maintained for a longer period with the mother country; but as the discovery and settlement of the more distant and isolated isles would in all likelihood be effected by the crews of vessels that had lost their way on the deep sea, their future inhabitants would necessarily remain completely isolated from the rest of mankind.

It would seem that the Indian Archipelago has been traversed from time immemorial both by the Chinese and the Malays. 'The Chinese, it is well known,' says M. de Labillardiere, 'received spices from the Moluccas many ages before these islands were seized upon by the Europeans.' And for ages past the Malays have had a fishery established on the north coast of New Holland, which they visit annually with a large fleet of proas, to the number of two hundred sail and upwards, in search of a marine slug, called *trepang* or *bêche de la mer*, which they cure for the China market. We are therefore warranted to conclude that the same adventurous spirit which had ascertained the existence of these distant regions, and rendered them available for the purposes of mercantile speculation, would not only lead enterprising individuals of the Malayan nation to the successive discovery and settlement of all the islands of the Indian Archipelago, at a comparatively early period in the history of the world, but induce them to launch out, like Columbus, in quest of unknown lands into the boundless Pacific. Maritime enterprise is the characteristic of islanders; and we are warranted to believe, from instances that have occurred within the memory of man, that voyages of discovery have in all past ages been undertaken by that adventurous race, whose offspring now inhabit the South Sea Islands, on the most indistinct idea of the existence of any land in the direction of their intended course. A solitary native of the Fiji Islands had been driven to sea by some sudden storm when fishing in his canoe on the coast, and had landed at length on the Friendly Islands, three hundred and sixty miles from his native isle. In such circumstances no European, unacquainted with the science of navigation, would have ventured to put to sea in search of the distant island from which the stranger had been accidentally driven. But the thoughtless Polynesian, fired by the spirit of adventure, disregards the suggestions of prudence, and fearlessly embarks on an expedition as wild as Don Quixote's. Stimulated, accordingly, by the intelligence he had received from the stranger, a chief of the Friendly Islands set sail for the Fiji Islands some time afterwards, with two hundred and fifty followers, in three large canoes, each of which must have carried eighty men with provisions for the voyage.

In such voyages, however, the unskilfulness of the pilot or the unexpected change of the wind, would often carry the adventurous islanders far beyond their reckoning; and in such circumstances they would either founder at sea, or perish of hunger, or be driven they knew not whither, till they reached some unknown and previously undiscovered island. In the latter case they would gladly settle on the new-found land, fearful of again trusting themselves to the ocean, and entirely ignorant as to what course they should steer for their native isle.

This mode of accounting for the gradual peopling of the South Sea Islands is accordant with known facts; for numerous adventurers have been known to leave their islands in those seas, on such hazardous voyages as the one I have just referred to, and have never afterwards been heard of. Nay, instances are frequently occurring in the South Sea Islands of canoes being blown off the land by a sudden squall, or driven out of their course by some other accident of a similar kind in their short voyages from one group of islands to another. During the last few years the New South Wales sperm-whale ships have repeatedly fallen in with canoes that had been thus accidentally driven out to sea, and that, but for their assistance and direction, would never have reached any land. In one instance of the kind that occurred within the last two years, there were two dead bodies in one of the canoes. These calamitous accidents have doubtless been aggravated and rendered unnecessarily fatal by the mental character and disposition of the South Sea Islanders; for, conjoining a remarkable proneness to despondency with their spirit of adventure, when the wind blew strong and adverse in their short and frequent voyages from island to island, instead of redoubling their exertions, they generally pull down all sail and extend themselves in sullen despair along the bottom of their canoes, abandoning themselves and their tiny vessel to the mercy of the winds and waves.

Scattered over the immense superficies of his writings, we meet occasionally with passages which show how easy it would have been for Dr. Lang to charm his reader as well as to convince him. Let his History of the Colony furnish one or two proofs of this assertion:

If a peach-stone is thrown into the ground in a favourable situation in New South Wales, a large quantity of fruit may be gathered from the tree that shortly afterwards shoots up from it, without any subsequent culture, at the expiration of the third or fourth year. A gentleman, to whom the colony is much indebted for the zeal which he long evinced in the path of Australian geographical discovery—I mean Mr. Allan Cunningham—was induced, from this circumstance, uniformly to carry along with him a small bag of peach-stones on his exploratory expeditions into the interior; and whenever he found a suitable piece of ground in the great wilderness, to dig it up and plant a few of them in it, in the hope that the future trees might one day afford a timely supply of food, either to the wandering native, or to Europeans who might accidentally lose their way in the pathless solitudes of the interior; for the reader is doubtless aware that the native forests of Australia afford nothing whatever in the shape of fruit for the sustenance of man. I was much struck with the circumstance when it was first mentioned to me, many years ago, by Mr. Cunningham; and while I could not help commending, from my very heart, the pure and disinterested benevolence it evinced, I could not help inwardly regarding it as a lesson to myself for the future, and a reproof for the past. Alas! how many spots have we all passed unheeded in the wilderness of life, in which we might easily have sown good seed had we chosen, and left it to the blessing of God, the dew of heaven, and the native energies of the soil! Such spots we may never revisit; and the opportunity of doing good which was thus afforded us, but which was suffered to pass unimproved, will never return.

And again, when he becomes descriptive:

With the exception of the open plains, which occur on the elevated levels in the interior of the country, and which, like the plain of Bathurst, are naturally destitute of timber, the territory of New South Wales is, in its natural state, one vast interminable forest. In many parts of the colony, and especially in the interior, the land is but thinly timbered; there being not more than three or four trees of moderate height, and of rather interesting appearance, to the acre. In such places the country resembles the park scenery around a nobleman's seat in England, and you gallop along with a feeling of indescribable pleasure. In general, however, the forest land is more thickly timbered, sufficiently so to form an agreeable shade in a hot Australian summer-day, without preventing the traveller from proceeding in any direction at a rapid trot or canter. On the banks of rivers, and especially on the alluvial land within reach of their inundations, the forest becomes what the colonists call a thick brush, or jungle. Immense trees of the genus Eucalyptus tower upwards in every direction to a height of from 100 to 150 feet; while the elegant cedar, and rosewood of inferior elevation, and innumerable wild vines and parasitical plants, fill up the interstices. In sterile regions, however, on rocky mountain tracts, or on sandy plains, the forest degenerates into a miserable scrub, as the colonists term it; the trees are stunted in their growth and of most forbidding aspect, the fruit they bear being literally pieces of hard wood similar in appearance to a pear, and their shapeless trunks being not unfrequently blackened from the action of fire. In such regions, the more social animals of the country entirely disappear. The agile kangaroo is no longer seen bounding across the footpath, nor the gaily-plumaged parroquet heard chattering among the branches. If anything with the breath of life is visible at all, it is the timid gray lizard hiding itself in the crevices of the rocks, or the solitary black snake stretched at full length on the white sand, or the busy ant rearing his slender pyramid of yellowish clay, as if in mockery of the larger monuments of the Pharaohs, and establishing his puny republic amid the loneliness of desolation. In such forbidding regions, the mind unavoidably partakes of the gloominess of nature; and the only idea that takes forcible hold of it is, that such must assuredly be the region on which the primeval curse has especially fallen.

CHARLES HARPUR.

AUSTRALIAN Poetry has found its first exponent in CHARLES HARPUR. This gentleman was born at Windsor in 1811, and received no education beyond that given him by his father, a schoolmaster. His life has been spent entirely in the interior,—a fact, indeed, which might be conjectured from his writings. For the last ten or twelve years he has been in the service of the Government as a Gold Commissioner.

In 1853, Mr. Harpur published a small volume of poems. His fame as a Poet must rest upon one or two of the pieces contained in it. Many of them are not likely to afford much pleasure to the reader, for their author appears to have little power over the heart, except as a describer of nature. There are two cardinal objections to his compositions which must largely interfere with their popularity. These are—the want of harmony in his verse, and the want of taste displayed in his selection of language. Popular poetry depends more upon these qualities than upon the depth or subtlety of thought displayed in it. The ear must be pleased before the heart can be conquered. Mr. Harpur always conveys an impression of power, and when he is treating a congenial theme, he writes well: but whenever he attempts the lighter graces of lyric verse, he suggests the idea of a muscular man dancing a clumsy minuet.

By far the best thing he has written is *The Creek of the Four Graves;* in fact, nothing else from his pen makes the slightest approach to it. It is a fine piece of landscape painting, and it contains at least one image that might be envied by any poet.

> I verse a Settler's Tale of the old times,—
> One told me by a friend, the kindly sage,
> Old Egremont, who then went forth with four
> Of his most trusty and adventurous men
> Into the wilderness,—went forth to seek
> New streams and wider pastures for his fast
> Augmenting flocks and herds. On foot were all,
> For horses then were cattle of too great price
> To be much ventured upon mountain routes
> And into brush-lands perilously pathless.
>
> So they went forth at dawn: and now the sun
> That rose behind them as they journeyed out,
> Was firing with his nether rim a range
> Of unknown mountains that like rampires towered
> Full in their front, and his last glances fell
> Into the gloomy forest's eastern glades
> In golden masses transiently, or flashed
> Down on the windings of a nameless creek
> That, fringed with oaks and the wild willow ran
> Noiselessly on, between the pioneers
> And those new eminences.
>
>   Wilder grew
> The scene each moment—beautifully wilder!
> For when the sun was all but sunk below
> Those barrier mountains, then, within a breeze
> That o'er their rigid and enormous backs
> Deep fleeced with wood, came whispering down, the wide
> Slant sea of leaves stirred in the slanting rays—
> Stirred interdazzlingly, as though the trees
> That bare them were all thrilling,—tingling all
> Even to the roots, for very happiness—
> So prompted from within, so sentient, seemed
> The bright quick motion.
>
>   Halting wearied here,
> Our travellers kindled for their first night's camp
> The brisk and crackling fire, which also looked

A wilder creature than 'twas elsewhere wont,
Because of the surrounding savageness,
And soon in pannikins the tea was made,
Fragrant and strong, the freshed-sliced rasher broiled
On the live embers, and as soon dispatched
By the keen tooth of healthful appetite.

   And as they supped, birds of new shape and plume
And strange wild voice, westward repairing by,
Oft took their wonder,—or between the boles
Of the upslanting forest trees they saw,
Perched on the bare abutments of those mountains,
The wallaroo look forth : till eastward all
The view had faded into formless gloom,
Night's front ; and westward, the high massing woods
Steeped in a dusk and deepening beauty, lay
Heaped all the more distinctly for their darkness
Against the twilight heaven,—a cloudless depth
Yet luminous from the sunset's fading splendour:
And thus for a brief interval they looked
Even like a mighty picture of themselves
Hung in some vaster world.

                       Their supper done,
The echoes of the solitary place
Came as in wonder round about to meet
Strange voices moulding a strange speech, as then
Lifted in glee—but to be hushed ere long,
As with the night, in kindred darkness came
O'er the adventurers, each and all, a sense
Of lurking danger.

                       But all settled soon
About the well-built fire, whose nimble tongues
Sent up continually a strenuous roar
Of fierce delight, and from their fuming pipes
Drawing rude satisfaction, grave discourse
Of their peculiar business brought to each
A steadier mood that reached into the night.

   The simple subject to their minds at length,
Fully discussed, their couches they prepared
Of the green tresses of the willows near,
And four, as pre-arranged, stretched out their limbs
Under the dark boughs of the forest high
O'erdoming and traced out against the clear

Wide gaze of heaven, and trustful of the watch
Kept near them by their thoughtful master, soon
Drowsing away forgetful of their toil,
And of the perilous vast wilderness
Around them, slept; whilst all things there as well
Showed slumbrous,—yea, the circling forest trees,
Their foremost bodies carv'd from a crowded mass
Less visible by the watch-fire's bladed gleam,
And even the shaded and enormous mountains,
Their bluff brows glooming through the stirless air,
Looked in their quiet solemnly asleep:
Yea, thence surveyed, the universe might have seemed
Coiled in vast rest,—only that one dim cloud,
Diffused and shapen like a mighty spider,
Crept as with scrawling legs across the sky,
And that the stars in their bright companies,
Cluster by cluster glowingly revealed
As this slow cloud mov'd on, high over all,
Looked thoughtfully awake.

      And now the moon
Up from behind an eastern hill was seen
Conglobing, till a mighty mass she brought
Her under border level with its cone
As thereon resting edge to edge, when straight
Its solid bulk seemed inwardly to grow
Impregnate with her radiance, whilst the trees
That fringed its outline, their huge statures dwarfed
By distance into brambles, and yet all
Clearly defined against her ample orb
Even to their sprays, out of its very disk
Appeared to swell in bold relief, as they
Were sculptured from her substance.

      Egremont
On all this solemn beauty of the night
Looked out, still wakeful, for sweet thoughts of home
Ingathered to his heart, as by some nice
And subtle interfusion that connects
The loved and cherished (then the most, perhaps,
When past or absent) with the beautiful
And lasting things of Nature. So then thought
The musing Egremont, when suddenly—hark!
A bough cracked loudly in a neighbouring brake,
And drew at once, as with a 'larum, all
His spirits thitherward.

 D

He listened long
With head bent forward, till his held breath grew
A pang, and his ears rung. But Silence there
Had recomposed her ruffled wings and now
Brooded, it seemed, even stiller than before,
Nested in darkness: so that he ere long
To his sweet mood of museful memory
Calmly recurred.—

But there, again ! and hark !
Oh God! have Hell's worst fiends burst howling up
Into the doomed world? Or whence, if not
From diabolic rage, could surge a yell
So horrible as that which now affrights
And upwards sends the shuddering air ?

Alas !
Beings, in their enmity as vengeful, come
In vengeance ! For, behold, from the long grass
And nearer brakes, at once, a semi-belt
Of stript and painted savages divulge
Their bounding forms !—full in the flaring light
Thrown forth then suddenly by the fire, as though
Even it had felt the shock the air received
From their so terrible cries !

A moment seen
Thus as they bounded up, on then they came
Closing with weapons brandished high, and so
Rushed in upon the sleepers ! three of whom
But started and then weltered quivering under
The first fell blow dealt down on each, by three
Of the most stalwart of their merciless foes !
But one again and yet again heaved up—
Up to his knees, under the crushing strokes
Of the huge nulla-nulla, till his own
Warm brains were blinding him : for he was one
Who had with misery nearly all his days
Lived lonely, and who therefore, after hope
Hungered, and thirsted for some taste of good.
And now he could not but dispute the fact
Of death even in the fact. For oft 'tis seen
That Fortune's gay and pleasure-pamper'd child
Consents to his untimely power, with less
Reluctance, less despair, than does the wretch
Who hath been ever blown about the world,

The straw-like sport of Fate's unkindliest blast,
Vagrant and tieless—ever still in him
The craving spirit thus graves unto itself:

"I never yet was happy—never yet
Tasted unmixed enjoyment, and I would
Yet pass on the bright Earth that I have loved
Some season, though most brief, of happiness,
So should I walk thenceforward to my grave
Whenever in her green and motherly breast
It might await me, more than now prepared
To house me in its gloom—resigned at heart,
Soothed and subjected to its certainty.
Even by the consciousness of having shaped
Some good in being. But to have lived and now
To die thus desolate, is horrible!"

And feeling thus by habit, that poor man,
Though the black shadow of untimely death
Hopelessly thickened under every stroke,
Upstruggled desperate, until at last
One as in mercy, gave him to the dust,
With all his sorrows.

                   Egremont, transfixt
With horror—struck as into stone, saw this,
Then turn'd and fled! Fast fled he, but as fast
His deadly foes went thronging on his track!
Fast! for the merciless yelled in the chase!
And as he fled, the forests beasts as well
In general terror, through the brakes a-head
Crashed scattering, or with madd'ning speed athwart
His course came frequent. On, still on he flies,
Flies for dear life, and still behind him—yea,
Nearer and nearer, hears the rapid dig
Of many feet!—

                   And now, what should he do?—
Abruptly turning, the wild creek lay right
Before him! But no time was there for thought,
So on he kept, and plunging from the brink
Sank to his middle in the flashing stream—
In which the imaged stars seemed all at once
To burst like rockets into one wild blaze
Of writhing light. Then strongly wading through
The ruffled waters he sprang forth, and clenching

With iron clutch a stake-like root, that from
The opponent bank protruded, up its dark
O'erjutting ledge went clambering, in his blind
And breathless hurry, when—O, surely God
Has a peculiar care of those for whom
The daily prayers of spotless womanhood
And helpless infancy are offered up!—
When in its face a cavity he felt,
The upper earth of which was held fast bound
By the close implication of the roots
Of two old tea-trees. Into this he crept,
Just as the dark forms of his hunters thronged
The brink whence he had plunged.

      Thereon a space
They paused, to mark what bent his course might take
Over the further bank, so to hold on
The chase more surely. But no form was seen
To shoot up from its outline, nought there stirred,
Wherefore they augured that their prey was yet
Somewhere between ; and the whole group, with that,
Plunged forward till the fretted current boiled
Amongst their crowded trunks from bank to bank,
And searching thus the stream across, and then
Lengthwise, along the ledges, one by one
Athwart the cavity they passed—so near
That, as they waded by, the fugitive
Felt the strong odour of their wetted skins
Pass with them.

    But the search was vain. And now
Those wild men marvelled, and in consultation,
Then coupling his strange vanishment with one
Of their crude superstitions, fear-struck all
And silent they withdrew. And when the sound
Of their receding steps died from his ear,
Our friend slid forth, and, springing up the bank,
Renewed his flight, nor rested from it, till
He gained the welcoming shelter of his home.

 Return we for a moment to the scene
Of recent death. There the late flaming fire
Now smouldered, for its brands were strewn about
And four stark corses, plundered to the skin
And brutally mutilated, seemed to stare
With frozen eyeballs up into the pale

Round countenance of the moon, who high in heaven
With all her starry multitude looked down,
As peacefully down, as on a bridal, there,
Of the warm living, not, alas! on them
Who kept in ghastly silence through the night
Untimely spousals with a desert death!

There afterwards, for many changeful years
Within a glade that sloped into the bank
Of that wild mountain creek—midway within
Its partial record of a terrible hour
Of human suffering and loss extreme,
Four grassy mounds stretched lengthwise, side by side,
Startled the wanderer;—four grassy mounds
O'erstrewn with skeleton boughs, and bleaching leaves
Stript by the wintry-winged gales that roamed
Those solitudes from the old trees which there
Moaned the same leafy dirges that had caught
The heed of dying ages: these were all;
And thence the place was called—passingly called—
The Creek of the Four Graves. Such was the tale
Egremont told us of the wild old times.

The following ballad of bush life, entitled "Ned Connor," is so well executed as to make us wish that Mr. Harpur had written more in the same style, instead of soaring into cloudier heights. Both this and the preceding poem are perfect specimens of local colouring.

'Twas night—and where a watery sound
  Came moaning up the Flat,
Six rude and bearded stockmen round
  Their blazing bush-fire sat,
And laugh'd as on some starting hound
  The crackling fuel spat.

And merrier still the log-fire cracks
  As night the darker falls,
While not a noisy tongue there lacks
  To tell of drunken brawls,
But most of battle with the Blacks
  Some bloody tale appals.

Amongst them then Ned Connor spoke,
  And up his form he drew :—
What is there in an open stroke
  To boast of? You but slew
Those who'd have done, each hell-black one,
  The same or worse to you.

But, lost among the hills, one day,
  Which then was well nigh shut,
I met a Black upon my way,
  And thus the matter put
Unto him :—" See ! this knife's for thee,
  Come, guide me to my hut."

His savage eyes grew huge with joy
  As on the prize they bent,
And leading, even like a boy
  He caper'd as he went :
But think you, men, to give the toy
  Ned Connor ever meant ?

An hour had brought us many a mile
  And then, as closed the day,
The savage pointed with a smile
  To where my station lay :
"There ! give to me the knife," said he,
  " And let me go my way."

I never meant that he should touch
  The thing, as I have said,
And when he stretched his hand to clutch,
  A thought came in my head :
I raised my gun, as though in fun—
  I fired—and he was *dead* !

The ruffian laughed in his pitiless mood
  When ended thus his tale,
But all the rest, though men of blood,
  With horror seem'd to quail,
And saw, though he stood boastfully,
  That Connor too was pale :

For through the moaning of the trees
  He seem'd to hear the sound
Of his own laughter in the breeze
  Keep roaming out till drown'd
In wild and bitter mockeries,
  Up-answering from the ground.

Now what to hear had made them fear
   Had also made them dry:
But strange! the water-pail that late
   Brimm'd in the corner nigh
Was empty! In amazement great
   There's not a drop! they cry.

Their thirst grew bitter, and they said
   Come, this will never do!
It is your turn for water, Ned,
   Then why not go? He drew
Full hard his breath, and from his head
   There dripp'd a sudden dew.

But shaming to be tax'd with fear,
   He seiz'd the pail and said
"What care I? Though the night be drear
   Who ever saw the dead?
And if I fail to fill this pail
   The devil shall, instead."

He sallied forth. A sudden blast
   Went sobbing by the door,
Through which they heard his footsteps fast
   Recede—and when no more
They heard them, round the fire aghast
   They gather'd as before.

"I would not go alone to-night
   The way that he is gone,"
Said one, "for all the gold my sight
   Hath ever fallen upon:
To slay that creature was not right,—
   I'd say't where he my son!"

And now impatient all and wild
   They wonder'd at his stay,
Till one outspake: "A weanling child
   Could not make more delay:
If longer slack in coming back,
   He'll bring with him the day."

But while they thus were wond'ring—hark!
   They hear a frantic shriek,
Then nearing footsteps through the dark
   Come waywardly and weak:
And as the dogs did howl and bark,
   They star'd but fear'd to speak.

> Against the door, that to had swung,
>   One rush'd then and 'twas split;
> 'Twas Connor! who amid them sprung
>   And fell into a fit:
> And long that night in ghastly plight
>   He struggled there in it.
>
> And when his sense return'd—again
>   The sun was rising bright,
> But shuddering as in mental pain
>   He turn'd him from the light,
> And pointing said—"To bed! to bed!
>   For death is in my sight!"

The poem does not end here in the original; it is continued for some sixteen or seventeen stanzas further, in which Connor relates his interview with the ghost of his victim. It is questionable whether the poem is at all improved by them. They seem rather to weaken the effect of the whole; destroying the dramatic effect produced by the last lines quoted above, as well as their deep suggestiveness.

Although Mr. Harpur may never rank very high as a poet, it is clear that he possesses a certain amount of genius. Suffering in the first instance from a narrow culture, he never seems, unfortunately, to have found out the limits of his power, nor even the direction in which it lay. Thus it is that he has written a mass of verse which will never recompense him for the labour it has cost him. Apparently disdaining the more common sources of poetical inspiration, he has striven to emulate the lofty flights of Wordsworth: and while he has grasped at objects placed beyond his reach by nature, he has left behind him those which might have been attained with ease. Nevertheless he may justly claim the honour of having laid the foundation stone of our national poetry.

W. FORSTER.

WILLIAM FORSTER was born in Madras, in 1818, and came to this Colony eleven years after. The early years of his manhood were spent in the bush as a squatter. While engaged in this occupation, he commenced a series of contributions on political subjects to the Sydney press. Many pieces of this kind, containing much satirical force, appeared in the well known *Atlas* of 1844. One of his productions made a considerable noise at the time, and has not yet been forgotten. It was a political satire, under the heading, *The Devil and the Governor*,—the Governor alluded to being Sir George Gipps. This branch of literature has been cultivated with a good deal of success by our writers, but the first piece of the kind which met with more than ordinary notice is the one now mentioned.

SCENE.—*An office: Governor discovered seated at a writing table. Devil advances.*

Governor (aside).—What fellow is this, whose footsteps rude
    On my private hours thus dare intrude,
    When doors are closed, and the desolate blast
    In the outward midnight is bellowing past?
    I hear the sentinel's step below—
    How the deuce he got in, I should like to know.
    'Tis an ill looking hound! that aspect hard
    With the sorrow of sin is deeply scarr'd;
    And the records of passion deeply streak
    With their infinite lines that iron cheek;—
    I'm really afraid for help to cry,
    For I shrink from the scowl of his glaring eye

     And feel in his presence a sense of awe,
     Like a felon caught in the clutch of law,—
     Would I could summon my slaves together,—
     Where's Riddell and Parker,—where's Merewether?
     Yet he rather looks like a gentleman, too—
     I'll speak to him first—what else can I do?
     His manners may please, though his look's severe;—
     (*Aloud*) My honest fellow, what brings you here?
Devil.—Ha, ha! my old boy! how soft and mild;
     Why, you talk in the tone of a well-bred child.
     Cheer up, cheer up; dismiss alarm,
     My time is not come to do you harm.
     We've been friends too long to be quarreling now,
     And I'm not the man for a foolish row.
     I doubt not my face is strange, but still
     You've borne me in deeds the best good will,
     Come, come, cheer up, don't look so blue,—
     I'm a Governor, George, as well as you.
Governor.—The *devil* you are!
Devil.—   The devil I am.
     'Tis an ugly name in one's mouth to cram;
     But ah! you sly dog! you guess'd it well—
     I govern the vast domains of Hell.
     Why start at the word? since, by the same token,
     'Tis not the first time you've heard it spoken.
Governor.—Dark prince of the deep! what want you here—
     Since mortals with you must meet in fear?
Devil.—I've come, my dear soul, for an hour or two,
     On passing events to chat with you;
     To render you thanks for the mischief you're brewing
     For the State you oppress and the land you're undoing;
     And also to offer—excuse my freedom—
     A few words of advice should you chance to need 'em.
Governor.—As for your praise, it might not flatter,—
     So let it pass, as it don't much matter,—
     Sit down. And I hope you've taken tea—
     The hour for that meal being past with me;
     I'd offer you grog, but I sadly fear
     My cupboard is lock'd, and the key's not here.
     My servants to roost, I believe, have fled,
     My aide-de-camp's out, and my Sec. in bed—
     Yet now I reflect, I can find you some—
     'Tis a bottle of best imported rum,
     Just out of a batch that was seiz'd in town—

Oh dear! how I miss that Hutchinson Brown;
The keenest fellow in any nation
Is he, for sniffing an information,
With the pounce of a cat, the eye of an eagle,
And a nose for a job, that would honour a beagle;
As for me, I don't drink it, 'twas brought as a sample,
But do not be guided by my example,
You can suck from a bottle, as I suppose;
Hold it well up, and take care of your nose.

Devil.—Pooh, pooh! such stuff mere children's sport is,
I now drink nothing but "aquafortis."
How long I may do so remains a question,
For I'm told it exceedingly hurts the digestion;
And such is the general spread of sobriety,
They've got up in Hell a Temperance Society.
Now, I make it a rule—though much trouble it brings,—
To patronize all those sorts of things.
A sober sinner is not the less
A sinner for want of drunkenness;
And they wrong me who say that I'm fond of riot,—
I like those crimes best that are done in quiet.

Governor.—You talk rather boldly.

Devil.—   Well, I'm wrong
To trench on your prejudice, if it's strong.
Your pardon I heartily beg—but stay,
I've wander'd from much I meant to say.

Governor.—Your advice, your advice,—'twere a shame to lose it,
Though I need not take it unless I choose it.

Devil.—I grant you the praise you've fairly won
By the deeds you do and the deeds you've done;
I know that as causes corrupt the mind
Like the chains by which tyrants have crushed mankind,
That the blighting touch of a despot's rod
Kills in man's spirit the breath of God.
That the purpose he bade your race fulfil
Is not for the meek slave's fettered will,
That the cherishing light of the holy skies
Falls barren and vain upon servile eyes,
That the weeds of evil will thrive their best,
Where the fair shoots of nature are clipped and dressed;
Yes, under those climes where the poisonous brood
Of error is nursed by servitude—
Where souls are bowed by the weight they bear,
Where their moral sky looks dark, and their air

Is thick with the filth that bondage breeds,
I scatter my foul and fertile seeds
Where most I am bent on man's undoing.
The tyrant assists my work of ruin.
In New South Wales, as I plainly see,
You're carving out plentiful jobs for me.
But forgive me for hinting your zeal is such
That I'm only afraid you'll do too much.
I know this well—To subject mankind
You must tickle before you attempt to bind!
Nor lay on his shoulder the yoke until
Through his habits you've first enslaved his will.
You're too violent far,—you rush too madly
At your favourite ends and spoil them sadly.
Already, I warn you, your system totters,
They're a nest of hornets these rascally Squatters,
Especially when you would grasp their cash—
Excuse me, George, but I think you're rash.

Governor.—Rash! d—n it, rash!

Devil.— . . . . Don't fly in a passion,
In the higher circles 'tis not the fashion;
And swearing, besides, you must allow,
Is neither polite nor useful now.

Governor.—Would you have me forego the rights of the Crown,
To be laughed at all over this factious town?
I'll teach these Squatters to pay their rent,
And don't care one rush for their discontent;
They've abused me in print, they've made orations,
They've their papers and pastoral associations;
To England they've sent their vile petitions—
They've their Agents in swarms like heathen missions;
They've gone to the length of caricaturing—
But I'll show them the evil's past their curing.

Devil.—Come, come, be cool or your aim you'll miss,
Your temper's too hot for work like this;
This people I say will submit the more readily
If you've only the wit to grind them steadily.
You've a snug little tyranny under your thumb—
But manage it well, or down 'twill come.
'Twere a pity to peril this rich possession
By a foolish rashness or indiscretion;
Wentworth and Windeyer are troublesome chaps,
And the Council's a thorn in your side, perhaps;
But let them grumble and growl their fill,

You know very well their power is nil.
Look at the schedules by which, 'tis clear,
You handle a monstrous sum each year;
Look at the patronage thrown in your gift,
To give any fawning friend a lift.
Didn't you find a berth for Therry?
What were his merits? vast? Oh! very—
When a fellow like that can be made a Judge,
They may prate of their freedom, but I say "fudge."
Look at the power you have to draw
On Stephen and Co., when you want a new law.
Look at the lands that are unlocated,
Where your devils of the Crown are so nicely created,
Then calmly proceed, and with prudence act;
"In the middle lies safety,"—that's a fact—
Subdue by degrees, and slowly oppress,
Or, I tell you, you'll get yourself into a mess.
While people petition, they'll find it "a sell,"
But don't push them too hard, they might rebel.

Governor.—Rebel! ha! ha! you're surely in joke;
Rebellion here—a mere puff of smoke.
What would the people of England say
A rebellion! how queer! in Botany Bay!
Pick-pockets, swindlers, thieves, and jobbers,
Cut-throats, and burglars, and highway robbers—
A mob that escaped the gallows at home
'Tis worse than the "the servile wars at Rome!"
A handful of troops would put them down,
And the higher classes would join the Crown.

Devil.—It might be so, but just mark, my friend—
Who come to be losers in the end?
No doubt there'd be fun well worth enjoying—
Burning, and plundering, and destroying;
Fighting for towns not worth disputing—
Skirmishing, robbing, and rifle-shooting
From bushes and trees, and rocks for barriers—
Murdering of post boys and plundering of carriers,
Storming of camp by midnight entries
Driving off horses, and popping off sentries—
Seizing of stock for purposes royal,
Pressing of men to make them loyal;
Some heroes might fall in that petty strife,
Whom bondage had taught a contempt of life,—
Some patriots leading in civil storms,

>   Might dangle on gibbets their martyr forms;
>   Or exiled afar, to return no more,
>   Might bury their bones on a foreign shore,—
>   Proscribed by the tyrants they dared to brave,
>   And mocked by the people they fought to save;
>   But not in vain would they bear or bleed,
>   This land would have gained what most they need.
>   John Bull from his drowsy indifference waking,
>   Would give some of you despots a terrible shaking;
>   You'd be robbed of your berth and your reputation,
>   For causing your masters so much vexation—
>   And the people your chains so closely bind,
>   A tardy justice would seek and find.
>   Take my advice, I offer it cheap,—
>   Why, as I live, the man's asleep!
>   George, George, your manners much want reforming,
>   But I'll give your nose a bit of a warming.
>   *(Tweaks his nose and vanishes.)*
> *Governor (waking up).*—Was this but a dream? or was it real?
>   There's a pain in my nose by no means ideal.
>   There might be some truth in what he told me—
>   This place seems getting too hot to hold me.
>   I can't remain here for ever, 'tis true,
>   But I'll leave my successor something to do;
>   If I can't turn the Squatters out of their stations,
>   I can ruin the scoundrels by proclamations;
>   So I'll write out a draft for one this minute—
>   And if it don't sting them, the devil's in it.

Mr. Forster has been a frequent contributor to different journals in the colony during the last twenty years. His writings are principally of a political character. He has rarely ventured in the field of pure literature, but has contented himself with applying his literary power to the development of political questions. His 'leading articles,' and his less serious efforts both in verse and prose, would probably fill several octavo volumes. The following article—a criticism on an 'Oration' by Mr. Fowler—touches upon a non-political subject, and gives a fair specimen of the writer's capacity for dealing with æsthetic topics. It appeared at a time when the daily papers were full of the most fulsome eulogies of the lecturer, and gave rise to a rather bitter controversy. In his 'Oration,' Mr. Fowler had set himself to 'imitate without parody,' the most celebrated writers of the present century. It need scarcely be said that the merits of the dispute were entirely on Mr. Forster's side.

What a fashion it has become to pamper colonial literary efforts with profuse and indiscriminate applause ! I presume with a view to the encouragement of local genius. We kindly give certificates to the merest neophytes and charlatans. This must inevitably tend to depress the standard of colonial literature. Surely true genius need never shrink from true and honest criticism. If encouragement and cultivation be required, which many doubt, are they not best afforded by sweeping away with unsparing hand the mediocrities which encumber the same soil, and rob the seedling we would cherish of air and nutriment? The success of Mr. Fowler's Oration has been pronounced by the Press. Perhaps the Press would do well to reconsider its verdict.

Criticism chiefly concerns itself with two enquiries. First—What is your author's aim? Secondly—How has this aim been attained? If high and difficult, the greater, of course, the glory of success, and *vice versa*. But on the other hand the disgrace or failure is measured by comparison of the author's design with his powers and means of execution. If his estimate of these be false or extravagant, if he conceive absurdities or grasp at impossibilities, he exposes himself to just and proportionate ridicule. Nor is an author's design always to be gathered from his own enunciation., It may be purposely obscured or concealed—may be hidden altogether from his contemporaries, and even from himself.

In the case before us the orator proposes to illustrate and exemplify the best modern English writers by professed imitations of their style and sentiments. Notwithstanding Mr. Fowler's "moral reasons," the plan seems to me unworthy a man of letters—one which could never have entered the head of a fervent worshipper—altogether inconsistent with due reverence for and sympathy with genius. Unconscious imitation is a tribute we pay, in spite of ourselves, to intellectual superiority. We become, as it were, assimilated with great minds, we lose our individuality in the enthusiasm they excite, but in general, if we be wise, we dare not knowingly seek to identify ourselves with their wonderful productions. There have indeed been imitations, such as Pope's, made merely for purposes of literary exercise and amusement. These pretend to little and must not be severely judged. Mr. Fowler's efforts are of a more ambitious order: they are expressly intended as illustrations—to show how Byron, Wordsworth, Coleridge, &c., thought and wrote. The lecturer himself calls them "specimens"—an inappropriate phrase, and, to my thinking, somewhat hyperbolical. In short, 'tis an attempt to pourtray genius by reflections from Mr. Fowler's mirrors or "lanterns"—magic or not, as may be—or whatever else he may please to term them, a species of literary trifling, I had almost said, of profane mockery, which however it may suit the egotism of pretentious patronage to dignify with fulsome eulogies, displays in the imitator only inordinate self-esteem, combined I fear with a very faint appreciation of the sacredness and beauty of those great originals, from whom Mr. Fowler draws his second-hand inspiration.

To what end are his imitations? If great writers were to be illustrated, why not have given us passages from their own works? Would not such "specimens" have answered the purpose better than Mr. Fowler's? He does not assume his copies to be equal to their prototypes—I quite agree with him there. But whatever their merits they are but as masks upon real faces. What do we want with them at all? Can they in any way assist our judgment? Why must we scale the empyrean upon ladders of Mr. Fowler's manufacture?

I take then the lecturer's real design to have been this—viz., to show how cleverly Mr. Fowler could do imitations. Mr. Fowler is rather hard on dunces, but is not particularly successful in his endeavours to rescue imitators from the low position assigned them by Johnson and Emerson. Utterly false and absurd is his apologetic adaptation of a remark of Shelley's—"That all art is mimetic." Most truly so, in her selection of details. But in her conceptions taken as a whole, quite the reverse. From Nature, of course, those materials must be taken, which Art, under altered arrangements and in nobler forms, sublimes into creation. The features and the limbs are human, but the statue grows into the shape and aspect of a god. The antique theories of cosmogony involved that of a primeval chaos, out of which Jupiter *created* the universe. Shakespeare's highest *creations*, though wonderfully human, were not portraits. The work of Art is to select, to perfect, to realise Nature, who in details of execution is seldom or never perfect. The ideal is the realization of Nature. Above all, the artist draws from Nature herself, whereas the imitator or artisan at best draws only second-hand from the artist.

Parodies and caricatures are more nearly allied to Art than such imitations as Mr. Fowler's, or, to adopt his own phraseology, "specimens that are not caricatures." The grotesque, though an inferior species, is yet a species of Art. 'Tis, as it were, a second rainbow, parallel with, only dimmer than the first. Caricature, no less than high Art, has its genius and its ideals. Its types simultaneously exist both in Art and Nature, and its creations are of the ludicrous instead of the beautiful. The mere imitator cannot but fall far short of the caricaturist, because the conceptions of the latter, even when they excite disgust, have always the merit of originality.

And now within the narrow limits I have ventured to assign him, how has the lecturer succeeded in his task? For my own part, if literary imitation be taken to consist in something more than mere external resemblance, that is to say, in rhythmical structure and versification, I must confess my impression, which I admit to be that of a comparatively unlettered person, that Mr. Fowler's copies are little better than failures. My judgment certainly labours under the disadvantage of being founded on the newspaper reports, which appear not to be complete, but from the "specimens" published, I should have had great difficulty in recognizing the writers. Mr. Fowler's portraits, however, are wisely inscribed with the names of their subjects. This method helps on the reader's lagging acquiescence in those cases where some faint degree of resemblance may be conceived to exist—and in these it appears to me as if only the most vulgar notion of the writer were conveyed by some commonplace contrivance. For instance, in the Byronic "specimen," which is certainly not the most unlike, we have the trite contrast of "regal brows with damp worms crowned"—the disruption of the sense in the penultimate line, and the prophetic mysteriousness of the last. Of Wordsworth and of Hood again we may bring ourselves to discern some faint elimination—of the first in mawkish inanity—of the second in a string of most intolerable puns. Poor Scott suffers a strange transfiguration. Seldom indeed are the comic pages of *Punch* adorned by a more ludicrous image than that of the heroic Donald, rushing about after the fashion of a *Bombastes Furioso*, now kissing his lady-love and now "holding the baffled foe at bay." The travesty would have been admirable had there been the least resemblance to Scott's style, which I must own all my efforts fail to discover. Moore's "specimen," devoid of melody and softness, is like the play without the character of Hamlet. "The metre of Locksley Hall" and "smiling frankly up the night" might perhaps have served to remind us slightly of Tennyson, did we not find the same metre and a similar quaintness of expression in Alexander Smith and a host of other poets of the same school, as it is called. Some of the other specimens appear to contain better poetry, but if possible, still less resemblance, which leads one charitably to hope that Mr. Fowler would succeed better as an original writer than as a copyist.

But, unfortunately, in the text of his oration, he shows himself somewhat of a happier imitator than in his so-called "specimens." The ambitious style of the essay, thick sown with epigrammatic and metaphorical conceits, has a palpable though diluted relish of Emerson. An instance doubtless of that unconscious imitation to which I have above alluded, and which is indeed a common fault—if fault it be—of young authors. Far graver errors—but these also years may correct—are the mistaken sentiments, the false metaphors, the inapt and even ludicrous comparisons with which the lecture abounds. For example, speaking of modern poets, he tells us—"We are as destitute of colour and fancy as a plaster cast." Now plaster casts are not necessarily destitute of fancy, and I rather think modern poets are not so wanting in fancy as imagination. The comparison of Tennyson with Longfellow is particularly absurd—and still more so that of Coleridge with Johnson. What have these, respectively, in common, save that all are—or were—eminent poets and writers? Then Emerson has "the *Ionic* grace and chaste simplicity of the old Greeks * * * all the convolvuluted richness of the *Corinthian* abacus, all the chaste simplicity of the *Doric* column"—quite enough of contradictions for one man in all conscience. Does Mr. Fowler really know the meaning of these scientific epithets? And how is the bewildered reader out of such hodge-podge to make out the order of architecture to which Emerson's style belongs? When Shelley's lyre is likened to "the sough of the pine forest, whose variety is its charm" one is tempted to ask—Has Mr. Fowler ever *heard* the sough of the pine forest? If he had, would he have praised it for *variety?* Again, it is not easy to conceive how Wordsworth's style, or any other style, can include the qualities of both summer evenings and winter mornings, nor how Moore could have contrived to "write with the scarlet beak of the crane," nor how the epithet "Spenserian" can be properly applied to any of Moore's love songs. Then we have an *Etrurian* tomb peopled with very strange and rather incongruous inhabitants, viz.: "stately bards and philosophers of *Greece*"—"soldiers, statesmen, and scholars of *Rome*"—"fantastic phantasms of the *Hindoos*," besides *Englishmen* and *Germans*. And why is the style of Keats figured by "Thessalian holly," which few of us have seen, in preference to English, which, judging from Mr. Fowler's own description, would have answered his purpose quite as well.

These are but a few samples of the many conceits and affectations which encumber Mr. Fowler's literary sketches to such a degree that it becomes almost impossible to judge of their descriptive merits. His pictures are obscured by their framing and gilding, and the likenesses, if any such there be, lost in meretricious ornaments. When Mr. Fowler learns to write in a plain style, which perhaps he will when he has acquired by practice more confidence in his own powers, and left off imitating Emerson, we shall perhaps understand him better, and do more justice to his powers of delineation. For the present he seems to me a dangerous model for still younger writers, and one which they might be induced to follow by certain glittering qualities which his style undoubtedly possesses, and by the public approbation he has gained.

Criticism of this kind, free as it was from undue severity, did good service to the cause of Literature. Neither its value nor its justice, however, can be fully appreciated, unless the reader is acquainted with the ludicrous eulogies pronounced by the daily papers.

A second satire from Mr. Forster's pen, of a less personal kind than the one already given, attracted considerable attention at the time of its appearance in the *Atlas*. It was entitled, *The Genius and the Ghost*, and had reference to the subject of Transportation. The characters in the dialogue were, the Genius of the City of

Sydney and the Ghost of Transportation. The latter, alluding to the free emigrant portion of the population, breaks out into the following invective towards the conclusion:—

> But ye who freely sought this southern clime
> Without the badge, if not the taint, of crime—
> Self-righteous, spotless, calculating host,
> Who make morality your modest boast,
> Who point, with cool and quiet self-applause,
> At cherish'd statutes and unbroken laws,
> Ye virtuous emigrants! who from the brink
> Of crime and woe so sensitively shrink,
> Among your saintly myriads are there none
> Who blush at former crimes in secret done—
> Know ye no moments past, however long,
> When your frail virtue falter'd into wrong—
> No times, ere heavenly mercy bade you mend,
> When fortune, more than virtue, stood your friend?
> Oh! think, may not some friend, more dear than life,
> Some father, brother, lover, sister, wife,
> Some cherish'd name that fills the eye with tears,
> Read in the pages of departed years?
> Oh! may not such, by strong misfortune driven,
> Herd with those outcast sons of earth and heaven,—
> Oh! may not such, beneath some bitter blow,
> Some sudden outrage of capricious woe,
> Beset by daily want, by daily care,
> In the hot impulse of his keen despair,
> Urg'd by the present wish, the prompting time,
> For once—once only—lift the hand to crime;
> Then by impatient justice snatch'd, and sent
> To share with crowds their hopeless punishment—
> Oh! may not such, when shivering at the last,
> That forlorn spirit shudders o'er the past,
> Upon your cruel heads, with gasping breath,
> Launch the irrevocable curse of Death,
> From you who bid the wanderer turn away,
> And wrest from hopeless guilt its comfort and its stay?
>
> I would, when nations hoist a moral name,
> That judge and jury might decide their claim,
> I would not ask alone what victims swell
> The bloated gang, or gorge the stifling cell—

What ragged rogues the indignant tipstaff locks
In midnight dens, or convoys to the stocks—
What nameless crowd some public gaol restrains,
With vulgar handcuffs and plebeian chains,
The horde of felons rear'd to deeds of ill,
Whom, scarce polluted by the blood they spill,
Malignant justice drags, with vain display,
To choke and stiffen in the blaze of day,
Or sends abroad, where she may chance to find
Some simple race of primitive mankind,
To spread, where no resisting force controls,
The rank contagion of corrupted souls.
I wish opinion to be sound and strong
Where justice flinches from the unpunish'd wrong:
I ask what system of your partial times
Bestows impunity on chartered crimes;
What guilt some vile expediency protects,
Politeness smiles upon, or fear neglects;
For splendid faults what sanctuary, and which
Shelters the showy vices of the rich.
What wealthy ruffian, hedg'd around by awe,
You cherish, scatheless by the arm of law.
If might can reach what merit would not dare—
If men are honour'd by the clothes they wear—
If patriots at the shrine of tyrants fall—
If hollow consciences truckle at their call—
If stubborn priests on liberty look sour,
Or base religion bow the knee to power.

When in his gay barouche, or tandem neat,
Some fat insolvent whirls adown the street,
Thinking the while, no doubt, what charming sport
He had with Law Commissioner and Court,
And meets some wretch his arts to ruin led,
Whom his false schedule robb'd of clothes and bread,
Who in his threadbare vesture shrinks, and feels
The sprinkled blessings of his chariot wheels;
When, he, rich rogue, whose keen commercial eye
Each passing object glances gaily by,
That weeping wretch, so pale and so forlorn,
Shall dare accost with fashionable scorn,
Or to his victim impudently dole
The base compassion of his knavish soul;
When he shall still be honour'd and caress'd
At social boards—a sleek and favour'd guest—

When crowds around him bend in servile style,
Aw'd by his frown and flatter'd by his smile—
When such the bays that crown a villain's brow,
I ask—is this your moral city now?
At midnight balls, where mirth is faint and hot,
See yonder flush'd and fashionable sot;
Behold him, staggering with his weight of wine,
Mid laughing crowds pre-eminently shine.
The devil that obscures his slender sense
Inspires a more than usual impudence.
Then see him boldly mix, with drunken skill,
In the mad polka or the stale quadrille—
See some fair creature's palpitating waist
By his hot arm lasciviously embraced—
See the soft cheek of virgin beauty blaze
With the wild babble of his senseless praise—
See aged dames his batter'd jokes beguile—
See sober matrons chuckle at his smile—
Hear sons and fathers praise his "cheerful mood"—
"A little swipy" or "a little screw'd"—
See next at church some slender victim stand,
Whose parents lik'd the honour of his hand —
See, too, her fond and drooping eyes approve
His worn-out vows of mercenary love—
Hear, in his praise, relations loud and warm,
"A little wild, but certain to reform."
Then turn away where stocks and dungeons bind
The wretched dregs and rabble of mankind—
Where the low sons of vulgar drunkenness
Are taught the guilt of unrefined excess,
And dare you still, without a pang of shame,
Your virtue and morality proclaim?

It is evident that Mr. Forster's writings are never wanting in pungency. Perhaps they are wanting in finish; but that may be accounted for by the fact that they were simply newspaper contributions, which seldom meet with much elaboration. Had he devoted himself with more attention to letters than he has done, it can hardly be doubted that he would have gained distinction. He has not made many serious efforts in poetry, nor does he make any pretension to the name of poet. The tendency of his mind is rather to subtlety of disquisition than luxuriance of imagination. He would have made an admirable Scholastic Philosopher in the thirteenth century,—on certain points, indeed, he might have put Duns Scotus on his mettle. For a mind of such a temper, the following Sonnets are very respectable productions. They were written at the time of the Crimean war.

I.

Ah me ! the world's a vault that History paves
With buried nations. Egypt's awful bones
Are blanched in deserts. Hark ! the dulcet tones
Of Asian winds come whispering over graves !
Greece only melts us as with odorous breath
Of churchyard flowers that make a friend of death.
Fair Italy in hollow accents raves,
Mingling reproach with anguish, as a ghost
Complains 'mid scenes in life she loved the most,
And Poland like a prison'd spirit sighs !
Far off how many a dusky nation lies,
Deep hid in woods, or in oblivion lost.
Oh, Heaven ! the end—shall this be ever so ?
And whither these have gone must England go ?

II.

Sebastopol ! that on the sable sea
Sitt'st with the blood of many nations bathed,
Now that war's waning tempest leaves thee free,
How proudly frowning from thy craggy steep,
With haggard looks thou dost survey the deep,
Sublime, though shattered—terrible, though scathed !
Oh ! more enduring monument than brass,
O marble shape, stern city ! thou shalt pass
From memory never—privileged to bear
The horrid brand and character of war
Imprinted on thy forehead, as a scar
Adorns a warrior. Oh ! for ever wear
Thy glory so. When noble foes are crowned
By our own hands, we make ourselves renowned.

III.

Why shout ye thus, unthinking multitude !
Why thus, with sulphurous stars and fiery glare,
Disturb the quiet night ? Why vex the air
With idle pæans ? Look you ! peace is good,

And therefore to rejoice in sober mood,
We owe to God, who blesseth us thereby.
But why, I ask you, giddy people !—why
Need Freedom's sons by heartless mirth insult
Their brothers in affliction—why exult
When tyrants only chuckle? Still, the sky
Looks down on nations trampled in the dust ;
Still, Poland yields her myriads to the lust
Of foreign foes ; still, Italy, depressed
With hopeless anguish, tears her bleeding breast.

IV.

'Twixt East and West, a giant shape she grew,
To both akin, and making both afraid.
Casting a lurid shadow on the new
And ancient world, her greedy eyes betrayed
The tiger's heart, and ominously surveyed
The peoples destin'd for her future prey ;
From Polar steppes and ice-encumbered seas
To where the warm and blue Symplegades
Darken the splendour of a Grecian day,
She stretched her long grasp, conquering by degrees ;
And when at length the banded nations rose
In armed resistance, their combined array,
With equal arms, she shrunk not to oppose,
But bravely stood, as still she stands, at bay.

In political life, Mr. Forster has gained a high reputation for ability and honesty. His speeches display no eloquence, but they are pithy and philosophical. He was Colonial Secretary and Premier in 1860, but his administration lasted a few months only. It was strenuously supported by Mr. Deniehy in the *Southern Cross*. Mr. Forster was again Colonial Secretary in 1863, when Mr. Martin was Premier.

JAMES MARTIN.

JAMES MARTIN was born in Ireland, in 1820, and arrived in this Colony in his childhood. He was articled to Mr. G. R. Nichols, an attorney who distinguished himself in politics as well as in law; and after his admission he practised with considerable success. On the introduction of Responsible Government in 1856, he became Attorney General in the first administration of Mr. COWPER, and a few days after was admitted to the Bar. Since that period, he has occupied the position of a leader in the profession, and is generally regarded as by far the ablest man in its ranks. This success is the more remarkable, seeing that Mr. MARTIN, from a very early date in his career, seems to have divided his attention equally between politics and law. He has been a member of the Legislature, almost without intermission, for nearly twenty years; and by no means either a silent or an inactive one. He may be regarded as the legitimate successor of Mr. Wentworth in the position which that distinguished politician occupied among his contemporaries. Since the departure of Mr. Wentworth from our shores, no man has appeared to dispute the palm of pre-eminence with Mr. Martin. He is the ablest debater in the Assembly, and the most effective advocate at the Bar.

In a remarkable speech made ten years ago, in answer to an ungenerous attack upon himself, Mr. Martin traced the outlines of his career. "He was surrounded," he said, "by those who had raised themselves to high position by their own honourable exertions—true sons of the soil, not in the narrow sense in which the term was generally understood, but in the sense of the old Roman satirist, who applied the expression to those who owed their success in life neither to wealth, nor pedigree, nor fortune. With these and him there were many things in common. He asked them, and he asked them confidently, not ungenerously and unjustly to desert him on this occasion. From his outset in life till that time, he had to achieve everything for himself, and from the humblest beginning he had fought his way almost to the highest point to which, in this colony, it was possible to attain. At every step he had been met with opposition, and had been compelled to make good his ground, and whatever he had achieved he owed not to the favour or affection of any man. He had never cringed, nor fawned, nor played the sycophant, and if his conduct was open to condemnation, it certainly was in a contrary direction. The lesson of self-reliance, of which he trusted he might be pardoned in regarding himself as an example, would not, he hoped, be shorn of its value by an unmerited reverse in the moment of final triumph. As he had borne up against and overcome many obstacles of greater magnitude than the present, he trusted that he should successfully bear up against this one also, and that, in the stand which he then took, the generous and spontaneous sympathies of the House would go along with him, and that the only effect of the present storm would be, like those of the physical universe, to leave the atmosphere of public life purer than before."

The current has now set the other way, and Mr. Martin has no longer any opposition to fear. Judging from the course of events during the last few years, it seems more than probable that his predominance will increase, notwithstanding the unpopularity of his politics. As long as he remains in public life, his influence over it must be a powerful one. So far as that is concerned, it matters little whether he is in office or out of office. In the one case, he is Achilles in the field, and in the other, Achilles in the camp ; but he is still Achilles.

Mr. Martin has, in past years, written a good deal in the public Press. Twenty years ago, he edited the *Atlas* for some time, and was a coadjutor of the celebrated Robert Lowe. His contributions were principally on topics of a political nature ; and if they cannot be pointed out as models of composition, yet they all bear the stamp of a cultivated and powerful intellect, which rarely failed to grasp the salient points in the case before it, and to place them in the most effective light. We meet with no effort at invention—no display of imagination—no exuberance of humour: but we have keenness, fluency, and force, in a marked degree.

The following is the "peroration" of an article entitled *The Parting Word*, written on the departure of Sir George Gipps. It is not a bad piece of historical portraiture :—

> It is unnecessary for us now to go through all the charges that might be made against Sir George Gipps. Perhaps no Governor ever had a finer opportunity of making himself popular and respected—of conferring greater benefits upon the people over whom he was placed, and certainly no Governor ever effected a greater amount of injury, or perpetrated a greater amount of injustice. Having been entrusted, amongst other matters of almost equal importance, with the task of introducing a system of representative Government amongst us, he voluntarily resigned all the credit which he might easily have gained by carrying that system out, and did everything in his power to counteract it. The subordinate officer of a limited Sovereign, who can do scarcely anything except through the instrumentality of Ministers responsible to Parliament, he claimed for himself, and attempted to exercise, the most arbitrary power. He invented prerogatives before unheard of, and drew a distinction, on all occasions, between the interests of the people here and the Government at home. He paid no respect to the wishes or the opinions of the colonists, or their representatives, but constantly disregarded them whenever they were at variance with his own. Instead of being firm, he was obstinate and perverse. Instead of taking pains to soften and conciliate, he did everything to embitter and disgust. Placed over a community of British subjects, he acted with the arbitrary spirit of a Turkish bashaw, and denied to his fellow subjects here the possession of rights which the meanest man in England enjoys. Having by his shameful misgovernment made the great body of the colonists hostile to his measures, he collected, by the most disgraceful abuse of his Sovereign's patronage, a horde of wretched sycophants and time-servers around him, for the

purpose of obtaining for himself the most miserable semblance of support. He did everything in his power to alienate the affections of the people of this colony from the parent state, and his success in this endeavour has been proportionate to his exertions. He never retracted a statement or an opinion, however false or erroneous—he never admitted the impolicy or the impropriety of a measure, however ridiculous, unconstitutional, or unjust. His own will was always his law—and in carrying out the worst measures, he displayed an obstinacy which, directed towards the achievement of better and nobler ends, might have been attended with the happiest results. He was rash, without being bold—headstrong, without being decisive—and harsh and unjust in detail, under the pretence of being generally impartial. In short, he showed himself to be possessed of every quality necessary for a bad Governor, with scarcely any one of the requisites of a good one, and his eight years' administration will be a sort of plague spot in our history.

As might be expected, the departure of this Governor has called forth no honourable tribute of public admiration or respect. Those public institutions which he occasionally assisted, have presented him with formal addresses, confined entirely to thanks for the benefits which he conferred upon them, without making any reference to his public conduct. The officials and toadies, whose good wishes he conciliated, have indeed procured signatures to an address of another description; but neither the names attached to it, nor the manner in which those names were collected, entitle that address to any consideration. Money, too, has been subscribed for the purpose of honouring him by the erection of a public statue; but should so injudicious a step be taken, the splendour of the tribute will only be surpassed by the meanness of the character which it is intended to transmit to posterity. "Non quia intercedendum," says Tacitus, "putem imaginibus quae marmore aut aere finguntur; sed ut vultus hominum ita simulacra vultus imbecilla ac mortalia sunt; forma mentis aeterna: quam tenere et exprimere, non per alienam materiam et artem, sed tuis ipse moribus, possis." And we can tell the friends of Sir George Gipps, that neither monuments nor statues will make that man memorable in after ages whose good deeds are not sufficient to render him worthy of this distinction.

The following comments on the society introduced to Government House by Sir Charles Fitz Roy afford a good specimen of the writer's style. It is generally distinguished rather by rhetorical power than by any other quality. The first article, headed *The Ball*, refers to the public entertainment given by the Governor soon after his arrival in the Colony.

Our late Governor, during the period of his most calamitous administration, kept two objects constantly in view. The one was, to exalt the royal prerogative into the supreme legislative as well as executive power, and thus repres-

everything that was liberal and constitutional. The other, which may perhaps be considered as a necessary adjunct to the former, was to level all social distinctions, and reduce to the same degradation, the educated and the ignorant, the elegant and the vulgar, the honest and the dishonest, the moral and the depraved. To accomplish the first, he issued his squatting edicts, supported his District Councils, and misappropriated the public money. To accomplish the second, he invited to partake of his and his lady's hospitality, people of all classes and every grade of immorality, and insulted such persons of social consequence and refined habits as he persuaded to visit him, by admitting to the same room with them, people, of whom Cicero's description of Catiline's associates presents a strictly accurate idea—or if it does not exactly correspond, it is only because it falls short in comprehensiveness—because the associates of the abandoned and profligate Roman, were more respectable than those of His Excellency Sir George Gipps.

When this miserable tyrant departed from our shores, whatever might have been our hopes or our fears upon public grounds, we at all events consoled ourselves with the pleasing anticipation, that the reign of swindlers and demireps was at an end, and that under the rule of a gentleman claiming relationship with some of England's proud and lofty aristocracy, we should be sure to see the rules of decent society punctiliously adhered to. But Sir Charles Fitz Roy's first party has tended very much to undeceive us. Without entering into particulars, which of course it is impossible for us safely to do, we can undertake to say, that Sir George Gipps never invited to his house a greater number of doubtful characters, than there appeared at our new Governor's first public ball. In making this assertion, and in thus bringing this matter so prominently forward, we do not for one moment desire to impute to Sir Charles Fitz Roy any intention on his part to insult, or annoy, or treat with contempt, any class of people whatsoever. He has been too short a time amongst us to know much about those who call upon him, and he must necessarily depend, in a great measure, if not wholly, upon the judgment and experience of those about him, who have been longer in the colony than himself. His aide-de-camp must, of course, have much left to his discretion, and to this gentleman, at present at all events, does the responsibility attach of introducing to Government House people who could not possibly be introduced into any reputable company elsewhere. To this gentleman, then, do we attribute the blame in the present instance. But while absolving the Governor from any share in the invitation of improper characters, we cannot acquit him of the folly of taking into his household the aide-de-camp of Sir George Gipps. The experience which this young gentleman had under his former master, must have been of a character calculated to do anything but improve, and having so frequently issued cards to the very dregs of the people—so far as position, education, and morality are concerned—it could not be expected that he would be very select in the exercise of any discretion that might afterwards be entrusted to him. The result has proved, that what might reasonably have been expected has come to pass, for not only were Sir George Gipps' worst guests invited to the house of Sir Charles Fitz Roy, but some persons also whom even Sir George Gipps himself never did and never would admit to his presence—dead as he was to any fear of contact with the disreputable and degraded. As this, however, was the first party of our new Governor, much may be overlooked, and many allowances may be made. We may disregard in the ruler of three weeks' standing, what it would be our duty to denounce in one who had been a little longer amongst us, but we hope that in future Sir Charles will be more cautious than to leave his hospitality, as his Sovereign's representative, in the hands of a young aide-de-camp, or in those of anybody else. It is in no unfriendly spirit that we give him this advice in a matter which he may think relates to him more in his private character than in his public capacity. But he may rely upon it, that it is of great consequence to the people of this colony that the visitors of the Governor should, at all events, not be notoriously disreputable. In all young communities society has to be formed and fashioned out of materials not the most pliant and tractable, and it must depend, in a great measure, upon the head of the Government whether virtue is to conquer vice, or honesty and decency are to yield to profligacy and wickedness. Charles the Second, by his vicious example, degraded the character of the British nation, and for a time made vice the rule of society, and virtue the rare exception, but the influence of his own conduct did not long survive him—public order and decency were speedily restored. Should, however, a gentleman claiming his descent from this most abandoned and contemptible monarch, by countenancing vice and profligacy and ignorance amongst us, weaken the respect of the community for decency and virtue, the evil might be of longer duration than it was in England, and we might, for years to come, have to deplore the sad fate that sent to rule over us a scion of the house of Stuart, with all that disregard of character and propriety of conduct which distinguished the most abandoned of his race, and with infinitely greater power of perpetuating the influence, and spreading the contagion, of his example.

The same subject was continued, in a subsequent article headed *The Dinners*. After quoting the previous article at full length, the writer said :—

"Such was the language used by us on a former occasion, in reference to Sir Charles Fitz Roy's first ball—such the terms in which we felt called upon to express our indignation at the manner in which he had then suffered *his* hospitality to be abused, and *our* sense of decency to be outraged and insulted. We thought that the mistake which he then made might have been the result of unavoidable ignorance, rather than deliberate design, and we cast upon others that blame which we were unwilling to charge upon him. We knew that he could then have had no opportunity of making himself acquainted with the history and character of those who sought admission to his society, and we confidently indulged the hope that the timely warning which we then gave him would not be entirely thrown away. In this we deeply regret that we have been mistaken. His conduct since that period has satisfied us that our liberality then far exceeded our justice, and that for the invitation of improper characters to his first party he is himself directly and indirectly responsible. We say nothing about his visits to the houses of people with whom, as Her Majesty's representative, it was discreditable for him to associate—we speak now only of those whom he invited to his own table—and amongst those might be enumerated some of the most disreputable characters in the community. Sir George Gipps, with all his faults, drew some distinction, however flimsy it may have been—but Sir Charles Fitz Roy draws none. Nobody is too low—nobody is too ignorant—nobody is too degraded, for his most familiar intercourse. The most shameless prostitution—the most abandoned profligacy—the most notorious immorality—oppose no barrier against admission to his house. He recognizes no beauty in virtue—no deformity in vice; but treats them both with an equal share of his regard. He introduces the one to the society of the other, and does his utmost to degrade it by the unaccustomed and repulsive contact. The most irreproachable he has invited to meet the most abandoned. In short, he has commenced a career which, unless it be at once checked by the powerful voice of public opinion, will upset the morality and decorum of the land. It is difficult to imagine upon what principle—with what views—or for what reason—he has thus acted. It may be that he takes this course because he despises us, or because he wishes to gain popular applause by breaking through all class distinctions.

In either case his conduct is equally disgraceful. Descending, or claiming to be descended, from what he may perhaps consider an illustrious ancestry—connected with princes and with nobles by the ties of consanguinity—he may consider himself so far elevated above the little world in which he is now placed, as to be able to treat any portion of it with contempt. Or, perchance, like one perched upon a lofty eminence, he is unable to distinguish the just proportions of those below, where all appears to his vision too diminutive for comparison. This may be so. But he should recollect that he is not now in a petty West Indian island, where education and morality are little known. Here, at all events, he will daily meet with his equals in social standing, and his superiors in ability and education. And these, we can tell him, are people who will not suffer him to treat them with contempt. If indeed it be his desire to establish a large party, favourable to his Government, by the liberality of his invitations—if he be only anxious to break through the absurd provincial pride which is but too prevalent amongst us, he ought to adopt some other course than the one which he has taken. He ought to patronise worth and honesty and merit, rather than the successful profligacy which he has selected for commendation. We do not consider ourselves to be in any way cruel or unkind in desiring the exclusion of those females, who have violated the laws of morality, from society. We are ready to forgive their transgressions and forget their faults, to look with pity and compassion, rather than with hatred and contempt, upon their errors and frailties, and instead of wishing to pursue them with vindictive punishment, we would rather rather say to them, "Go and sin no more." But we would not allow them to associate with those who had never fallen—we would preserve our wives and daughters safe from the contagion which they might spread. These considerations, however, in no way influence the proceedings of Sir Charles Fitz Roy. He may say with the Roman satirist :—

> Nam vexant limen et ipsi
> Nobiscum. Da Prætori, da deinde Tribuno.
> Sed libertinus prior est: prior inquit, ego adsum.

Society is no longer pure—the most profligate now jostle the most virtuous, and those who have lost all character take precedence. In the days of Charles the Second and his concubines, this might have passed without much comment or observation. Nell Gwynne and Barbara Villiers and the Duchess of Portsmouth might appear at Whitehall and Windsor Castle without outraging the feelings of the noble dames with whom they mingled. In England—in great and virtuous England, however,—these times and practices have long since passed—two centuries have almost swept away the memory of those disgraceful scenes, and the principal actors have long since returned to the dust from which they sprung: but though the mortal part of Charles the Second and Barbara Villiers has perished—though the example which they set in the courtly palaces of our parent land, now finds no imitation there—their spirit, we regret to say, still exists in this remote corner of the world, in the person of their inglorious descendant.

The following article on *Dr. Leichhardt* affords another specimen of the writer's powers, in a different style. It may be mentioned that Mr. Martin was 26 years old when he was editing the *Atlas* :—

The return of this bold and indefatigable traveller, after having fully succeeded in accomplishing the object of his expedition, is one of the most gratifying facts that we have ever been called upon to record. It is no less pleasing than it was unexpected. When, on the 13th October, 1844, he left the last station on the Darling Downs with nine other persons, having with him only sixteen head of cattle, seventeen horses, and four kangaroo dogs, with a small supply of flour, tea, and sugar, his expedition was looked upon by many people as almost hopeless. The smallness of the party, the inefficient manner in which it was equipped, and the great length and supposed difficulty of the country to be traversed, were looked upon as insuperable obstacles in the way of success. Some few weeks after the return of Mr. Hodgson, vague rumours were circulated that the whole of the party had been destroyed by the blacks, and these rumours had so great an appearance of truth that an expedition was equipped, at some expense, to proceed on Dr. Leichhardt's track and ascertain his fate. That expedition returned without having met with any traces of his destruction, but still the general opinion was that the travellers had been murdered by the aborigines. The return of the Doctor was still looked upon as a thing beyond the range of probability, and a touching and beautiful funeral dirge was written by one of his friends, and set to music, no less beautiful, by another. In all circles he was beginning to be forgotten, otherwise than as one of the martyrs in the cause of science and discovery. As a living being he had passed away from the public mind. But, to the surprise and joy of everybody, while the plaintive melody in which his supposed fate was commemorated was resounding through our drawing-rooms, and calling forth from time to time a transient feeling of regret, he returned in health and vigour to contradict the friend who had consigned him to a solitary tomb in the wilderness, and to furnish the world with another memorable example of what human energy and ability are able to accomplish. In the brief and hastily written journal which he has been able to place before the public, we find nothing stated as to the hardships which he and his party must necessarily have endured. On this point his modesty has made him silent. But it is not difficult to imagine what must have been the sufferings of these travellers in their long journey of nearly 3000 miles, through the lonely wilds of this continent, during a period of fourteen months, living nearly all that time on sun-dried beef or such game as accident threw in their way. The Doctor says that they lived *well* upon this description of diet, but we must, while according him all praise for surmounting such difficulties as these, take the liberty of doubting the entire truth of this particular statement. Very little mention of the blacks is made in the journal, and we therefore presume that the Doctor's intercourse with them was not frequent. It does however seem wonderful that he could, with his small party, have traversed so vast an extent of country without having more than once fallen into collision with the aborigines. Wherever he met with them it appears that he entered into friendly intercourse with them, and procured their assistance instead of provoking or inciting their hostility. The nature of the country, and the exact direction of his route, cannot be sufficiently known until the full account of his adventurous journey is laid before the public. Enough however has been already disclosed to convince us that there is in this continent an immense tract of land in every way adapted for the purposes of civilised man. The interior of course is still unknown to us, as Dr. Leichhardt's route lay all along within a comparatively short distance of the coast. Whether the rivers which he passed over rise far in the interior, and whether they are navigable, and to what extent, he does not in his published journal tell us. He may, however, give us more ample information on this point hereafter. When we contrast the triumphant success of this expedition with the signal failure of that conducted by Captain Sturt, the superior ability, and perhaps the superior fortune of Dr. Leichhardt, at once become very conspicuous. With a large and well-appointed party, fitted out at an expense of £5000, Captain Sturt set out on his journey of discovery, and returned baffled and disappointed, without having accomplished any one beneficial object, or in any material degree added to our previous knowledge of the country. Dr. Leichhardt, on the contrary, with seven persons only, and without either flour, or any provisions other than his sun-dried beef, succeeded, in the short space of fourteen months, in reaching his original point of destination at Port Essington, and by that means acquiring a knowledge of the country which intervenes between that place and this colony. Whether Sir Thomas Mitchell will meet with equal success it is impossible to conjecture, though the well-known ability of that gentleman as an explorer, would lead us to anticipate the happiest results. Being better provided with the means of traversing the wilderness than Dr. Leichhardt was, the knowledge which he may acquire may be more extensive, but in a mountainous country, destitute of water, his baggage may be a hindrance instead of an advantage to him. It is to this absence of the *impedimenta* usually judged necessary for a regular exploring expedition, that Dr. Leichhardt owes much of his success, for baggage could not have been transported over many of the places which he had to traverse. The adventuring on such a journey, however, without this baggage, serves to render the Doctor's merits more conspicuous, inasmuch as his dangers and his hardships were thereby indefinitely augmented. The task which he has now successfully accomplished entitles him to be ranked amongst the most distinguished travellers—to occupy a niche in the Temple of Fame beside Ledyard and Mungo Park. The same spirit which led the latter to penetrate to the banks of the Niger, and induced the former to cross the inhospitable regions of Siberia, with a view of traversing the American Continent, with no other arms than his hatchet, impelled Dr. Leichhardt to undertake the hazardous expedition from which he has just returned with such triumphant success. It now remains for the people of this colony to show that they estimate the distinguished services of this gentleman as they deserve—that however great may be our apathy in other respects, we are yet prepared to render due honour to one who has risked so much to extend the knowledge and enlarge the happiness of his species. With small means, and in the face of fearful dangers and privations, this scientific foreigner has done a great public service to this colony—and the honour of the colony requires that that service should be adequately acknowledged. Our Legislative Council will, we have no doubt, do its duty on this occasion, and the Executive, we should hope, will not be backward in co-operating with it—but on the people at large does it in an especial degree devolve, promptly, handsomely, and in a spirit of generous liberality, to unite in presenting those pioneers of the wilderness with a reward worthy of the wealth and standing of the country, and of the great merits of those to whom that reward is to be presented. It has ever been characteristic of the British Nation to honour those who have conferred services on the public, of whatever creed or country they may be—let us now show that in our hands the national character is worthily and honourably maintained—and let not Dr. Leichhardt leave our shores without having been first convinced, that the high respect for heroic daring in the cause of science, and that liberality in rewarding it, for which our parent-land is conspicuous, are also to be met with in equal force in this remote corner of the Empire.

Three years ago, at a time when bushranging seemed a triumphant and established curse among us, a criminal trial occurred which gave rise to much angry comment upon the administration of the law. This was the trial of the Escort Robbers. Three or four young men concerned in a murderous attack upon the Escort were brought to trial, and convictions were obtained against them. The evidence for the prosecution was mainly that of an accomplice, and as this evidence was not supported by unimpeachable testimony, it was argued that the convictions obtained by its means were not in accordance with English practice. The daily papers were full of letters and leading articles on the subject—petitions were addressed to the Executive Council and the Governor in favour of the prisoners—and the impending execution was openly denounced as a murder. At this crisis in public feeling, Mr. Martin addressed an elaborate argument on the subject to the Governor, and published it in the leading journal. It concluded in the following terms:—

A large number of persons, I understand, including some, if not all, of your constitutional advisers, are of opinion that, notwithstanding any irregularities or illegalities in the trials, the public security requires that now that there is a chance of making an example, the example should be made. If any such mistaken policy should be adopted, it will be the surest indication of our falling away from the standard of British law. It is only in revolutionary, semi-barbarous, or unsettled times, that criminals are offered, not in vindication of the laws, but as a sacrifice. If one irregularity is to be overlooked because of the presumed guilt of the party implicated, then why not ten? —why not a hundred? Once admit the propriety of so overlooking an irregularity in any case, and that precedent will justify the same course in every other. The security which the law has cast around every one, by requiring guilt to be made manifest according to certain known and inflexible rules, will be shattered to atoms. An illegality intended to touch the guilty only, may at any time be applied with equal force to the oppression of the innocent, and Law, the proud distinction of all orderly and civilised societies, will cease to exist.

For these reasons, I trust that your Excellency will again consider the case of the men now under sentence of death, and whose fate depends upon you, and you alone. Your Executive Council may advise, but if their advice does not correspond with your deliberate conviction, you will betray your trust, and commit a great crime if you do not disregard it. In this matter of life and death you cannot, in accordance with your duty, allow any one to lead you to act against your own individual and deliberate opinion.

The prisoner Manns, against whom there was corroborative evidence, who was not tried at the first trial, and who in open court expressed a wish to plead guilty, stands undoubtedly in a different position from that of the other prisoners. His execution would violate no rule of law or practice, but it will scarcely satisfy the public mind that he alone, who may be thought not more clearly guilty, in point of fact, than the others, should be the only one to suffer. The law knows nothing of vengeance any more than sacrifice. The object of punishment is to deter from crime. Will that object be more successfully accomplished by the hanging of Manns than by his imprisonment for life? There can be no reason for supposing so : while, if he be executed alone of all those who were tried, the public sympathy for his fate will go a long way to mar the good which the extreme punishment might be expected to accomplish. The offence, too, is one for which I believe no one has for many years been executed in England, and by law the judge might have directed sentence of death to be recorded. Considering the hard and irregular way in which the case has been pressed against all the prisoners, and the ill effect which the execution of one only must necessarily have with the great body of the public, who will be unable to understand the distinction between the case of Manns and that of the other prisoner Bow, it will, I feel assured, be more in accordance with substantial justice to deal with both prisoners alike ; and above all, to let the whole world understand that here, amidst all our democratic irregularities and mistakes, the fate of the meanest or most atrocious criminal is treated in that spirit of calm impartiality which deals at all times, under all circumstances, and with all individuals alike, and allows no feeling of hate or vengeance or terror to influence, in the remotest way, that even course of justice which should be tempered with mercy, never more than when the people, or any portion of them, are seeking for a victim.

This is the noblest protest against an Executive blunder ever uttered by a public man in this colony. Although couched in language "worthy of a Somers or a D'Agesseau," it was, unfortunately, without effect, and the writer's prediction was more than verified. Manns was executed, not only in defiance of this protest, but in defiance of public feeling; and the circumstances attending his execution were such as to excite horror throughout the community. A more painful miscarriage of justice than that which occurred in the case of the Escort Robbers, has seldom occurred in any country.

In June, 1862, took place the inauguration of Mr. Wentworth's statue. It was a public ceremony. A large number of people was assembled in the Hall of the University, and Mr. Martin was called upon to pronounce an address on the occasion. He gave a concise account of Mr. Wentworth's services to his native country, and concluded thus:

> The next and the last of his public acts that I shall on this occasion advert to, is the establishment of the Sydney University. With that noble institution his name is for ever associated as its founder. Whatever may be the fate of our political institutions, how great so ever may be their vicissitudes, here, at all events, is an institution likely to endure. Allied exclusively with no single form of religious faith, its doors are open, with a wide and comprehensive liberality, to the members of every creed, class, and condition; and within its portals success is to be achieved only by the most deserving. Within these walls, wealth, fortune, pedigree, are of no account. Elsewhere eminence may be reached by a thousand devious ways—the warrior may be the favourite of a court;. the statesman may be the tool of a faction—but here, there is but one road to renown, and that road, with the most democratic equality, is open to the lowliest as fully as to the proudest amongst us. To the elevating and ennobling influence of such an institution no limits can be set. Hitherward, in future times, will turn the steps of those who feel the promptings of a generous ambition. Conquerors in the realms of mind, they will go forth into the world, vivifying the dull elements around them, and arousing, as by an electric shock, the sons of toil and trade and commerce to a conception of the true glories of the Universe. To the man who, in this early stage of our history, placed these splendid opportunities within our reach, it cannot be thought remarkable, even if he had done nothing more, that the honour of a public statue should be offered. Accordingly, eight years ago, his friends, comprising not only those who had witnessed but some also who had aided him in his labours, met together on the eve of his departure from the colony for a time, and determined that, in acknowledgment of his many services, that honour should be conferred upon him. The announcement was made at the moment of his embarkation amidst the cheers of his friends, and the disapprobation of

a few who regarded him as an enemy to the country. He who had done so much for the people, and had so often been greeted with their loudest huzzas, had before that encountered their hootings and revilings; but no one knew better than he did the inconstancy of popular favour. But, although they break their idols as often as they make them, the people in the long run learn to do justice to their benefactors, and Mr. Wentworth has enjoyed the singular good fortune of living to see conferred on him an honour which is usually witnessed only by a man's posterity, and to see it conferred with the assent and amidst the applause, not only of those who have ever been his friends, but of those who were amongst the most bitter of his opponents. He has outlived the envy, hatred, and malignity which inevitably cross the path of every man who becomes eminent in public life; and now, in his green old age, with his mind still clear, and his faculties still unclouded, he has been allowed a foretaste of the posthumous renown which awaits him. The memorial which we have raised to commemorate his services, is suggested by the graceful practice of classic times. It is a memorial which cannot be raised without the aid of Art in its highest form, and one which preserves, as long as the frailty of all things human will permit, the image, the face and aspect of those whom the world would not willingly let die. It is erected in this noble Hall, where he himself desired to see it placed; and surely no more appropriate site for it could be found. Here, under this magnificent roof, where gilded ornaments, elaborate tracery, and painted windows carry us back to the dawn of a purer Literature than that of ancient times, and of an Art applied to holier and better purposes than of old, we feel conscious of a link which unites us to the past and to the future; and we flatter ourselves that there is something akin to immortality in fame. Enclosed and overshadowed by this his noblest monument, let us hope that his statue will remain, for ages to come, not only as a memorial of great public merit, appropriately awarded, but as a perpetual incentive to honourable ambition.

In January, 1865, Mr. Martin wrote and published a lengthy address to the electors of various constituencies with which he was politically connected. He was then Premier and Attorney-General, but his administration was not popular, and was soon after brought to an end on a cry of free trade. In the course of this address he alluded to the most prominent political topics of the day, and sought to justify the policy which he had adopted. No one who is free from political prejudice can read it without admiration; it is a manly and eloquent vindication of his public acts.

In the following passage he reviewed the course of political affairs since the introduction of Responsible Government:

> When, eight years ago, responsible Government was conceded to us, the concession found us without party organization of any kind. There were the partizans of the old nominee Government, and there were the opponents of that Government, and that was all. Administrations were formed, not by the leaders of great sections of the people who held certain principles in common, and were bound together by the usual party ties, but by such accidental combinations as might appear to be able to command a majority in the Legislature. The Donaldson, the Cowper, the Parker administrations were thus constituted, and this state of things continued until the era of free selection. Free selection, as everybody knows, was carried under the auspices of Mr. Cowper, who had always opposed it until he saw that it was inevitable, and who never was at at any time a believer in its virtues. But it was (as it might well be expected to be) a most popular cry, and on the strength of that cry a singular legislative body was called into existence. I am sure that I shall not be considered as overstepping the limits of truth when I say that the persons then elected were not fair average samples of the wealth, intelligence, or respectability of the country. With their advent the floodgates of corruption were thrown wide open. Votes were bartered, seats were bought and sold, high patriots were purchased for low bribes, the magistracy was degraded, sinecures were created, useless offices established, the most profligate expenditure was indulged in with the most imperfect means for ensuring efficiency or preventing fraud, electioneering and parliamentary hacks of the most contemptible kind were thrust into important appointments, and in every way, so far as the Legislature and the Government—which was the faithful reflex of the Legislature—could accomplish it, the public administration was degraded. From such a Government, supported by such a Legislature, no statesmanship could be expected. Corruption and incapacity went hand in hand, until at length the imminent bankruptcy of the public finances brought about a change of Ministers.

Alluding to the necessity for cultivating our internal resources, he said :

> I thought then, and I think now, that this most magnificent territory, teeming with the elements of every kind of wealth,—mineral, pastoral, agricultural—was intended for other purposes than a sheep walk, like a vast Asiatic steppe, or a mere commercial emporium, like some small city of the middle ages. With a territory larger than the greatest European kingdom, and a population no greater than a sixth-rate European town, I thought that there was an ample field to which the starving thousands of the mother country might be

removed—to the great relief of that country—to the great advantage of this.
I knew that the skilled artizan of Britain could not be honestly asked to come
to a country where the necessaries of life were dear, and the articles in the
manufacture of which he was an adept were imported at a price with which he
could not compete ; and I felt that his position was not mended by the opportunity afforded of taking his wife and children to some remote gunyah on the
Namoi or the Darling, or settling down on some alluvial patch, the fruits of which
might, at any time, be reduced in price below the cost of their production by
imports from foreign countries. There is a limit to the number of shepherds
and bullock drivers, dock labourers, porters, warehousemen, and mercantile
clerks, that are required, and there are many other occupations equally desirable
and equally ennobling. I knew that the greatness of England arose not from
commerce, not from manufactures, not from agriculture alone—but from all
combined. By the opportunities which a wise legislation afforded for every
kind of industry and enterprise, those small islands became the habitation of
the greatest and the wealthiest people on the globe. The coal, the iron, the
copper, the lead, the wool, the fertile soil, which constitute the foundation of
England's greatness, are here as well as there, and in a larger measure ; but
while the British Islands support their thirty millions, this colony is unable to
maintain in comfort four hundred thousand. I knew that such a state of things
was most unnatural. I knew that, however lucrative it might be to supply
cotton silks to the nobility of the Sandwich Islands, and shoddy cloth and
Brummagem rubbish of all kinds to the simple savages of Oceanica, but a very
small number could participate in those advantages. We might by trade of
that kind constitute a rude, barbaric, bastard sort of Antipodean Venice, with
nothing of the greatness or grandeur of its prototype ; but we could never by
those means reproduce here a manly, vigorous, numerous British population.
I wished to see this country largely peopled with such a population. And
with that object I strove rather that every one should be comfortable than that
a few should be rich—that there should be fair scope for every man to follow
himself, or to bring up his children to, that pursuit to which his judgment or
his fancy inclined him ; and that no man should be found starving in a land of
plenty, or begging, and begging in vain,

> A brother of the earth
> To give him leave to toil.

Certain unpleasant particulars in our social history were thus
referred to :

For myself I am in no way solicitous as to the fate which may attend the
Government of which I am a member. I have sustained much loss, much
annoyance, much inconvenience by my tenure of power. I look upon office as a
means not of livelihood, but of conferring great services upon my fellow-citizens.
For years past the true functions of the Government in this country have been

utterly disregarded. In a degrading squabble for the acquisition or the retention of office, the true interests of the country have been overlooked. With a boundless territory and a small population—not the fiftieth part of what the country is capable of maintaining—we have had, and still have, an amount of distress and of crime which is positively disgraceful. In a country and with such a population as ours, distress and crime ought to be reduced to a minimum. I make every allowance for the improvidence and vice which will be found more or less in every community, but I cannot account for the deplorable state of the country except by some perverseness or want of foresight in our legislation. I am not now referring to protection. I leave that to a more fitting opportunity, and to that not far distant period when it will force itself upon men of thought, and through them upon the masses. But I speak of the absence of any real or substantial effort to afford assistance to those who are unable to assist themselves. Year by year, hundreds of children of both sexes are growing up, uninstructed and uncared for, with scanty clothing, insufficient food, and miserable shelter, surrounded from the first dawning of reason to manhood with scenes the most revolting and companions the most vicious and degraded ; and the Government has never yet been in a position to stretch out a helping hand to rescue these poor creatures from the doom that inevitably awaits them. The private beneficence of individuals has done something to grapple with this gigantic evil. We have ragged schools and asylums for the destitute, but they are utterly unequal to the full performance of the noble task, which it is their object to accomplish. It is in dealing with evils such as these—instead of agitating for changes in the constitution, and lauding with drunken and insensate clamour vote by ballot and universal suffrage—that our legislators would find the best field for the gratification of their ambition, and reap their richest reward. To duties such as these, our loud-mouthed patriots have never yet directed their attention, but have rather devoted their energies to the injury or degradation of the wealthier, than to the protection and elevation of the poorer, classes of the community.

The conclusion was as follows :

For these and other objects connected with the development of our resources, and the ameliorating the condition of our people, it is worth the while of those who wish the country well, to undergo much labour, receive much obloquy, and make many sacrifices. If I could see my way to their accomplishment, I would be content still to encounter an opposition more wearying than any I have yet experienced. The "friends of the poor man"—in other words, the most ignorant, worthless, self-seeking, and dishonest of our demagogues—have made it a part of their vocation at all times to stigmatise me as an enemy to the working classes. If to have ever been desirous to promote the welfare of the people constitutes me their enemy, then these demagogues have rightly described me. I know no nobler task to which any man can devote his attention than the task of diminishing the distress, augmenting the employment, extending the comfort, and promoting the contentment of those who constitute the great bulk of the community. . I have never been their flatterer,—I have often been their servant. I know as well as any man their prejudices and their infirmities, and I have had as large an experience of their enmity as of their favour. But I hope I never shall forget that they constitute the bone and sinew of the country, and that in the proportion in which they are prosperous so will the country become great. "The mob," says Victor Hugo, "is the human race in misery. The mob is the mournful commencement of the people. The mob is the great victim of darkness: Sacrifice to it! Sacrifice thyself! Let thyself be hunted; let thyself be exiled. Sacrifice to it thy gold, and thy blood, which is more than thy gold, and thy thought, which is more than thy blood, and thy love, which is more than thy thought; sacrifice to it everything except justice. Receive its complaint—listen to its faults and the faults of others. Listen to what it has to confess, and to denounce to thee. Stretch forth to it the ear, the hand, the arm, the heart. Do everything for it excepting evil. Alas! it suffers so much and it knows nothing. Correct it, warn it, instruct it, guide it. Put it to the school of honesty. Make it spell truth, teach it to read virtue, probity, mercy, generosity. Hold thy book wide open." I desire to act at all times in accordance, as far as I can, with the principles here so eloquently expressed. I wish to see our legislators turn their attention to real reforms, which have a direct influence upon the condition of the people. I wish to see the people better housed, better clothed, better taught, and better fed. I wish to see crime checked in the bud, and where it cannot be so checked I wish to see it promptly punished when fully developed. I wish to see all enjoy equal rights and equal security. I wish to see a gradual elevation of the poor, and not a rapid degradation of the wealthy. I wish to remove all causes of enmity and misunderstanding between those who are prosperous and those who are not. And, above all, I wish to see the affairs of legislation and government in the hands of men, who, by character, intellect, temperament, and culture, are not unworthy of such a trust; who will neither truckle nor domineer, who will do what they conceive to be right, regardless of consequences—and to whom office can hold out no attractions nor give any gratification one moment longer than it affords the means of conferring benefits upon the country.

Without possessing any distinctly literary faculty, Mr. Martin has all the qualifications of a clear, vigorous, and eloquent writer. His compositions are evidently those of a man who has studied oratory. We seem to hear them rather than to read them. They are suggestive of loud tones, flashing eyes, and animated gestures,—with an excited audience in front, and busy reporters in the gallery. This, perhaps, is unavoidable in the case of a man whose life has been almost spent in speaking. Mr. Martin has never written a line of verse, and with the exception of a few essays published in his youth, has made no attempt in literature, except as allied with politics. It is in what might be called the "State Paper" department of Literature that his intellect is qualified to shine. It is decidedly practical in its tendencies. Eminently fitted for legal discussions as well as political debate, he has capacity enough for much higher questions than either politics or law generally give rise to. In constitutional law, in political and in economical science, he has given abundant proof of his powers—not only in the familiarity he has displayed with the greatest writers on those subjects, but in the arguments he has brought to bear upon them. Evidence on these points may be found in his speeches.* It is enough to say that the range of his attainments is incomparably greater than is usually found either in lawyers or politicians : and that this, united as it is with great intellectual powers directed to unselfish aims, would make him a distinguished man in far higher society than that in which he moves at present.

Mr. Martin was Premier and Attorney-General in 1863, and holds those offices at the present time.

HENRY PARKES.

HENRY PARKES was born in England in 1815, and arrived in this colony in 1839. The death of his father at an early period in his life threw him on his own resources. Without friends and almost without education, he was compelled to earn his living by manual labour. During his stay in England he suffered much privation,—his life being a perpetual wrestle with poverty. For some time after his arrival here, his circumstances were hardly bettered. He obtained employment in some industrial establishments, and afterwards became a Custom house officer. This appointment he did not hold long. A letter appeared in a certain newspaper exposing some malpractices in his department. It became known that he was the writer, and he was immediately suspended. He soon after sent in his resignation, and then established himself in a shop. In 1850 he commenced the publication of the *Empire*, and carried it on for seven years. At the time of its appearance there was but one daily journal in the colony, which, so far as political theories were concerned, was in opposition to an immense majority of the population. This majority, powerful as it was in one way, was exceedingly helpless in another. It had no recognized organ calculated to exercise the slightest influence on the course of legislation; and at that time legislation was in the hands of a body which did not altogether possess the confidence of the people. The establishment of the

Empire worked a revolution in the political existence of the colony,—just as the establishment of the *Australian* worked a revolution twenty years ago. Whether we regard the difficulties encountered in this enterprise, or the results accomplished by it, it may be said without exaggeration that he could scarcely have devoted himself to a nobler or more arduous task. Few indeed can form any adequate conception of the difficulties, although every one may form his own opinion as to the results. Mr. Parkes was without capital when he began his career as a journalist, and no speculation depends more upon capital for its success than a daily newspaper. Competition between two papers merely raises a question as to which has the most money. The paper which gives the earliest and fullest intelligence—or which, in other words, best meets the requirements of a commercial community,—is sure to have the largest circulation. But intelligence cannot be procured without a lavish expenditure of money. The endeavour to overcome this difficulty involved Mr. Parkes in still greater difficulties; and at last, when the *Empire* had apparently secured its prosperity—when its circulation as well as its political influence was largely increasing—the proprietor was compelled to abandon it. During its existence under his management, it was decidedly one of the best papers out of England. It was well printed, well written, and well edited. Perhaps no man was better qualified for the duties of an editor than Mr. Parkes. An editor, properly so called, does not mean a man who writes leading articles, but one whose business it is to direct the literary management of a paper. He makes himself acquainted with the events, political and other, of the day—decides what particular subjects shall be treated in the next issue, and assigns to each contributor his particular task. It is obvious that there is no other manner in which an important daily paper can be properly carried on. Here, however, the practice is different, and the result is of course prejudicial to the character of our Press. Mr. Parkes understood the *rationale* of journalism better than any other journalist in the colony, and endeavoured to carry it out so far as circumstances permitted. He could not command the services of an efficient staff, but he numbered some of the ablest men in the country among his contributors. Among others, there were Mr. Martin, Mr. Forster, Mr. Deniehy, Sir Thomas Mitchell, Mr. Evelyn, and Mr. Butler. He himself was a very frequent contributor.

It is interesting at the present time, when so much distress exists among the working classes, to refer to a Parliamentary Paper on that subject, published six or seven years ago. Mr. Parkes had moved for a Select Committee to enquire into "the condition of the working classes" in Sydney. The matter was investigated thoroughly; startling facts were brought to light; and an exceedingly able Report was drawn up by Mr. Parkes. This is one of the many proofs afforded by that gentleman of his ability to deal with topics generally shirked by politicians. In the scuffle of political life, matters of vital importance to the social progress of the people are rarely attended to; but these are the subjects to which Mr. Parkes has especially devoted his attention: and it is not too much to say that more has been done—or at least attempted to be done—by him, in the cause of social science, than by any other politician amongst us. As regards his capacity as a writer, the following extracts from the Report in question will furnish satisfactory evidence.

The general facts of the case are thus put:

> A large number of persons belonging to the working classes are at present, and have been for some time past, suffering much distress from want of employment. In too many instances this is attributable to intemperance or improvidence on the part of the sufferers; but, supposing these cases to be undeserving of or beyond relief, there are still left several distinct forms of distress, arising from want of employment, which cannot be so easily explained, and ought not to be found in a well-ordered and progressive state of society. As might be expected in so large a city as Sydney—the principal seaport of a new country—there are many persons of better education and social habits, who are reduced to much suffering for want of any kind of employment for which they are fitted, and who make their distress the more severe by their struggles to conceal it.

And of this class there appear to be competent clerks and accountants, who cannot obtain situations. Since the discovery of gold, the unsettled courses of many working men, and their frequent absences from home, seeking their fortunes at the diggings, have left numbers of women and families in Sydney without protection or any regular means of subsistence, and the consequence is a large amount of destitution and misery. Still more unfortunately, we find that there are many men, both mechanics and labourers, of good character and sober habits, able and willing to work for their "daily bread," who, nevertheless, cannot obtain employment. There seems to be among those who have resided for any length of time in the city a feeling of unwillingness to accept employment as labourers in the country, which is not accounted for by some of the witnesses, and is variously accounted for by others. Some raise objections because there are no schools for their children; others have heard unfavourable reports from the interior and are apprehensive of ill-treatment; and others again prefer the cheap and ever present enjoyments of the town to any advantages that are remote and contingent. It is also shewn that some men will not accept reduced wages even when expressing their anxiety to obtain work; but the refusal appears to be dictated by the fear of permanently injuring their class by the reduction, and a feeling that they would not be more secure of future employment themselves if the lower rates were submitted to. But in the face of this evidence there is the fact that wages have greatly receded—in some cases to about one-third of former rates—during the last few years; and it is admitted on one hand that neither the desire to keep up the present standard nor the feeling of reluctance to leave Sydney operates in all cases, while on the other the prevalence of such feelings is strongly denied.

Facts are then given as to the actual amount of suffering among the unemployed. Upwards of 3,000 persons were in a state of destitution. The Report proceeds to point out the various features of the prevalent suffering; and in the first place, it dwells upon the miserable character of the house accommodation provided for the working classes. This is an evil which has not since been mitigated in the slightest degree.

The house accommodation of the working classes of Sydney is admitted on all hands to be deplorably bad; even in the more recently erected dwellings the means of drainage and ventilation are almost entirely neglected, and many of the older tenements are so unfit for the occupation of human beings, that one witness declares them to be "past remedy without a general fire." The suburbs to a great extent are as unhappily situated as the city; in both cases, one general description of the lowest class of houses is applicable. A block of twenty or twenty-five wretched hovels affords shelter for perhaps a hundred human beings. The rooms, two in number, are ten or eleven feet square, and scarcely high enough for a man to stand erect; the floor is lower than the ground outside; the rain comes in through the roof, and filth of all kinds washes in at the door; the court or yard, that is common to all, is covered with pollution that must be endured by all; and, inside and out, everything is an object of disgust, and wears a look of loathsomeness that would terrify men away, if it were possible to meet with its resemblance not familiarised to their senses through being created by themselves. In smaller groups there is no provision for greater comfort. The houses are constructed as if they were not intended for homes; and, strange as it may appear, nothing has been gained by experience, except in a very limited degree, to lead persons in occupying new ground, to make better provision for health, cleanliness, and comfort. In many parts of Woolloomooloo, which have been built over during the last fifteen or twenty years, there are narrow lanes of houses with all the evils inseparable from improvident construction, insufficient living room, confined space outside, and want of drainage, in forms as aggravated as in the old cities of Europe. Nor does it appear that any of the superior contrivances for domestic convenience, such as indoor sinks, fitted pantries, suitable stoves, and clothes' closets, which are so great a comfort to the humble housewife in England—have been generally introduced into the better class of working men's houses, which, it is gratifying to learn, have been lately erected in some parts of the city.

The buildings, originally so ill-adapted for human habitations, are rendered still more unhealthy and wretched—in frequent cases to a degree perfectly frightful—by the general system of over-crowding which has been induced by high rents. Some cases that are stated in detail, it is hoped, may be considered abnormal even in the condition of social life described. A den of two rooms is occupied by seven men and seven women; seventy human beings are found herded together in a common lodging-house of six rooms; and no fewer than 315 Chinamen are lodged in one building. Leaving the haunts of vice and promiscuous association, still we cannot leave behind us the types of similar misery and disease. Necessity often forces honest and striving families into dwelling-places so inadequate to their wants that their jostled and overloaded existence may be supposed to be lightened only by their higher range of moral qualities. The instances appear to be few where one of these miserable tenements is allotted to the exclusive use of one family. The consequences of this state of things to the moral and physical well-being of the inhabitant is forcibly stated by two of the medical witnesses. "The want of proper accommodation," says Mr. Aaron, "has a direct effect on the moral sense of the occupants, because they are obliged to do everything in public, you may say; and the state of bodily feeling which is induced by the absence of sanitary conditions, no doubt, induces many of these people to resort to intemperance. They sleep in ill-ventilated and over-crowded apartments—get up in the morning, especially in the summer time, unrefreshed, and want something to rouse them. It is not, therefore, to be wondered at that they should go to the public-house for a morning dram." Such is the effect on the hard nature of the men; but there are others—the weaker members of the abject household—who are constantly exposed to the gradual process of human slaughter that is silently going on. This is the evidence of Mr. Roberts : "I should say it would be utterly impossible for a housewife to keep a bad house tidy. When she is placed in such a house she soon ceases to strive to preserve order and cleanliness in her house ; the husband does not care about coming home to his wife ; she becomes careless and neglects her children ; their diet is also neglected, and they are allowed to expose themselves to the sun. This all re-acts, not only upon the health of the man and the woman, but also upon that of the children, and ultimately upon the habits of the people. A large number of the deaths of children arises indirectly from the same cause."

A second ulcer in the body politic is thus alluded to :

The streets of Sydney are infested by a large number of vagrant children, or children entirely neglected by their parents ; and some of the relations of juvenile depravity are appalling and almost incredible. According to the evidence of an intelligent officer of the Metropolitan Police, the traffic in female prostitution has extended its meshes around unhappy children scarcely above the age of infancy, and the closest ties of nature are converted into the bonds of their perdition. Cases of such extreme depravity, it is hoped, are rare even among those precipitated into courses of early wickedness, but it can no longer be doubted that such cases are to be found among the many hideous forms of ignorance, squalor, and sin, that fill some of the lanes and alleys of this wealthy city. Female prostitution itself seems to have increased in undue proportion to the increase of the population during the last few years, and the accelerated increase has been largely fed by the sacrifice of girls of tender years. The vice is fostered by system, and there are wealthy persons who refuse to let their houses, except for its purposes. The number of boys in a vagrant state is variously estimated, and it may be doubted that there are many entirely destitute of home and kindred ; but the evidence abundantly shews that a large class exists to whom the possession of parents is of no value in giving direction to their lives, and who are growing up to be an incumbrance and a curse to society. In the language of one witness, they are "floating about the streets and lanes like fish in a pond." It has not been found practicable to obtain a classified return of these unfortunate children, but it is assumed, from the information collected, that the moral features of their condition which are susceptible of reformation are much the same in all cases.

Your Committee have considered it their duty to present, without softening the deepest colours, the worst features of the disordered state of things, which is fast undermining the social happiness of the community. It is lamentable to discover the darkening mass of physical and moral disease—much of it obviously arising from preventible causes—in a city where the natural aids to beauty and sanitary precaution in its streets and structures, the variety of land and water, and the brilliancy of climate, are all in favour of the largest amount of health and enjoyment; where wealth abounds, and the luxuries and refinements of Europe have been extensively introduced. It would seem, that in the short space of a lifetime we have reproduced all the criminal enormities which have grown up through centuries of ignorance, pestilence, arbitrary government, and civil war in the cities of the old world. But there is another side to the picture: the region of depravity and moral death is limited. The highest calculation numbers our destitute children at one thousand; and that would seem to indicate, though imperfectly, the extent of the worst state of human existence, as these 'pariahs of the streets' must be supposed to belong to the most abandoned classes. These dark features do not belong to the character of the labouring classes of society. The witnesses who have had the best opportunities of forming correct opinions concerning them, concur in assigning to the general body of the working classes in Sydney—the mechanics and others permanently settled as citizens—a high character for honesty, intelligence, and sobriety.

The causes of this misery are next dealt with. From the fact that a still greater amount of distress exists at the present time, it may be inferred that the absence of 'facilities for freehold occupation' is not the chief cause, as stated in the Report.

The diminution of the comforts of life, and the positive distress which prevail among the well-ordered portion of the working population, are attributed to different causes,—but chiefly, and by the greater unison of testimony, to the mal-administration of the public lands. If the land policy of the colony had offered facilities for freehold occupation to the industrious and thrifty, it is contended that the continuous withdrawal of such families from the wages-receiving masses of the city would, by leaving fuller employment to their necessitous fellows, and by creating new demands for labour in their own operations, have obviated much of the evil. This view is taken, alike by witnesses who are thorough free-traders and by those who are decided protectionists, in their opinions on purely fiscal questions. One witness, consistently with his free-trade opinions, traces the mischief in part to the "Government tampering with the labour market," or, in other words, supporting immigration from the public treasury, and maintains that the law of supply and demand in regulating labour, as in all other things, would work most healthily by being left entirely to itself. In answer to what he terms the "spasmodic demands" for labour in particular localities, he says, if the want was real, "immediately men found there was something worth coming for, they would come. Others consider that nearly all the social derangement has been produced by the operation of the principles that regulate our trading intercourse with other

J

countries, and argue that the only effectual remedy would be the imposition of protective duties, to foster our infant manufactures, and to sustain a remunerative market for our agriculturists against foreign competition. In support of these views they point to our perished manufactures of cloth, cordage, nails, pottery, and tobacco, and to our farmers unable to obtain for their wheat and potatoes the cost of carriage.

In respect to the evil of intemperance, which extensively aggravates the prevailing distress, Mr. Justice Wise and other witnesses, who appear to have bestowed much study on social subjects, consider it frequently rather the effect than the cause of the discomfort and misery in the houses of the poor. The remedies they suggest are increased means of public education, greater sanitary provisions for the regulation of buildings, more rational modes of popular recreation, and more active sympathy in the intercourse of classes. But your Committee cannot resist the conviction that intemperance has been a prolific instrumentality in producing the distress complained of, and they are of opinion that the present licensing system requires complete revision. The subject, however, is so vast, and involves so many subordinate questions, that they consider it should be referred for further inquiry.

The connection of cause and effect is in some measure to be traced between the fiscal laws of the colony and the existing social evils, and a revision of our entire taxation is a matter of necessity. We have the authority of eminent economists in support of raising revenue in a new country by the imposition of duties that would tend to foster manufacturing enterprise, and such encouragement to our own people, within well considered limits, would not be inconsistent with practical freedom in our commercial intercourse with the world, while no nation affords us an example of the establishment of manufactures without such encouragement. But it is respectfully submitted that we are not to follow blindly the course of other countries, but to be guided in our economical arrangements by such principles as are most applicable in the peculiar circumstances of our own. An original thinker in the department of Political Economy observes, even of the Mother Country:—"England, I say it with regret, but without the very slightest hesitation, is not to be taken as a safe specimen of the career of a people developing their productive forces. Untoward events have dogged the progress of the nation; some connected with faults of legislation and administration; some arising out of circumstances over which neither legislators nor administrators exercised any influence, and which escaped perhaps any timely attempt to control them, because the annals of the world gave no warning of them, and afforded no opportunity of observing them elsewhere. If this suggest many regrets for the past, it still gives better hopes for the future. The evil that has mingled with our institutions or our habits, may be weeded out; the good influences we have missed may still be won to purify and protect us, and other nations, if they assume our economical organization and power, may escape many of the evils that have afflicted our progress, or from which we suffer now." The spirit of these reflections should be infused into any efforts to improve our institutions and laws, if we are to make the best of the resources placed at our disposal.

Various suggestions for dealing with these social evils are then thrown out:

The improvement of the dwellings of the working classes appears to be a matter that admits of no delay, and cannot be over-estimated in importance. Accepting the definition of wealth—to which the expositions of economical science all tend—as the means of human happiness, and regarding the action of good government as directed to its attainment, for all the members of society, it cannot be for a moment questioned that the moral and physical well-being of the greatest number of our households should be an object of the highest public concern. Not in a spirit of false philanthropy, but with an enlightened view of the end of civilization, every danger should be anxiously eradicated which threatens the mental power and bodily vigour of the race. The members of the future nation can never be strong, if the springs of life are suffered to be vitiated. Manly and contented citizens can hardly be expected to rise up from the arms of unhappy and unwomanly mothers. Attachment to the soil is of too delicate growth to receive its nourishment from the desecrations of the family hearth.

Much may be done by legislative measures in mitigation of this evil. No apartment in houses within the city should be allowed to be built under certain dimensions, determined to be necessary for the preservation of health in a close and constantly respired atmosphere, and without sufficient means of ventilation. Blocks of houses should in all cases have adequate outdoor conveniences, including space for the exercise of children. Public baths and washhouses should be established in different parts of the city. Common lodging-houses should be licensed and regulated by law. Some more effective means should be devised for the suppression of the odious traffic in vice which has been described.

If searching improvement could be carried into the homes of the adult population, it is believed that one effect of it would be a decrease of the juvenile destitution found in the streets. But the evil is one pregnant with the most dangerous consequences to society, and should be combated wherever it is met; and your Committee strongly recommend the early establishment of a Reformatory for juvenile delinquents. At present it appears that these young offenders are frequently discharged by the magistrates because there is no place for their confinement except the common gaol, where they would be associated with the adult prisoners, and the knowledge of this among the police often saves them from apprehension. The great success of reformatory establishments in Europe does not leave the question in doubt as to the value of such an experiment here. La Mettray, near Tours, opened by M. De Metz in 1839, and Rauhe Haus, near Hamburgh, founded by Dr. Wichern in 1833, are about the oldest and most celebrated; and the many hundreds of young profligates who have passed through those establishments have, with few exceptions, been thoroughly reclaimed, and become respectable members of society.

As one means of reclaiming our vagrant children, which at the same time would meet a growing want in the maritime trade of the colony, your Committee recommend the establishment of a Nautical School, separate from other educational institutions, in accordance with the report of a Select Committee of the Legislature in 1854, where boys with a propensity for the sea might be trained in all the arts of seamanship, and apprenticed out under respectable masters.

These observations have not lost their value in the six or seven years that have elapsed since they were penned. They will not lose their value for many years to come. We are still suffering from the evils so emphatically dwelt upon by the writer. The dwellings of the working classes are still built upon the same principles—the streets are still crowded with vagrants—the great vice of modern cities still flourishes in our midst. No attempt to do away with these abominations was made by the Ministry in existence at the time when this Report was presented to Parliament. It is gratifying to record, however, that the matter has not been left out of sight since Mr. Parkes has himself been in office. Among other measures for the improvement of our social condition, an Act for the establishment of a Juvenile Reformatory has been passed. Nothing is more imperatively needed than this. From the prominent manner in which Mr. Parkes has identified himself with these topics, there is reason to believe that more will be done in the shape of social legislation during his tenure of office than has been done during the last ten years.

But Mr. Parkes is a man of letters as well as a social reformer: and the interest he has already displayed in the intellectual advancement of the people will doubtless lead to some practical measures in that behalf. This city is perhaps the only English city of any importance which does not possess a Free Public Library. As yet, we can hardly be said to possess any public Library at all worthy of the name. We have two Circulating Libraries with some 30,000 volumes between them; but it may be doubted whether they do much to assist our mental progress. They certainly feed an appetite for fiction, but they have not the means of cultivating scholarship.

As a prose writer, dealing with topics of practical importance, Mr. Parkes exhibits not only vigour of style, but comprehensive and logical habits of thought. He throws a net round his subject from which nothing of any value can escape. He is not eloquent —he is not imaginative—he is not ornate. Qualities of this kind are not in keeping with those branches of investigation for which nature has fitted him. We do not look for airy flights of fancy in the *Wealth of Nations*, or for subtle imagery and graceful diction in the *Principles of Political Economy*. Mr. Parkes has certainly published two small volumes of poems, but they exhibit the feeling of a poet without an adequate power of expression. He has never been able to master even the trifling difficulties of rhyme, and his versification is consequently as rugged as if it belonged to the sixteenth century. We read of great men amusing their leisure hours with carpenters' tools, and we never imagine that the results of their handiwork displayed much skill. Mr. Parkes has amused himself with iambs and anapæsts instead of saws and chisels.

Mr. Parkes has been a prominent member of the Assembly for some years past. In 1862, he was appointed by the Government to lecture throughout Great Britain on the advantages of this colony as a field for emigration. Soon after his return, he was again elected a Member of Parliament, and is now Colonial Secretary. The biographies of self-taught men rarely exhibit so marked a triumph over difficulties as his.

D. H. DENIEHY.

DANIEL HENRY DENIEHY was born in Sydney, in 1828. When a child, he went with his parents to England, but his stay there was not a long one. On leaving school he was articled to Mr. Stenhouse, and subsequently enrolled as an attorney. He practised a short time in Sydney, and afterwards in Goulburn; but his devotion to literature was too intense to admit of the necessary attention to business, and unfortunately he soon became equally devoted to politics. His first appearance in public life took place in 1853, at a time when the new Constitution Act—framed by Mr. Wentworth, and adopted by the Council—was a subject of absorbing interest. His speeches on this occasion gained him a great reputation for eloquence, and naturally led to his election as a member of the first Representative Assembly. He achieved no success as a politician; and as a man of letters, he has left little behind him to convey a just idea of his extraordinary powers. He contributed to several newspapers; with one, the *Southern Cross*, he was especially identified, and in its columns and in those of the *Freeman's Journal* of eight years ago, we must look for whatever may be worth preserving. It was in the former journal that the most elaborate production of his pen appeared,—a political satire, entitled, *How I became Attorney-General of New Barataria*. As a piece of literary workmanship, no other production of the kind can be said to surpass it.

There has never been any man in this country whose knowledge of books was more extensive than Mr. Deniehy's: and it may be added that there has never been any one who possessed a finer critical capacity. The range of his attainments was not less surprising than the depth and penetration of his criticism. All that was best worth knowing in modern literature was familiar to him, and the zest with which he appreciated it may be judged from the language he employed. The following waifs will give some proof on these points. They are, alas! but the spars scattered on the sea-beach, when the hurricane has subsided and the ship gone down for ever. They cannot do justice to the splendid faculties with which he was endowed: to his power of imagination as well as fancy; to his intense admiration of Beauty, both in Nature and in Art; but they will afford some indication of these qualities, and suggest to critical readers how much might have been accomplished under happier circumstances. Let it be recollected that what is here given was not the result of studious elaboration. These extracts were simply a series of hasty contributions to a newspaper, of so little account in the writer's eyes that he scarcely seems to have taken the trouble of correcting them.

During the years 1857 and 1858, Mr. Deniehy contributed a series of critical papers to the *Freeman's Journal*. The following is one on *The Elder Roscoe and his Poems*:—

Charles the Fifth once caustically remarked, that although Scripture abounded with precepts to pardon our enemies, we were nowhere directed to forgive our friends. How many a distinguished writer, laid for his last long slumber in cathedral marble, or folded in the green rural sod, could he rise again to walk the world's ways, would echo bitterly the imperial *mot!* Enthusiastic executors and legatees empty the waste-paper baskets of departed genius into the compositor's hands, and conceive that they are supplementing the glories of the calm thinker,—so calm *now*, would men leave that little terrene immortality he worked for wisely and won well, but rest as he left it. Unfortunately, these assiduous friends have a passion for publishing in one dangerous direction for the integrity of a great man's fame—that of verse. They seem beyond all things anxious that the world should be benefited by the *nugæ metricæ*, of however doubtful quality, of the illustrious dead. In youth, as experimental efforts, or occasionally as a solace in melancholy hours,—

> Smoothing the raven down of darkness till it smiled,

men with purely the faculty and afterwards the fame of great prose-writers, have written verses—trifles traced to amuse and vanish, like a child's inscription with his father's staff on the moist sands of the retiring sea. The thought that, after their reputation had been built up and they themselves had departed, those attempts would be paraded before the public eye as a claim additional on the remembrance of mankind, would only—and reasonably enough—have horrified them. And who, besides, cares for such an embodiment of the axiom *non omnia possumus omnes*, as the hymns of so grand a prose-writer as Jeremy Taylor, the verses of Burke, or the jingles of poor Gerald Griffin, a master in the province of prose fiction, or the sterile rhymes of women with the wonderful imaginative powers of the sisters Bronte? Indeed, here is a reason, and a philosophical one, why people should care *not* to see them. They go far to impair that ideal of plenary strength which every genial reader finds comfort in cherishing, of a great writer who has taught and purified him. An ideal which is beneficial, too, because it widens belief for the man who feels it in the capabilities of human power. No book has fully done its office that stops with satisfying you as a work of art; it should enrich and exhilarate the spirit, by suggestions flowing from the very fact of the existence of a man who could and did produce it.

A collection of the poems of William Roscoe, the historian, made within the present year, has just reached Australia. Roscoe belonged to an order of modern writers, of which Hallam is the archetype. A class this, with the qualifications of solid learning, clear vigorous understanding, and an honest purpose to find out and tell what it believes to be true. We have every respect for this class—the *positif* of literature, and every recognition of its value. But it altogether wants the philosophical and imaginative endowments which this age (so loudly abused as "shallow") more than any preceding era, severely exacts in those who pretend to teach it. Within the range of facts, and in judgments upon facts, they can be pretty safely trusted. But in matters perceptible only by loftier and subtler faculties—such, for instance, as the *sociological* value of the Christian institution of a sisterhood of virgins, as giving a basis for the independence of women unknown in Pagan society—the scholastic philosophy,—or the real nature and actual worth to mankind of Art and Ideal Literature,—what they say, when they do say anything, is worthless enough. With William Roscoe, Italian literature was a passion, and his strength lay altogether in it. Latterly, the pretensions of Roscoe have been assailed by one of the highest critical authorities of modern times. But it is, nevertheless, questionable, if any English writer was on the whole as well fitted as Roscoe, by specific cast of mind, united with the necessary attainments, to execute the Medici biographies. A man of Roscoe's temperament, breathing so ungenial a moral atmosphere as that of Liverpool sixty years ago—with an enthusiastic though an unintelligent eye for the finer world mirrored in pictures and prints,—a keen sense of those elegances of life which in his earlier days lay at a distance from him, and above all, with that intense appreciation of the particular sections of wisdom locked within books, and the technical appliances of literature, which belongs specially to *the self-taught man*, was pre-eminently the person to see the great Pontifical reviver of letters and his magnificent father, from the right point of view—a point of view from which most men won't consent to survey them. The growth of Roscoe's own inner life was perhaps largely the social growth of the Augustan age of Italy.

In saying this, we by no means endorse all the admiration with which it is conventional to speak of Roscoe's biographies. Horace Walpole praised them enthusiastically, and so did Dr. Parr, and the historian Gillies. "Pursuits of Literature," Matthias grew lyrical on reading them, and blew a complimentary flourish on his scholastic cowhorn. For the critical powers of these "grave and reverend signiors," we profess no very extraordinary respect. But we have, as behoves us, for their scholarship great deference. It is easy to see that what called for and obtained the praises of those notabilities, was that Roscoe's information was derived from fontal sources, and that his books, instead of being shadows of other books, were new and genuine contributions to historical knowledge. A historian of the greatest age of Art since the era of Pericles, and of the world's most magnificent *connoisseurs*, Roscoe labours under cardinal defects. We allow him—with the respect and gratitude due to one who has instructed us—to be genial, learned, and impartial. But his æsthetical criticism is valueless. It is doubtful if he had any higher idea of the creations of Art than as "objects of taste." He had never caught a glimpse of the calm majesty so sorrowing and so yearning, of that strong spirit who dwells in the palace called Beautiful, while yet the mystery of doubt and the mystery of death prowl without at the gate that looks far over into the world. Unlike the German mind, and the mind of England and France, the Italian intellect has alone in plastic Art adequately revealed all its grandeur and creative capacity. Dante, and at a later period a few of the great composers of hieratic music, throw themselves across this rule as exceptions. The man who cannot see—and see without a misgiving, that the business is mainly one of ornament or superfluity—with an eye at once pious and philosophical, into manifestations of power and character through Art, will be unable to tell what is best worth hearing about the times of Lorenzo and Leo. He can, in fact, *know* little of the great men upon whom the Medici fame rests, like an airy *baldacchino* of golden tracery upon the stupendous jasper columns of some august sanctuary. Mrs. Jamieson's brief notice of Correggio in her little book on Italian Painting—that he was "a true servant of God in his Art" —above sordid ambition, and devoted to truth—not only gives you a master-key to the higher criticism of Correggio, but opens a historical idea that

K

reaches like a corridor into the heart of Correggio's age. A proof of how imperfectly Roscoe appreciated the masters of Italian painting, is furnished in the following lines from an Ode, in the volume before us, on the Foundation of a Society for the formation of the Fine Arts in Liverpool. The theme is a parallel of Poetry with Painting:—

> Opposed to Waller's amorous song
> His art let wanton Titian try,
> Let great Romano's free design
> Contend with Dryden's pompous line,
> And chaste Correggio's graceful air
> With Pope's unblemished page compare.

Scarcely as much ground is there for any parallel here drawn as for one of Homer and Horace Vernet,—*they* both paint fighting men. What *could* a man like this, who looked upon his Italian engravings through spectacles that might have been forgotten on the table of Button's coffee house or Wills', really perceive of the triumphant strivings of grandly endowed and religiously earnest human beings to bring out and bequeath the divinity within them? He has nothing to tell you of their relation to the great problem—the evolution, as far as may be, here below, of what is finest and purest in human nature. In the memoir of Lorenzo, after a few biographical details, he gets rid of Michael Angelo, by an anecdote of a French painter, long incredulous of the master's powers, who exclaimed, after gazing at two statues Cardinal Richelieu had brought into France, "*J'ai vu Michel Ange; il est effrayant*"—I have seen Michael Angelo; he is terrific! Roscoe's own criticism flows in a runnel of this kind:—"Of the sculptures of Michael Angelo some yet remain, in an unfinished state, which strikingly display the comprehension of his ideas and the rapidity of his execution." Get an idea of your own out of *that*, reader, if you can! "Such," he proceeds, "are the bust of Brutus and the statue of a female figure in the gallery at Florence. In the latter, the chisel has been handled with such boldness as to induce a *connoisseur* of our own country to conjecture that in the finishing it would be necessary to restore the cavities." This "jargon of the *connoisseurs*" is the substance of what Mr. Roscoe gives you as the genius and art of Michael. And he quotes from a wretched *silhouette* of a book on pictures, written in French by a poor arid creature named Richardson, who stands in much the same relation to painting that old Nichols or honest Joseph Spence, the anecdote-mongers, do to Poetry. A judgment on Buonarotti as a Painter is, in effect, avoided, and we can do nothing better than place what Mr. Roscoe says before the reader. "Already it is difficult to determine whether his (Michael's) reputation be enhanced or diminished by the sombre representations of his pencil in the Pauline and Sistine Chapels, or by the few specimens of his cabinet pictures, now rarely to be met with, and exhibiting only a shadow of their original exellence! All the highest criticism on those great epic ornaments of the Leonine age has been produced, and they have shed their grandest inspiration upon the hearts of poets, since Roscoe's day. Besides, Michael was no colourist; men of his Miltonic cast never are. The late gifted David Scott, who so worthily dwelt within the sublimer austerities of Art, for instance, was not. Men of this kind have the *sensuous* faculties too much subjugated. Be this a comment on as much of the question of preservation as lurks in Mr. Roscoe's remarks. The essence of the criticism, however, leaks out at the word "sombre." It is, in reality, objections to the conception and the *genre* that Mr. Roscoe echoes. "Sombre!"—why by the *sombreness* of the thing—of the Last Judgment, or, as the matter might be more fairly or more boldly put, the dark apocalyptic grandeur of it—the *shadowing out* of doom, would the supreme Michael himself, be content to stand. And the improvement Michael Angelo's works effected in public taste, is summed up as the claim upon posterity of that marvellous man who ranks with Shakspeare and Beethoven, as arch-exponents of that awful *potential* world that lives in the depths of our common nature—world of grandeur and of sorrows so sublimated as to be worthy the endurance of angels, of pleasure abysmal and ineffable, and of victorious and everlasting beauty that pierces the soul as flame the living flesh!

Roscoe's reputation should have been left to stand upon a cippus of modest historical prose. William Stanley Roscoe, and Mrs. Sandbach of Liverpool, had done sufficient, with whatever amount of success, to represent the poetical pretentions of the distinguished family of Roscoe. The unlucky verses before us display scarcely an original idea of any kind—scarcely a single gleam of native fancy, or even a memorable felicity of expression. They are echoes of the tinkles of Pope and Shenstone and Dyer, without even an approximation to the merits of that meagre music. Pope, like Boileau, had the good sense of a man *comme il faut*, and melody beside; and poor Shenstone held his varnished crook as prettily, and looked the sentiment *et ego in Arcadia* as nicely, as any gentleman that flirts in pastoral costume beside the sculptured fountain-basins of Watteau. How the name of Dyer evokes images of schoolboy years —of the dim, secluded, somewhat sleepy, schoolroom in Phillip-street, in that dear city of Sydney, with small old-fashioned windows enchased with grape-vines and honeysuckle, and darkened by antique and bowery lemon-trees, in which, of sunny mornings, with many a lapsus, we were wont to recite octo-syllabic praises of "the Groves of Grongar Hill," from "Enfield's Speaker." Dyer had a good eye for "still life," and his modest landscapes have many a touch of sunshine and tender colour.

"The Wrongs of Africa," the longest composition in the volume, though dull enough as a poem, recalls one of the noblest of the many noble episodes in Roscoe's beneficent life—a life beautiful and unobtrusive withal. He took an early and intrepid stand against the slave-trade, and that in one of the chief marts of that horrible traffic—in a city·"every stone in whose buildings was bought and cemented with the blood and marrow of the kidnapped and murdered African," as George Frederick Cooke—pointing his phrases with hiccups, in one of his fits of sublime drunkenness, once took occasion from behind the foot-lights to remind a Liverpool audience.

The poem of "Mount Pleasant," produced by Mr. Roscoe between the ages of sixteen and twenty, might have been very well left without republication. It contains such an instance of equivocal grammar as this:—

> At intervals the red-breast's throat
> Pours the clear warblings of his closing note.

And the writer also alludes to a polar region,

> Where the faint sun scarce liquidates the main.

The word, besides being a synonym for pecuniary payment, means certainly also to clear and to make smooth. But it strikes us as pretty plain, that the poet means liquefies. This image also occurs in Mount Pleasant—

> So stands some lake amidst the sheltering vale,
> Its waves unruffled by the rising gale ;
> On the green surge are poisonous insects found,
> And putrid vapours spread black mists around.

But the criticism is not worth a cowrie, that leaves the poorest poem without endeavouring to find, if not a flower, yet some cool green leaf worth carrying away. Here are two tolerable things—four lines about the portraits of friends—the third bombastic enough, the fourth good.

> The sparkling eye, the blooming face,
> The shape adorned with every grace,
> To Nature's self scarce yields the doubtful strife,
> Swell from the deepening shade and ask the gift of life.

Let us also show these lines about Burns ; the two first enclose a striking image; the two last are very queer stuff—

> And let Despair with niggard light
> Disclose the yawning gulf below,
> And pour incessant on his sight
> Her spectred ills and shapes of woe.

The writer of this essay had evidently studied something else besides books. Painting and Sculpture were no "lands unknown" to him. His very style seems to have been largely influenced by his appreciation of the Fine Arts. This is one of the most remarkable features in Mr. Deniehy's mental character. Nearly his whole life having been passed in his native land, he could have had little or no opportunities for making himself acquainted with the works of the great Masters. His personal knowledge could have been little more than recollections of his childhood. Yet his criticisms betray no sign of defective knowledge: on the contrary, they convey an impression that he was just as competent to criticise a painting as a book.

The next paper is on Gray:

Gray, in the degree to which taste and scholarship flowed about and fed the root of his poetical faculty, eminently resembles Longfellow in our own day. But Longfellow has enjoyed wider opportunities of culture—the spiritual element shooting down from German literature, and the privilege of following instead of preceding the great modern poets. Both, to use Dryden's illustration, see Nature for the most part through "the spectacles of books." Indeed, were one to judge from Longfellow's poems, one could scarcely say he had ever observed external nature for himself, much less loved it with a poet's passion; but there is evidence in his prose that he had,—in some charming passages of "Hyperion," and above all in "Kavanagh," our favourite among all Longfellow's books. "Roaring Brook" is a sketch transferred from among the living woods and the living waters. Longfellow digs, *dilettanti*-wise, into the mines of the Minnesingers, as Gray loved to quarry in the bardic strata of the Scandinavians and the Welsh. Both are never happier than when working up other men's gold. Supply them the metal, and they bring fancy and artistic finish of their own. The result is a beauty of design all men can appreciate, and appreciate, too, at a single glance. In the process of re-casting, no writers were ever so successful. As La Bruyere remarked of the felicities of Boileau,—they seem to create the thoughts of other people. In Gray, the reflective faculties altogether overpowered the perceptive. He picked up his images in the grounds of all sorts of people, and had no objection to say so. Indeed he was often not as much indebted to others as he led people to believe, —" The curfew tolls the knell of parting day "—for instance, owes very little, if anything at all, to Dante's *squilla di lontano*. No man ever had the judiciousness of artistic taste in a higher degree. Who but Gray would have expunged from the Elegy one of the loveliest verses ever written in English—a verse which *he* with his scant store of imagery was likely to appraise to the last iota of its value—simply because its happy morning radiance and sweet dewy freshness of colour might beat up and *spot*, as it were, the sombre tone and dim shadowy *breadth* of the composition:

> There scattered oft, the earliest of the year,
> By hands unseen, are showers of violets found:
> The red-breast loves to build and warble there,
> And little footsteps lightly tread the ground.

This circumstance of flowers strewn upon a grave by "hands unseen," is the most exquisite thing in all Gray's poetry. The "hands unseen" is a touch of the true poetical gramarye—a gleam from the Spirit Land. Lord Byron has borrowed it without acknowledgment in a famous stanza of "Don Juan." He has made, by the way, as able use of it as Gray himself ever did with any of his own peculations, or Milton with the wonderful epithets he was now and then—to old Gifford's unspeakable disgust—in the habit of borrowing from the elder dramatists. Lord Byron has given the words historic dignity :—

> When Nero perish'd by the justest doom
>   That ever the destroyer yet destroyed,
> Amidst the war of liberated Rome,
>   The shout of nations and the world o'erjoy'd,
> Some *hand unseen* strew'd flowers on his tomb ;
>   Perhaps the weakness of some heart not void
> Of feeling, for some kindness done when power
> Had left the wretch one uncorrupted hour.

Gray's sensibilities were exquisite. He had a fusing power, borrowed from the melancholy light under which things presented themselves to his eye. It did for him, to a very considerable degree, what imagination does for greater poets. A pensive, tender, moralising sadness, born of the temperament of the man—native, in his spirit, and not expressly put on with his "singing robes"—coloured, harmonised, verified all reflections and fancies into one whole of melancholy grace, just as the evening horizon melts together and atones all things into grave repose—making earth look for awhile a pensive but a happy place ! You have this in the Ode on a prospect of Eton, as well as in the Church-yard Elegy. The essence of the sentiment lies in Burke's saying—"What shadows we are, and what shadows we pursue."

I remember my accomplished friend, Mr. Frank Fowler, in a collection of sparkling thoughts and images published some three months since in the *Sydney Morning Herald*, conceived he had found the root of the first stanza of the Elegy in these lines from the thirteenth book of Pope's Homer's "Odyssey :"—

> As the tired ploughman, spent with stubborn toil,
> Whose oxen long have torn the furrowed soil,
> Sees with delight the sun's declining ray
> When home with feeble knees he bends his way.

My friend's praise of Gray's verse is as charming as a rural sunset of Cuyp's —"calm, evening-like, and beautiful," he calls it. But I can see nothing but a coincidence in the verse from the Odyssey and Gray's—the use and to some extent the necessarily similar treatment of one of the most obvious circumstances of country life. The weariness of the ploughman "plodding" homeward must have struck every rural loiterer for centuries. Surely that vesper image of rest from toil had so often met the eye as to suggest use of it, if neither Pope nor Gray had ever existed, to all English poets of rustic life—to Thompson and Bloomfield, and Bowles and Bamfylde, and Crabbe and Clare, and Hurdis.

Hard fighting men, and men of the world, have ever loved Gray's "Elegy." Wolfe praised it passionately, shortly before he expired on the heights of Abraham. There was, perhaps, a strange feeling stirring in his breast when, as he gazed from his boat on the dark, swift tide of the Canadian river, imaging the stars "thoughtfully awake," he whispered to himself—

> The paths of glory lead but to the grave.

In his last moments Daniel Webster gasped, "Poetry—Gray's *Elegy*"—when in the evening of age, as in the morning of childhood, the feeble tongue could only enunciate the *nouns*, and leave those around to fill up and complete the structure of the sentence.

Under the title of *Books and Things—a Table Talk*, he strung together a series of critical and philosophical remarks, which are well worth reading:

"I cannot," said Dr. Arnold, "enter fully into these lines of Wordsworth's—
> To me, the meanest flower that blows can give
> Thoughts that too often lie too deep for tears.

There is to me something in them of a morbid feeling—life is not long enough to take such intense interest in objects in themselves so little." Sad sort of talk this for so great a man as Thomas Arnold, of Rugby. His remark might, to some little extent, apply to a mere maniac entomologist, or to a man midsummer-mad in field botany. Wordsworth, though, according to the most illustrious of his critics, he saw by some rare quality of organization in the eye every natural object under forms of sublimated beauty unknown to mankind generally, was the last man to take an intense interest in a little object purely for the object's own sake. He gives no extraordinary attention to the trivial thing itself, if any product of God's handiwork can, rightly viewed, be called trivial. The flower may be "little," but who shall say the "thoughts too deep for tears" which it gives, are little? And why should Dr. Arnold have assumed that *such* thoughts must of necessity be altogether about the flower itself, when reflection wakened in its tenderest moods by the lowly blossom may, when arrived at that stage of intensified pathos to which the poet refers, be a thousand leagues away? "The meanest flower" is only impressive to Wordsworth from the suggestive function it performs. Only in the profound heart and the Æolian sensibilities of a meditative poet would a stray meadow flower stir ineffable things that dwell below the source of tears. The homely memories of by-gone life "departed never to return," not less than the yearning questions passionately, and as Wordsworth himself says, "obstinately" whispered by the soul, as to the meaning and purpose of this glorious equipage of physical creation which has so much to do with that soul, may have been thus called up. And what Wordsworth implies is, that he as a poet is endowed with a range of sensibilities so *wide* as equally to touch the grandeur of the mountain valley, with the rainbow resting, as it were, the basis of an aerial architecture in its elemental walls, or the tropical heaven, amid the thunders of the typhoon, opening up its apocalyptical abyss of ethereal fire, or any other image of terror, of beauty, or of splendour, alike with the fairest blossom of the fields. Not in a handful of violets gathered from Arnold's early home at Laleham, simply as violets, would Arnold have felt the only interest about which a true poet would care to speak; but in the tender thoughts they would give, perhaps, of the time when Thomas Arnold took his bride to that happy home of Laleham.

The distinguishing faculty, I think, of recent great American statesmen, is not what we ordinarily call *genius*—great originality of ideas, or splendid action under the direction of speculative wisdom, with the higher form of eloquence as concomitant—so much as a clear common sense faculty, altogether exquisite in its perceptions of the real palpable relations of things, as things happen to be in this world, and the best way of managing them. This, I think, applies to men ranging from Webster down to George S. Hilliard; even to Edward Everett with his rhetorical robes on. They have inherited the mind of the great printer who represented the Infant Republic at the Court of Versailles; they are Franklins, *with the advantage of having been at college*. Their's is intellect of the type of Paley's and Whately's; they only see ordinary things, but to see them as *they* see is a rare and precious gift; and sophistry has for them no more a principle of resistance than a smoke-wreath for the rushing arrow.

The best and the briefest definitions of wit and humour that I know of, occurred some years back, in a notice of Leland's translation of Heinrich Heine's "Reisebilder," in that most brilliant of London weekly publications, the *Leader*. The notice is, I presume, Mr. Lewes's. "Humour affirms all that is generally human instead of denying it, and it is, in fact, an *exuberant sympathy* acting in company with a sense of the ludicrous, while wit is the *critical intellect* acting in company with that same sense."

"Life's Problems" is a little book, much in the tone of the Essays of Arthur Helps—the feelings and opinions of a thoughtful, thoroughly cultured mind put into pure and simple English. In his papers, "Sexual Difference in Mental Constitution," he approaches the real solution of that vexed psychological question of the superiority of the intellect of one sex to that of the other. "Created apart," he says, "with separate individualities, counterparts to each other, alike in what they have and have not, it was most palpably designed that neither should live alone, or singly achieve that which, united, follows in the order of Nature. Each, mentally and physically, is the complement of the other. Two halves, both are necessary to make a perfect whole, and in their union only can each find its own most perfect development as an individual." The two last sentences are, in substance, the property of Wilhelm von Humboldt, less known, but a man of greater native intellect, than his illustrious brother Alexander. Humboldt alone satisfactorily answered the question of a superior intellect in either sex. According to him, there is an ingenitely masculine and feminine mind—two hemispheres of one orb ; and to compare them is to compare things which, as the logicians say, are *disparate* and admit of no comparison. In that extraordinary book of the extraordinary Count de Montlosier, *Des Mystères de la Vie Humaine*, there is this striking passage which, as regards human existence, is perhaps, not unworthy of note—"We shall know one day that the distinction of sexes belongs to the whole of nature ; *we shall know that the sex resides in the principle of life*, and not, as is generally believed, in the external form."

That charming writer, Robert Aris Wilmott, once said that, in Southey's biographies, the departed were laid in "tombs of crystal." The figure is beautiful. But did Mr. Wilmott, who knows and loves the rich elder literature of England better than almost any of his cotemporaries, extract his gem from this pebble-like conceit of Drummond's of Hawthornden, in the lament for Mœliades :—

> The Muses, Phœbus, Love have raised of their tears
> A *crystal tomb* to him, through which his worth appears.

The greater part of Madame de Stael's philosophy and criticism, bears much the same relation to what is genuine in both, that roses in *buhl* do to the living flowers. The mechanical copy has a flush of colour of its own about it ; and the ingenuity that makes the artificial singularly *like* the real, ought perhaps in strictly equitable appraisals of talent, to be taken into account. The only approach, as far as my memory goes, that Madame made to a sound philosophical sentiment, is an expression in her recantation of her early ideas on suicide. When she first wrote, it was with the vivacity and the impertinence of youth—'*mais à quoi servirait il de vivre, si ce n'etait dans l'espoir de s'ameliorer ?*' What would be the use of growing older, if it were not with the hope of growing wiser ?

There is a certain thoroughly imaginative subjection of the perceptions in the presence of supreme feminine beauty,—an atoning of all surrounding things at one point, which only belongs to the movements of passion in the highest poetry. This is really the *piu nell' uno* of the Italians. I have met with two notable instances of it recently. One in N. P. Willis's tragedy of "Bianca Visconti," and the other in Aubrey de Vere's graceful volume of sketches in Greece and Turkey. The Condottierro Sforza in the play, speaks to his bride, a young Milanese Duchess, on their wedding night—

> I remember
> The fair Giovanna in her pride at Naples.
> Gods ! what a light enveloped her ! She left
> Little to shine in history ; but her beauty

L

> Was of that order that the universe
> Seem'd govern'd by her motion. Men look'd on her
> As if her next step would arrest the world;
> And—as the sea-bird seems to rule the wave
> He rides so buoyantly—all things around her,
> The glittering army, the spread gonfalon,
> The pomp, the music, the bright sun in Heaven—
> *Seem'd glorious by her leave!*

Mr. de Vere paints a picture of an Eastern beauty he had the rare fortune of seeing unveiled at Constantinople, with a mixture of Etty's luxurious feeling and the purity of Stothard. "The favourite wife was a Circassian, and a fairer vision it would not be easy to see. Intellectual in expression she could hardly be called; yet she was full of dignity as well as pliant grace and sweetness. Her large black eyes, beaming with a soft and stealthy radiance, seemed as if they would have yielded light in the darkness; and the heavy waves of her hair, which, in the excitement of the scene, she carelessly flung over her shoulders, gleamed like a mirror. Her complexion was the most exquisite I have ever seen, its smooth pearly purity being tinged with a colour unlike that of flower or of fruit, of bud or of berry, but which reminded me of the vivid and delicate tints which sometimes streak the inside of a shell. Though tall, she seemed as light as if she had been an embodied cloud, hovering over the rich carpets like a child that does not feel the weight of its body; and though stately in the intervals of rest, her mirth was a rapture. She, too, had that peculiar luxuriousness of aspect, in no degree opposed to modesty, which belongs to the East; around her lips was wreathed in their stillness an expression at once pleasurable and pathetic, which seemed ever ready to break forth into a smile; *her hands seemed to leave with regret whatever they had rested on, and in parting to leave something behind;* and in all her soft and witching beauty she reminded me of Browning's lines—

> No swan-like woman, rubb'd in lucid oils,
> The gift of an enamour'd god, more fair."

What a fine wit L. E. L. had, though life *did* seem to her fancy like an etruscan vase—*folâtre* figures running on a back ground. Do you recollect her making lady M. W. Montagu, in "Ethel Churchill," remark that she found, "with great mortification, she was every day getting wiser!"

How touchingly true is that remark of a female friend of John Kenyon's—"To be happy, we must not only forbear to anticipate the future, but must teach ourselves to forget the past!"

There is a good lesson, notwithstanding the dash of sadness about it, in the fact that the powers and achievements of genius are bounded by the merest material circumstances. The being born a quarter of a century, sooner or later, often makes huge difference in what the gifted effects in his day. What could not Bichat, the Napoleon of modern medicine, have done with the microscope, so ineffective in his time, as it became a few years after his death? And again, think of the harmonic grandeurs and splendours, such as human ear hath never heard, which the genius of Mozart would have evoked from those recent colossal appliances of orchestral instrumentation, upon which, as on a plinth of Theban proportions, rests so much of the fame of Meyerbeer and Berlioz!

How beautiful to contemplate Genius, undistracted by ambition or envy, perfecting itself for the life to come amidst the quiet daily discharge of duties! I know one such instance—a person in whose society I have never spent an hour without leaving it a better man, with aims purified and elevated. Who would expect that a man of encyclopædiac learning and the finest perceptions of beauty—who could throw truths in exquisite forms, such as I am about to quote—

Easily as the oak looseneth its golden leaves,

was content here in Sydney to toil through diurnal drudgery, at a conveyancer's desk, satisfied to maintain those dear to him, and endeavour to keep himself, in St. James's words, "unspotted from the world?" Is not this, which I once took down from my friend's lips, truly beautiful? "In seasons of grief, the effect of those grand passages of poetry which shake the soul to its very foundation, is merely that of the storm which leaves behind it a wreck without any purifying influences; but the effect of that poetry which is based on Christian solaces, resembles the commotion in the pool of Bethesda, which indicated that, with the disturbance—healing virtue had been communicated to the reposing waters, *by the presence of an invisible angel.*"

"The down on the breast of an eagle." What a beautiful image of Charles Drake's that is—in allusion to those gentle humanities which are never so tender and so pathetic as in the strong heart of a hero. With rough old Zachary Taylor, the green waving wheat field was one of the sweetest things on God's earth, and visions of the autumnal uplands must have been his cheer through the crush and carnage of his splendid Mexican campaign, whenever the tense brain relaxed from attention to the matter of the moment. Priceless were the tears that coursed down the "iron cheeks" of Pitt, that terrible night in the Commons, when 216 votes were given for, and 216 against, the impeachment of Lord Melville, and the Speaker, after ten minutes' pause, recorded his casting vote with the ayes.

Most people know something of Henry Taylor's "Philip van Artevelde," but I am surprised that his "Notes from Life" are not more generally read and more frequently quoted. For pure, ripe, weighty wisdom, the book is surpassed by few in our literature, and it foreshadows much of the tone which belongs to the writings of Taylor's friend—Arthur Helps. Is not this passage remarkably fine? "If there be in the character not only sense and soundness, but virtue of a high order, then, however little appearance there may be of talent, a certain portion of wisdom may be relied upon almost implicitly; and that they will accompany each other may be inferred, not only because men's wisdom makes them good, but also because their goodness makes them wise. Although, therefore, simple goodness does not imply every sort of wisdom, it unerringly implies some essential condition of wisdom; it implies a negative on folly, and an exercised judgment, within such limits as nature shall have prescribed to the capacity." 'One of the best commentaries on this noble passage will be found in the female character. There have been hundreds of worthy, high-principled women,—simple, unassuming, and without a shadow of pretension to being "clever"—who never *could* fall into the fallacies or perpetuate the follies of their lax though brilliant brothers and husbands.

In Balzac and Thackeray, you have a deal of what may be called in a good sense, the Pre-Raphaelitism of literature.

There is largely in literature and life, a practice of praising by comparisons, and the criticism, like the vehicle it employs, is odious. One celebrity can only be praised by some people as it operates to depreciate another; one achievement is lauded just as the eulogist conceives it throws another achievement into shadow. In the heyday of Mr. Lever's popularity, one stupid periodical could only indicate its heaped up and overflowing admiration of "Harry Lorrequer" by exclaiming "We had rather be the author of this book than of all the 'Pickwicks' and 'Nicklebys' in the world." This is a side-thrust at Mr. Dickens. Now, I cannot see why the rollicking dashing fun of Mr. Lever's book could not have been enjoyed without a gird of abatement at the rich humour of "Pickwick," or the tragic power and delicate pathos which are the higher characteristics of "Nicholas Nickleby." There is not only room enough in the world for perfectly new and dissimilar beauties, but for beautiful things that resemble each other in a great many respects. Ever after the mighty explorations of De Quincey into that psychical realm which obeys a law of material stimulants, there is place for the experiences of luxury and terror of the American *Hasheesh* (or hemp-eater). Bailey's idea of the Graces is welcome, even after Canova's has for half a century ruled our conceptions of a perfect embodiment of that exquisite myth. I felt much annoyed lately by meeting this kind of criticism in a notice of Stothard in Leigh Hunt's "Table Talk." Stothard is there placed above Flaxman. Except in the divine purity of their ideal of the female face and form, the two men are utterly unlike; and it would be as unfair to back one against the other as artists in a general sense, as to contest if Milton or Spenser were in the abstract the greater poet. The genius of Flaxman was epic; Stothard's was idyllic.

Most men, when praising others warmly, are unconsciously praising images struck from the *die* of their own *ideals* of themselves.

Criticism should be gentle; all life, literature, politics, are but processes of approximation. "Even solar time," said Julius Hare, "is not true time." But it does.

The hope that suggests, and the achievement that embodies, our youthful endeavours bear the relation to each other of the Baptistry at Florence, and the gates of bronze Ghiberti moulded for it. The building and the achievement are alike excellent things in their way, though

> A thousand such there are elsewhere
> As worthy of your wonder.

But the young hope, and the portals of breathing imagery, "*they*," as Michael Angelo said of the latter, "are worthy of Paradise!"

Mr. Deniehy was of Irish extraction, and when very young, he spent a few months in Ireland. This was but a small foundation for such a structure of patriotic feeling as he contrived to rear upon it. How intense his sympathies were with everything connected with Ireland, the following paper, headed *John Mitchell as a Literary Man*, will sufficiently shew:—

A sad stage in the later career of so brave and gifted a spirit as that dashing North of Ireland attorney who threw himself, like another Arnold of Winkelried, on the spears of Anglo-Irish policy,—who, by an act, to say the worst of it, of heroic precipitancy, solved the question if there was to be anything in the Young Ireland movement besides fervid and picturesque writing and bold and brilliant speaking,—was his advocacy of American slavery, and uncharity and abuse—all the worse because in the dark hours of defeat, and amidst the ruin's of a life's purpose, of him who, if not chief, was a loyal and lofty brother in arms. Of course I think and write of the men and deeds of Young Ireland as one who, out here in Australia, must form his judgment mainly from what he reads, partly from what he has heard. Among the *litterateurs* of an organization which largely and on principle operated in literary forms, Mitchell seems to me to have been *le beau sabreur*—the Murat of the movement. Duffy, with devotion deep as the foundation of his soul, to the cause, not alone of Irish political welfare, but of the whole regeneration of Irishmen, shewed a literary character broad, abundant, luminous as a river, and yet chequered with soft sad autumnal hues, with that wisdom which is ripened by mournful convictions and sad experience brings; and its movement had "the deep rush," to use in a higher sense what Sheil so finely said of Yelverton's eloquence. In Davis, you had the archetype of Young Ireland culture, and of the masculine purity of genius hallowed to lofty purposes. He, in the true meaning of the word—in Fichte's, and not the grammar-school sense—was the scholar of his party. And he was their poet too. Neither his imagination nor his fancy was remarkable—though in the "Sack of Baltimore" there are gleams of the former, the "starry trance" of the hushed landscape and the waters, for instance—of exquisite subtlety and delicacy; and of the latter, the bane of Irish poets, if he possessed much of it, his nature was too earnest and too strong to play with the pretty things it might have moulded for him. His real power as a poet lay in that principle which is at the heart of all lyrical power—passion. Analyse Burns, analyse Beranger, and you get a similar result. Not in flashes which reveal, as in ethereal fire, objects which for most lie self-withdrawn in psychical darkness, not showing ordinary things in that tempered and tender atmosphere which is to the atmosphere of logic and the understanding what the rarified and roseate morning of Alpine peaks is to that of the lowermost valleys. Passion pulses through every lyric of Davis's—alike in the "Surprise of Cremona" or "Fontenoy," and the "Bride of Mallow," or that song which would have kindled every capacity of splendour in the eyes of Burns, "The Girl of Dunbruce"—

> I never can think upon Bantrey's bright hills,
> But your image comes up and my longing eye fills,
> And softly I whisper, Again, love, we'll meet,
> And I'll live in your bosom and lie at your feet.

This vital current rushes as powerfully and as fast through "Native Swords," or any other copy of verses justifying the political sentiment of the hour, as the proud stanzas of the "Convention ot Dungannon," or that heartrending *caoine* at the grave of Wolfe Tone, which itself ranks with "The Burial of Sir John Moore," the "*Convoi de David*," and "Who Fears to Talk of Ninety-eight" —the noblest elegiacs of modern literature. "*Cet homme ira bien loin parcequ'il croit tout ce qu'il dit*"—that man will go great lengths because he believes in what he says,—a remark applied to a very different person, might have been said not only of Davis's life, but of the promise that burned in all his literary efforts. What are Southey's Life of Nelson, Stanley's Dr. Arnold, Crabbe's Life by his son, or any other recognized biographical master-piece, Carlyle's Memoir of Sterling excepted, and John Mitchell's Hugh O'Neill, compared with Davis's Life of Curran? It has the fire and the living and lucid splendour which a statue of the Orator, struck by necromantic force from molten lava, might present. It has the shadowed freshness and purity of the holy well under the twilight hawthorn, when the little offerings, affixed to spray and twig by peasant piety, flutter in the dying breeze—

> The summer evening's latest sigh
> That shuts the rose.

His studies in Augustin Thierry, in Scott and the glorious old *repertoire* of Scottish ballad, suggested, and his archæology and picturesque learning aided, in imparting to his poetry costume and local colouring, correct and effective in an extraordinary degree.

Mitchell's, it strikes me, is an intellect of noble and robust type, under the control of an arbitrary and ill-disciplined will. A man, methinks, born under some particular star presiding over revolutionary genius; ready at all points for wars of independence,—to talk what the Crown lawyers call "seditious and inflammatory harangues"—to write articles in which the essence of all the rebellion of all the hereditary bondsmen on the face of the earth, is condensed and intensified within *vade mecum* dimensions,—to govern "clubs"—beard Judges—spit upon juries—lead armies—patent novel and readier types of barricades,—ransack arsenals,—and experiment with infernal machines on the naval property of Her Most Gracious Majesty, with a hand as cool as if he were addressing, before all Ireland, *battant le chien devant loin*, letters to my Lord of Clarendon, and his logical and rhetorical Grace of Dublin.

With a strong, keen, swift intellect, disciplined and even philosophically cultured in one or two directions, there are pretty broadly defined imaginative and spiritual characteristics about his thinkings. Lonely and narrow we should think, but deep as a tarn and mountain heather, is the ideal vein in his nature— poetic feeling of his own, fresh, genuine, and thoroughly idiosyncratic, as poetic feeling always is in the man of *caractère*. Not the result of mere æsthetical results or hyper-refinement, as in the majority of scholars and critics, but the endowment nature only refuses to every Strong Man for some reasons like those for which she sends imperfect physical developments into the world. A vein this which Robert Browning, the everlasting struggle and the obstinate questioning of the race, in the person of a poor heart-broken quack, who strutted and fretted his hour in the sixteenth century amidst college classes and cliques in Switzerland; still less creates the dream lands of Morte Arthur, or Kubla Khan, or gives, like Clarence Mangan, a wild song of "Boating on the Bosphorus,"—"Youth at the helm, and Pleasure at the brow,"—sadder than an epicedium, yet

Bright as fever, or the dreams of wine.

But it is the faculty which, when the lonely man broods over and reminds you, as he sits a lonely exile—chained but not conquered, one might say, on the hot, white crags of Bermuda—of the dear scenes in the land he "loved not wisely but too well," till the moan and murmur, the gliding whisper, and the swirling glee of sylvan waters, and the blossoming bushes, whose noontide photographs on the quiet stream are ever and anon broken by the darting trout, and the melancholy sunset that bathes the stretch, mile after mile, of heather, come before you, so sweet, so soft, so dear, so *old* in the intense shade of pathos, affection attaches to that simple word applied to persons and places, as to make the eye fill and the heart quicken its pulses. Ever to me, an Australian, who spent but a swallow's season in Ireland, there are passages in Mitchell's "Jail Journal" that affect me, I scarcely know why, and set my memory re-touching Irish landscapes, as I remember the chorus of Tom Campbell's noble song, "Erin mavourneen, Erin go bragh," did one night, sung by one of the peripatetic Minnesingers of London, in a strong Munster brogue, to a harp of dilapidated pretensions, on the *pavé* of Ratcliffe-highway. They conjure up the places I know best in Ierne, however unlikely the spots they refer to—the brimming Lee with a midnight flash of the mill-wheels at Dripsey, Gongena Barra with its "pomp of waters unwithstood," sung by poor Jerry Callanan in strains where, as often in martial music, the victorious mingles with the plaintive, and the black-waters shimmering by the home of Raleigh, and those sacred shades—wizard woods of Kilcolman, that with useful and shadowed beauty closed in about the visions of the dying Spenser. It scarcely enters within the scope of these desultory remarks to say much about Mitchell's journalism. His articles were written at a desperate period, with a view of bringing about the crisis, and under feelings not only of desperate excitement, but of that headlong bitterness which must always belong to the chief of an organization wherein, from the very nature of things, there must be in some quarters vacillating hesitations and perhaps conflicting counsels. The power, too, which Mitchell hated, as only a revolutionary tribune can hate, was also, he well knew, attempting to precipitate action before things on his side were altogether ready. As there was little time for preparing weakened Ireland for her work, the stimulants applied were accordingly as powerful as might be. I suppose the world has seldom seen as strong leaders as those of *The Irish Tribune.* As literature, they come up marvellously close to Milton's canon of poetry; they were "simple, sensuous, impassioned." Splendid sarcasm, vitriolic in its specific quality as a destructive; argument close and conclusive, couched in eloquent execration, taunt, and curse, and defiance, jest and jeer, as grim in their way as attainders or excommunications. But above all, history—Irish history, pointed out week after week, in such a light as from the flames of a burning church one might see the inscription on mural tablets a minute ere the slabs crack and drop into the blazing chaos. The "thunderers" of the *Times* were, compared to them, weak rum and water to Russian quass or the Tartar distillation from equine milk. The denunciations of Junius, the flimsy pretensions of which to power as political literature De Quincey has, among a host of similar services, shown the world were as lemonade—and inferior lemonade, too—beside the arrack of the Mitchellian diatribes.

I have alluded to evidences in Mitchell of philosophical thinking and culture. I myself was certainly not prepared for anything like the criticism of Lord Macaulay's remarks on the Platonic and Baconian philosophy, in the shape of entries in the patriot-felon's journal—trenchant, sparkling, but sound and solid. The jaunty, devil-may-care tone might perhaps seem unsuited to the dignity of philosophical argument; but otherwise, after hearing the eminent essayist's case, and the advocate for Plato in reply, I think even Plotinus or Schleiermacher would certainly declare their illustrious teacher amply vindicated. I myself believe little in the prevalence of Platonic Greek; I am prepared to believe that Mitchell has read and can read it nevertheless; but perhaps the brilliant defender had sharpened his victorious blade not a little on those Alexandrian stones with which Emerson has paved his noble temple for the worship of truth and beauty. It is a rare sport to see how the Irish attorney knocks about the learned and luxurious man of letters—the historian, critic, poet, essayist, orator, literary artist *par excellence* of the generation. The Ulster rebel, too, slates his Lordship on points on which, as involving the superiority of the eternal and super-eternal· to the material and temporary—excellent and absolutely indispensable as many things in the latter category are—no man with a just sense of what is demanded from a philosophical thinker would like to be worsted. Facts rather than truths, and forms the most fascinating and brilliant for the presentation of the former, seem to be alone within the domain of Lord Macaulay's intellect. Mr. R. H. Horne, now of the neighbouring city of Melbourne, has shewn, in some volumes of masterly criticism, how incompetent Lord Macaulay is to appraise the specific power upon which the intellectual character of a great poet is based.

When the first number of the "Month" appeared, in July 1857, he wrote a complimentary *critique* in the journal from which the previous articles have been taken. It was as follows:

We are glad to see Mr. Fowler at the head of a literary journal. A respectable publication specially devoted to literature and art has long been a desideratum in the Australian metropolis. Into no hands could the management of it more happily fall than Mr. Fowler's. His taste and knowledge—his practical acquaintance with those literary technics so necessary to raise a project of the sort above the pointless and purposeless quality of an amateur's miscellany—and beyond all, his sparkling talents as a prose-writer, pre-eminently qualify him for the editorship of a serial of this kind. Mr. Fowler's delightful sketches in the daily newspapers are the only local productions, within our observation, which present the brilliant finish of English Magazine writing of the first class—with all its virtues and, it is but fair to add, a dash of its vices. But the vices are not the peccaneies for which "Prometheus" has been recently "pitching into" Mr. Fowler in the *Empire;* and the cleverness of "Prometheus" is cleverness of the wrong sort ever to point out where the disorders—and they are not very grave ones—are seated. We earnestly hope our readers will patronise this periodical. As a matter of personal gratification, they can scarcely spend a shilling better than in the purchase of fifty-six pages of reading so pleasant, and of so elevating and refining a character, as this first number of the "Month." As a public duty, we know none more important—for parents particularly—than to aid in the cultivation of native literature by encouraging projects like Mr. Fowler's. Young men begin to see a living fact in literature, reaching at and touching themselves, when they find it, with all its power to win minds and hearts—all its splendid fascinations—produced in the place they live in and by men they meet daily in the street or market-place. Fires of emulation are in this way very quickly kindled, and fanned in many a genial bright young heart. And then look a

M

little further on at possibilities. The little packet of juvenile manuscript dropped with a nervous hand and beating heart into the slit of a letter-box at a publishing office, may prelude grave and noble labours in riper years—labours which may perhaps make men speak with a lingering note of kindness in their voices of Australia, for the sake of things done by the hand, once so shame-fast and so small, that quivered at a letter-box one afternoon long, long ago.

From the initial number of a periodical of this kind, one ought not, perhaps, to expect even a close approach to perfection; but the typography and general appearance are anything but pleasing. There is a slop air about the mechanical part of the publication. It is printed on indifferent paper, generally with a shabby thin type, in some places with a mean ill-cut brevier, anything but worthy of the contents. The rich images and delicious pictorial touches of Mr. Fowler's own Lecture on Coleridge are made palpable through a paltry little type, that suggests the print of those limp loose leaves of testification to the virtues of a quack's panacea which, in the days of our European travels, sallow melancholy men were wont to thrust into our hands at street corners. The wrapper is the best part of the *brochure*, and that might be vastly improved by the substitution of some elegant medallion on wood for the miniature month-almanac. The consummation of effect in a jewel does not more depend on the setting, or the hue and freshness of a beautiful face on a judicious bonnet-lining, than purely literary writing on its visible embodiment in typography. W. J. Fox, a man by no means of that *connoisseur*-class which regards Baskerville and Whittingham impressions as among the most valuable items of a scholar's personalty, has a philosophical remark or two on this subject, in one of his Finsbury Chapel lectures, worth quotation. Speaking of the cheap reprint of Lord Bacon's Essays, the fine old teacher of the people, who has recently been taught a lesson as old as the days of Socrates, says—" I think it requires something for the eye as well as the mind. Until a man is satisfied with the coarsest food that will support existence; until a man is satisfied with the coarsest kind of clothing that will shield him from the vicissitudes of the weather; until a man is satisfied with the poorest shelter that will form a dwelling and screen him from the storm, it is not reasonable nor desirable that he should be satisfied with the very cheapest and coarsest kind of printing and of publication. He will desire something more, on which the eye can rest with satisfaction, *and which may help truth to find its way with more facility and gracefulness into the intellect.*" We do not mean to say that the "Month" is printed in the very coarsest form—we merely cite the observations to justify the importance here attached to typographical details in *belles lettres* publications. The "Month" comes from one of the best printing houses in the city, and we are inclined to place the shortcomings of the Magazine to haste, and want of this specific matter rather than to lack of executive taste and ability.

The paper, "Art Education in Australia," is ably written. But the suggestion for establishing professorships of painting and design, in connection with the mechanics' institutions of towns likely to be incorporated, betrays some very *naive* notions of the state of the institutions in question, and of society in rural towns. Our own idea about those institutions is, that, for the present, they should be mainly taken into the hands of the government, as educational establishments—schools for the adult. They should be placed under the Secretary for Education—when we have one—as a portion of the hierarchy of establishments for public instruction, reaching from the university to infant schools, and including museums and public libraries. Each town should, under this *regime*, elect trustees as a local executive council, for the advice of the Minister. The article is full of fresh and vigorous thought; and our readers will thank us, we feel sure, for extracting these remarks : [a passage is here given, and the writer continues :]

Eloquent and true. We shall never forget the delight with which, in childhood, we first beheld a few well-known sites in this wild native land of ours, pictorially rendered by a few poor lithographs. The vignettes on wood in Braim's "New South Wales" were a fascination for our school-boy eyes. In riper years, Claxton's sketch in oils—full of fine warm colour and vigourous handling—of the Valley of the Weatherboard, immersed in the glory of sunset, helped to strengthen a love of country which had lacked the food on which that love best thrives—Home, shewn in

> The light that never was on sea or land,
> The consecration and the poet's dream.

"My Ferry Boat" consists of a few hasty random strokes from a hand that has drawn and *can* draw with the humour of Doyle or Gavarni. There is an excellent notice of Mr. Norton's Australian Essays ; and a review of some illustrated books, in which one can see the charming pen of the Editor, as you trace the hand of some elegant woman in the draping of a curtain. Here is a group of the book-furniture of a drawing-room table, finished with a *luxe* that would even have satisfied Balzac. [Extract given.]

We invite the reader's attention to the exquisite beauty of diction in this passage. Every epithet has been chosen and applied as a mosaic-worker employs his crystals and tinctured stones. There is really a feeling in the selection of the words profoundly artistic. And after the strange talk we have lately heard, of Mr. Fowler's diction being but a "dilution of Emerson," we cannot resist remarking that the extract goes far to prove, what we have always believed, that the writer has that not very common endowment, a *style* of his own.

The "World of Books" is a series of those notices of what is doing in Literature in Europe generally, which forms so striking a feature of the "Westminster Review." Like most good things, it has its drawback. It makes unlettered bores and idle sparks, with a spice of tact, look walking libraries—learned in books they never saw the covers of. An impudent jackanapes can, thus equipped, sometimes abash honest scholars, whose conscientious pride of sterling acquirements makes them refuse to speak of works with which they are unacquainted, except with the proviso that they have but heard of them, or seen notices in the periodicals. We shall have sharp police-office attorneys, after twenty minutes' perusal of the "Month," speaking of the new Paris edition of Plotinus, the Abbe Lamennais' translation of Dante, and entering into the question of Alexander Smith's annihilation, and Dobell's failure to prevent the catastrophe. Nothing so much tends to retard real culture, in a young community almost wholly engaged in money making, or living very fast, than these facilities for the factitious. Who would labour hard to put a single silver *epergne* on his sideboard, when for a few shillings he may safely display a whole service of nickel or albata, seeing that few can detect an *imitabile fulgur*, and few are provided with detective tests. We should, at whatever loss of general information, much rather see critical articles on specific books. Those who *did* quote the "Month" on such occasions, would be more likely to have *some* ideas, and sound ideas, about the works they mentioned. With several of the notices in the "World of Books" we differ. Mrs. Browning's "Aurora Leigh" is full of loveliness and power—in every sense a fine poem. But it will not "precipitate her fame" beyond Tennyson's, or that of her husband, "the noblest Roman of them all." Critics should guard against this practice of finding every new production, however really charming, the most beautiful thing ever written. We know the temptation; we know what it is to write or speak with the spell of novel beauty upon the heart and the imagination. But, irrespective of improving the wise considerateness which should characterise the literary judicature, it is the over-lauded writer himself who suffers most by this; the rebound is often terrible. A case in point is Alexander Smith's. Upon that author's appearance, legions of the hyper-enthusiastic newspaper-writers of Great Britain warned Tennyson to hide his diminished head. Even the *Nation* cannot praise Thomas Irwin's graceful "versicles" without placing the writer on a level with the Laureate, and claiming higher merit for him than belongs to Smith and Robert Lytton Bulwer, or to a truer poet than either, Matthew Arnold. Again we doubt much if that spoiled child of the critics, the aforesaid Alexander Smith—never particularly a favourite of ours—has been "utterly annihilated as a literary man by the 'Athenæum's' article of the 3rd of January." Heaven help literary men! Devout indeed should be the prayer, *pereant qui ante nos nostra dixerunt*, if the sixty "glaring plagiarisms" pointed out by the critic of the "Athenæum," crush the character of a writer like Mr. Smith, who, though not a great poet, is nevertheless a young man of genius, who *has* done some things with glowing grace, and *may* do others of higher beauty. Are history and biography never to preach wise charity and fostering forbearance? Comes there from that early urn of Keats, amid the Roman violets, no mournful prayer for his boyish successors? Is it not just possible the "Life Drama," with its auroral flush of fancies—fancies everywhere and little else—may be to the works of Mr. Smith's matured years, what that voluptuous midsummer dream of *Endymion* was to Keats's last volume of poems? "No genius," says Sir Egerton Brydges, with his quiet thoughtful elegance, "when he feels the feebleness of his first steps, can guess the mighty course he is capable of running at last, by the aid of energetic and long enduring exercise!" And in a profound recognition of the truth embodied in this saying, lies the modest hope that is nearest our own heart. If the sixty passages put upon their trial by the detective police of the "Athenæum" were altogether "glaring plagiarisms"—which, to a very considerable extent, with the critic of the *Leader*, we deny—still, enough remains the *bona fide* property of unfortunate Mr. Smith to give him a place among English poets. Where, for instance, could he have stolen the first thing in the "Life Drama"—that exclamation of the reckless man of genius, waking out of the splendid waywardness of his sins at the strong words of the poor repentant girl—

> Thou noble soul,
> Teach me, for thou art nearer God than I.

The number contains some verses by the late Mr. Evelyn, full of that manly purity and delicacy of feeling which is the very *aroma* of love poetry. The painful affair in which Mr. Evelyn, some months since, appeared in connection with Mr. Parker, the present First Secretary, will be present in our readers' minds. The young poet died at the age of twenty-seven; and never, we believe, has a purer or more graceful spirit descended into the austere peace—peace nevertheless—of an early grave. "Whom the gods love, die young!"

[After quoting the verses referred to, the critique concluded with a few comments on Mr. Fowler's Lecture on Coleridge, a report of which was published in the "Month."]

We have left ourselves scarcely more than sufficient space to express simply our admiration of Mr. Fowler's glowing Lecture on Coleridge. A part only is given of it this month. It is full of charming things, and displays all the fine keen brilliant qualities of the lecturer's writings. It is all keenness and point, under a surface of delicately-wrought enrichment—like a damaskened sabre—imagery of glowing gold on a blade of polished steel.

On the publication of "Peter 'Possum's Portfolio"—a collection of miscellaneous articles written by Mr. Richard Rowe—the following *critique* was written by Mr. Deniehy:

Alas! for poor Peter 'Possum. With one frailty—one that, to use Bishop Hall's expression, too frequently "hung plummets on the nobler parts," a finer being never existed. Genius (we use the word advisedly), a heart princely in its abounding generosity, a lofty sense of honour, and a modesty rare in these days, were all Peter's. There was no principle of adhesiveness in Peter's coin; half his last shilling would have been held "in trust" for his friend—half a shilling earned by labour, may you never know, reader, how bitter.

We have accredited Peter with genius. Writing for his daily bread, commenting upon passing events—upon men and things so small and so commonplace that Heaven only knows by what ingenuity poor 'Possum ever screwed a comment out of his brain upon them at all—the author of the volume before us had little opportunity, and unfortunately cared less, for writing up to the higher mark of his powers. His humour, that when some donkey in position came athwart it, broke fresh and glittering in a thousand atoms, as the phosphorescent wave of these southern waters at the stroke of the midnight oar, was of the finest quality. The specimens in the book before us give faint idea of it. Peter's facetiæ sparkled most about transient topics. He would enchase with jokes some ninnyhammer's absurdity of the hour, as a jeweller enriches an emerald with brilliants in the bezyl of a ring. The aim in the "Portfolio" has been to reprint his papers of a more permanent interest. His faculty for poetic translation was something wonderful. There are in the book some specimens of northern poetry—"Gam le Norge," the national song of Norway, "Nostalgie" from the Swedish, and a charming copy of verses, called "Birds of Passage," originally contributed to this journal—which were rendered from versions of the original in French prose. Now it hath never entered into the heads of man to conceive anything more barren, balder, or more dreary, than a French translation in prose from foreign poems. An Irish bog is in comparison a lively suggestion of Eden. Blair's sermons, or the old English prose translation of honest Solomon Gessner's death of Abel, are but incomplete types and feeble foreshadowings of the thing. A broomstick or the piston of a steam-engine is not more devoid of ornament, than Peter's media for northern song, of poetry or music. And yet these translations, in common indeed with all Peter's, are almost equal to Clarence Mangan's renderings from foreign tongues, and quite the peers of Thomas Smibert's in "Chambers's Journal"; and this those who know anything of the writers named will consider no mean laudation. Peter, with his really fine imagination and his opulent fancy, was not a poet. The original verses in the volume, except "Farewell to the Bow," "Don Francia," "Death," and the really powerful "Soul Ferry," are below the writer's powers. In some of the chapters of "Arthur Owen" it is that a glimpse of what was in the writer, and a vindication of his claims to rank as a man of genius, are alone, we think, obtained.

The "Portfolio" contains some nineteen prose pieces, and forty or fifty poems, original and translated. We know few ways in which our readers could better invest a few shillings than in the purchase. "Arthur Owen's Biography," which originally appeared piece-meal in the "Month" is, in its collected form, worth the whole sum demanded for the book. Some of the prose papers are remarkably fine—thought and feeling genial and graceful, sparkling with novel images, and always characterised with felicity—frequently by very high beauty of style. The opening, for instance, of the pleasant paper, "Johnson's Chambers," is, to our mind, delightful prose; it is a sketch of a classic locality in London. [Extract.]

Addison's courtly lips would have relaxed into a smile of pleasure at that delicately sketched full-length of his own Sir Roger. Honest Dick Steele—who has left on record how nobly, how chivalrously, how reverentially, a scamp can love his wife ('Even a negro has a soul, your Honour')—honest Dick would have sallied forth, had this sketch appeared in his day, and after the Lake Tchad sort of exploration necessary to find Peter at all, carried him to Wills's, with a view to what the missives of attorneys designate " further proceedings." But we protest against a peccadillo of Peter's in the matter of recasting "Johnson's Chambers." As it originally stood in the *Sydney Morning Herald*, we liked it better. A paragraph in truer keeping with the general treatment of the subject, occupied the place of that quoted above. We are firmly convinced that all literary *rechauffées* are failures. From Leigh Hunt's "Rimini," this holds good down to the new edition of Father Faber's poems—where one of the deepest cries of anguish ever uttered over a lost Beloved, is made to apply to a sister, not only with very bad taste, but in defiance of all canons of Art; for men never mourn sisters in the way the passionate strain of the poem laments the catastrophe.

The *magnum opus* of Peter 'Possum, however, is "Arthur Owen." A degree of passion and imaginative power, a pathos and altogether exquisite delicacy of feeling, a perception of, a faculty for, reproducing rural beauty in artistic forms, is shewn in this remarkable story, of which there is not an inkling in all the author's minor sketches—with all their versatility, their humour, their graphic talent. It is, in fact, the Autobiography of a Childhood. The story is that of a Deformed Boy, morbidly alive—as what deformed was not and is not?—to his misfortune, and making it tinge and shape the medium through which he sees and hears all things. Out of the hewn sandal-wood and the bruised herb, however, comes sweetness; and though hideous malformation only provoked the bitterness, the woe, in "Arthur Owen," that ended in madness—to Mrs. Marsh's exquisite story, "the Deformed," in "Two Old Men's Tales," we refer our readers for the psychology of depravity "figured" from another point of view. Not that we hint at anything wrong in the conception of "Arthur Owen," by this comparison; both are right; and both are pieces of high class fiction. But Mrs. Marsh's tale, we think, for many reasons, a fitting *pendant* to that before us. Arthur Owen, the son of a clergyman, is born in Wales, and pictures of the scenery of truly imaginative kind, that is, coloured with deep human feeling, are given, which no sketches of the beautiful principality have ever excelled, save those in Mr. Downe's "Mountain Decameron." He loses his father in early childhood, and the circumstances connected with this ruling event of his life for misery—the death-bed, the funeral, the changes in the household, the men and women drifted in upon the almost broken-hearted child's field of vision by reason of the catastrophe, are described with marvellous pathos and power. The boy's sufferings at school, his escape from the thraldom, his wanderings in dens and through depths of darkness—his glimpse of one creature *who had been kind*, to whom he yearned—for whom he felt in his lonely shattered soul capacities of love—carry the autobiography down to chapter xviii. where it abruptly breaks off in some disjointed fragments altogether lyrical in their passionate eloquence, hinting the author's madness and his return to a drear sanity—to "a sluggish calm."

Samples of inadequate extent we can alone give our readers of "Arthur Owen." Did space and time permit, the entire transference to our columns of the second chapter—one charming and highly finished series of landscapes,—would best evidence the literary excellence of the story and the genius of the writer. Here however is an incident told with touching grace: [Extract.]

It is scarcely necessary to recall the reader's attention to those lonely images —"the blackbird in the hazels *cooling* the air with his *gushing* song," and the niche in which "the empty robin's nest" was "half-hidden with primrose leaves." To more delicate, albeit very circumstantial, touches of imagination would we point :—the thought how things would look when the boy came down; the gray cromlech glowing warm in the evening sun; the impertinent intrusion of a ludicrous image (that of the wagtail's resemblance to the squire's lady) on what was felt to be holy ground; the black park-trees in the twilight "stretching out their arms, as if they were ogres" about to snatch him from his father, "over the dim wall"; and the omen that came with the night, and descended with that paraclete—the unlooked-for assiduity of affection in his father's heart. Another and a different scene we shall now present, the catastrophe and close of which—particularly its workings on the thoughts of the boy, and the "environment" of circumstances and images all tinctured by his sense of what had taken place—we regard as manifesting very high qualities in the writer. [Extract.]

We shall now turn to the poetry. To this we have already, in general terms, alluded. Our estimate of the original pieces, though they are often graceful and musical in expression, is, we feel certain, much what Peter's own is—not a very high one. The translations, as we have already hinted, are of the very first order. Perhaps, no poet has ever been so often translated, alike by sage and schoolboy, as Horace. Yet, to our mind, nothing has ever equalled 'Possum's versions of the ode to Pyrrha, and the *duet*, Horace and Lydia, given below. And his translations from the Greek Anthology have a warmth and colour unknown to the scholarly and correct, but frigid renderings of Bland and Merivale—are more compact, and have, therefore, more of the special character of the Greek epigram than the sprightly translations of William Hay, published in "Blackwood's Magazine," some years ago. [Extracts from Possum's poetical writings are here given, and the notice concludes with a friendly farewell.]

In the *Southern Cross* he published a series of obituary notices of eminent men of letters. In the years 1859-60, many illustrous names were enrolled in the records of Death. The great writers

of the last generation followed each other to the grave in quick
succession. Among these were De Quincey, Macaulay, Leigh
Hunt, and Mrs. Jamieson, and on each of these, as the news
reached here, Mr. Deniehy wrote a few critical comments. The
following article on De Quincey has a special value, inasmuch as
it throws some light on the mental growth of the writer :

The mightiest master of the English language, and one of the mightiest
masters of style in any language, has passed away. All the opium excesses of
his youth, and the unappeased and pursuing grief and misfortunes of his life,
notwithstanding the small, frail, world-worn organization—" Life in its house
of bones"—with that thin luxuriously sweet voice which R. P. Gillies said
"seemed as if it came out of Dreamland," had survived to an age far beyond
that usually allotted to the sons of men. To ourselves, personally—who are
under intellectual obligations to De Quincey's writings greater than we are to
any modern author—the intelligence was literally a shock. The great critic
said, in his earlier papers on Wordsworth in "Tait's Magazine,"—in one of
those sentences no man but De Quincey ever framed in English, having that
harmony subtle as organic beauty, when compared with the mechanical forms,
however clever, which are generally termed Style, that the deeper admiration
of Wordsworth would be found to grow in the hearts of men and women
located in the austere melancholy loneliness of the American and Australian
Continents. It was one of the dearest hopes of our heart that we should ourselves one day live to see the great Master of philosophic criticism, and of all
forms of the expression of Thought, Imagination, and Passion, and pour at
his feet the whole enthusiastic treasures of a life-long admiration, and a life-
long gratitude, of one whose mind the illustrious writer's influence had done so
much to mould here in Australia,—and to contemplate and understand all
literature and philosophy from stern majestic summits of the ideal and spiritual,
which, but for him and that pure and pathetic medium of deep human affection
through which he loved to contemplate all things, would never have been
afforded us.

To us, one of the saddest lessons in modern literary history, is the slow and
reluctant acknowledgment of the paramount claims of De Quincey. Not simply
by the public at large; that is easily explained; but by literary men and critics.
For years, the most omnivorous of readers knew little more of De Quincey than
that he was the person who had written *The Confessions of an English Opium
Eater.* To dozens of grateful persons with some real pretensions to letters we
have, ourselves, had the pleasure of introducing a Prince in English Literature
with claims as unknown to his natural subjects as the Russian verses of Puschkin
or the *Diablo Mundo* of Espeonceda. Dean Trench, in a foot-note to one of
his books on the English language, couched in terms of the profoundest admira-

tion, recommended De Quincey's writings. But the only worthy "appraisal," —to use a pet phrase of his own—of his pretensions, was in the *Leader* newspaper, from the pen, we suspect, of that masterly critic, G. H. Lewes, and also in a paper which appeared some years ago in "Hogg's Instructor," purporting to be the experiences of a German scholar in his study of English Literature. The *Leader* said boldly that De Quincey was the greatest of the masters of the English language. And the writer in Hogg remarked, with keen critical truth, that it was literally impossible to know the capabilities and resources of English, without an acquaintance with this great writer's productions. Perhaps, one way of accounting for this obscurity of position under the magnificent proscenium of literary fame, was that De Quincey's writings were scattered through periodicals, and so embedded in strata of comparatively ephemeral and comparatively valueless matter. It *is* a fact that till very lately—till the American corrections and the author's own reprint in serial volumes, De Quincey's writings had alone this disadvantageous form of book-existence. But where were the critics and intellectual teachers of the people not to disclose the existence of this treasure— to quote what had been said on specific subjects by De Quincey better than any man, living or dead, had before spoken ; and to show there was a grandeur and a glory of expression, a music, a disciplined but almost lyrical passion in the English language which—and we know exactly what we are saying—we defy the national literatures of the world, ancient or modern, to parallel. At the close of last year a stupid pedagogue in Edinburgh, hight Mr. Demaus, brought forth a class-book of English Literature, most elaborately arranged in historic periods, and so ostentatiously exhaustive as to range its modern specimens of great English writers from Carlyle to Mr. Austen Layard,—*his* claim to the honours of a classic in the richest of literatures being the book on the Nineveh excavations. But De Quincey,—in a work published in the city, where, in the intimacy of John Wilson, the most brilliant episodes of his literary life took place, is not even mentioned. Even Mr. Robert Aris Wilmott, one of the best judges living on what is majestic and profound in alliance with beauty and nobleness of form, has no niche in his beautiful "Parlour Table Book," ranging from Hooker, Sir Phillip Sydney, Taylor and Donne, to Coleridge and Landor, for the most powerful vindicator of Christianity in our language—for what Mr. Gilfillan has aptly called, "the most gifted of scholars, and the most scholarly" of men of genius!

The range of De Quincey's acquirements was, as has been before remarked, literally encyclopædiac. Seldom has imagination so grand and poetic—so much passion and sensibility—been mated with learning and knowledge so profound, so various, and so accurate. Burke's case is scarcely an exception. Burke is rather comprehensive than deep, though unquestionably among the greatest thinkers. But he had neither the subtlety of De Quincey, nor his philosophic instincts. De Quincey sees a truth at once; Burke searches, and reasons himself into seeing it. Besides, with all the florid quality of his style, and his opulent fancy, he had not the Miltonic breadth and massiveness of De Quincey's imagination. Often, in a word, this faculty of the Opium Eater's appears, as when speaking of the element of cruelty in heathen worship, he says of the Gods, "their eyes *smiled darkly,*" on human sacrifices. There are few things Burke has done that De Quincey could not have done. But Burke could not have written De Quincey's philosophic criticisms of poetry, nor, under any possible circumstances, the raptures, deep as the principles of love and grief in the human heart, of the *Suspiria de Profundis.* We think that De Quincey's mind had more of the Roman than the Greek quality. Power and grandeur were rather his chief mental attributes and the objects of his sympathy, than the forms of pure beauty, of repose, and pleasure. In this, it strikes us the contrast with his great friend Coleridge, whose main haunt and region, when he was not discussing theology and metaphysics, stood among the luxuries of Beauty. De Quincey had a virility that would have made him a politician and a statesman; Coleridge, with his "Conciones ad Populum" and his "Manuals," never would have made either.

The masterly writer in the *Leader* already referred to, notices what must have struck every reader of De Quincey,—the *excursiveness* which is so frequently a character of his essays. He has a habit of wandering away from the main line or paths, that diverge or rather travel off from his subject. The critic of the *Leader* suspects in this an infirmity of the Will, arising perhaps, more or less, from a morose paralysis induced by the use of that drug with which the Prince of Dreamers has for ever connected his fame. In this, the writer sees, too, a clue to the somewhat fragmentary character of most of De Quincey's performances. Will in character he can scarcely be said to have lacked, for he conquered perhaps the most fascinatingly tyrannical, the most inexorable in its charms, of all evil habits,—Opium eating. And, as a dear and honoured friend of De Quincey's remarked to us, some days since, there must have been Will, and plenty of it in the man who, a refugee within the precincts of the Abbey of Edinburgh, under pressure of misery so terrible as to approach positive want among those he loved so dearly,—those to whom allusions of majestic tenderness threw such tender shades of pathos as never before fell over prose literature,—would nevertheless contribute to "Blackwood" masterly disquisitions—the most calmly and deeply considered, and the most philosophic *de omnibus rebus,*—and to "Tait" all the Ionic beauty of his Lake reminiscences. Then, as to the excursiveness,—though we think it very frequently mars the effect of much of De Quincey's historical, critical, and polemical writing, for *directness* is, in all speaking and writing, one of the prime elements of *power,*—we think it may be accounted for in another way. Where a very able writer indeed would see but one or two sides to his subject, the unique subtlety of De Quincey's mind would see sides and angles numberless,— examination of which *he* deemed collateral aids to the *approfondissement* of the theme. Then making the divergences from the main point of inspection more signal,—it is the nature of human character that the collateral question, once started, a mind, not only wealthy in speculative thought, but so richly furnished with almost all that could be known on the subject—thoroughly a master of the facts and opinions on the point of those who preceded him—so full of illustrative anecdote and historical suggestion, should employ it to a perhaps inartistic augmentation of a mere appendage. It was as if over zealous and over wealthy Piety should lavish its appliances on making the side chapel in a cathedral so rich and so unduly large, as to leave what might have been an additional circumstance of beauty and state an excrescence on the mother fabric. As to the fragmentary character, it must always, more or less, belong to all writing for the serials of the day, executed to order, almost under the pressure of immediate demand, and still worse, of immediate wants in the executant himself. Think of De Quincey sitting calmly and comfortably down surrounded by the magnificence and light of mountain and lake scenery, in the seclusion of Lausanne, as Gibbon did, to write, as the object of a life, some great cardinal history of a nation. How much fairer if, once so situated, he did no better than his still superb papers on the Cæsars, it would be to seek for a key to the fragmentary character of his Essays in psychologic causes. Besides, we have a suspicion that all human speculation, so lofty and so grand as those in which De Quincey's intellect loved to dwell, as the eagle on lone cliffs that look out evermore on the mysterious and melancholy sea, and, indeed, all the loftier exercises even of the imaginative faculty—leave on the mind a subconsciousness (the word is De Quincey's own) of the incomplete and the fragmentary. We do not now refer to the unfinished character of so many of this great writer's magazine papers, where the causes are much nearer the ordinary circumstances of life, and the meaner necessities and characteristics of our common nature. One thing we cannot help alluding to, before closing,— the pathetic profundity with which the religious conviction and the unfaltering belief in Truth, of De Quincey, everywhere shew themselves. Even to one rejecting the writer's belief, this quality gives his speculations a deep and touching beauty.

O sad ! sad ! the life-story of this grandly endowed being—this man so gifted, as seldom, in all the ages, God gives to His creatures powers so exquisite and so vast ; and capacities of suffering co-equal in their exquisiteness and their vastness. When we think of the lonely boy a fugitive in the streets of London, and rescued from starvation by the generosity of the poor street-walker, Anne, her that he wished to follow, were it possible, "into the darkness of the grave, to waken her with an authentic message of peace and forgiveness and genial reconciliation!" Then his lonely life in his eyrie at Westmoreland, his thoughtful visits across the hills at midnight to Wordsworth. His domestic bereavement, his deep sorrows ; the interregnum of actual happiness and peace which must have stretched from the date of his commencing to his resigning the use of opium—a season of darkness, ploughed at times by weird lightnings and Elysian ineffable glimpses of beauty through the rifts of the abiding clouds, come before us mournfully. Equally melancholy, with all the surpassing splendour of his intellectual activities and his services to literature—

his growing old, unappreciated, while the Macaulays and the Hallams, with all the sparkle and finish of the one, and the dry, weighty literature of the other—but runnels and fountains compared to the stately Danube of De Quincey's intellect, were among the *dii majores* of the nation! One recollects, too, his deep devotion and his fervent admiration of Wordsworth—for whom his noble criticisms do more with "thinking hearts" than anything else that has ever been written about him—and for Coleridge. And the reader, with an eye and an ear for the grief which is too noble for the slightest cry of resentment, hears in the occasional moan, as it were, of a self-sequestered sorrow, how bitterly the deep omnificent spirit had been stricken by the coldness—cold, albeit as pure as his own Skiddaw,—of Wordsworth, and perhaps the selfishness of Coleridge. Both were good and great men, but there were those with infinitely less intellect and a good deal less of the severer virtues, we should be inclined to love more. But the end has come, and the august dreams of the Unseen which girdled his way through life are long since, we trust, realised for De Quincey. And one thing is certain—that wherever the literature and the language of England exist, as that of one of the noblest of her intellects, will the memory of Thomas De Quincey be cherished, and his writings regarded as one of the grandest of the national possessions.

The following article on Macaulay was written and published at the same time:

Perhaps no name is more intimately identified with what is classic in English Literature than Lord Macaulay's. To perfect mastery of facts, and the whole field of opinion as connected with the subjects he treated, Lord Macaulay added the charms of a style in some senses the most brilliant in the language. The purely rhetorical graces of composition—everything that *mind* could do, divorced from an impassioned temperament—were manifested in the writings of this distinguished man. His *magnum opus*—his "History of England"—of course remains unfinished; but it is questionable whether any literature presents a work so unique. The noble author did not realise the ambitious project he announced in the opening chapter of his book, in phrases not unworthy of Cicero or of Gibbon. But he did not achieve this: for the first time in history a man appeared to depict national progress, who had not only political science and vast learning, but who, with a knowledge of facts and events elaborately extracted from sources the most recondite—muniment rooms, private family journals, and forgotten books and pamphlets, printed when there were persecuted travelling presses in England, which no man in his generation but Lord Macaulay knew of,—combined a pictorial power of realising and presenting scenes and actors never before possessed by a historian. The reader who wishes to see what the Painter would term high art and low art in Literature, should pass from one of Lord Macaulay's *tableaux* in the History of England—for instance, the death-bed of King Charles II.—to what is generally termed the "graphic" portion in the writings of the very best novelists of the day. You turn from an Italian master to Wilkie or Mulready. Both are "true;" but the grandeur and the dignity which men associate with historic truth belongs to the one. The other gives the every-day *vraisemblance* of town and village life.

But Lord Macaulay's reputation will be most enduring as the Essayist. His papers upon historical subjects are rather what the French call *etudes*, than what we English ordinarily understand as Essays. Everything that is known on the subject is exhibited—and exhibited in a masterly way, and sound critical inferences are uniformly drawn. But then the defect comes; fine writing, great learning, exquisite handling of what *has* been handled: but no such turning over the topic in a fresh and unsuspected light, such as one would have had from Coleridge, or Carlyle, or De Quincey, or even John Sterling, and many an "inheritor of unfulfilled renown." A gifted man Lord Macaulay was in a very high sense, and especially the type of an accomplished man, but his success in letters among his countrymen proves and illustrates the salient quality of the Anglo-Saxon mind. Lord Macaulay could deal brilliantly with anything, but he took care always to deal with facts; and *there* lay the secret of his success. English readers, with small taste for abstract truths, who have the privilege of reading Emerson and Julius Charles Hare in their own language, preferred to either the American or the Englishman, the point, the decision, the character of being posted up to facts, and the muscular grace with which Macaulay handled things on a level with every reader's intelligence. Lord Macaulay could be a slashing critic, too—and he extinguished Robert Montgomery—but as the noble Lord had no pretensions to philosophical criticism, *he* could be extinguished in turn. One distinguished contributor to the pages of the *Southern Cross*, Mr. R. H. Horne, of Melbourne, uprooted and scattered to the winds for ever, in a notice of Macaulay's Essay on Milton, in the *New Spirit of the Age*, the pretensions of the brilliant essayist to the character of a critic in æsthetics. Lord Macaulay had said that some degree of madness was inseparable from the poetic character in its higher manifestations. Mr. Horne triumphantly shewed that a man who really had pretensions to the sacred name, must base his claims, not upon some Sybilline frenzy, but upon a finer and clearer sense, —a keener and profounder perception of great truths, than belongs to his cotemporaries.

We have to say a word or two of Lord Macaulay in his characters of Orator and Poet. And first as an Orator. Perhaps the speeches smell too much of the lamp. And we all know that he wrote and got them by heart before he delivered them. So did Sheil—so did Plunkett, whom Lord Dudley and Ward called the first speaker in the House of Commons of his day; so did the old Greek Orators. But read them; and there are no speeches in print so finished and so felicitous as Macaulay's speeches on Parliamentary Reform and the Government of India.

Lord Macaulay in earlier life,—if we recollect rightly, in Knight's "Quarterly Magazine,"—produced some brilliant verses. The noble Lord could be always brilliant, but never poetic. Still it is a question if there is anything finer in the language than the *Armada*, and what heart has not thrilled to the ballad of the fourth French Henry at Ivry?

> Press where you see my white plumes shine amid the ranks of war,
> And be your Oriflamme to day the helmet of Navarre!

But Lord Macaulay's most ambitious production was the "Lays of Ancient Rome." The book showed that Lord Macaulay, though not a poet, was poetic, and unquestionably a scholar in whom the older literatures had kindled and become a fire. He himself has brilliantly described triumphs such as the laureation of Petrarc at the Capitol, but here was the triumph of a scholar with the average endowments of fancy and feeling. So close, with all the art, and the lore, and the versified rhetoric, did it bring the author to the true poet, that the best judges were at times puzzled as to which was the true Dromio.

Gone to his grave. Perhaps his fame reposes on the exercise of those faculties which literary men, using philosophic terminology, call Talent as distinguished from Genius. But it is much to be questioned if any names of recent days will go down to posterity with higher prestige than that of Thomas Babington Macaulay. Young men of Genius, mark the moral! Men of the most splendid faculties and the richest endowments,—William Maginn, for example,—have passed and left poor traces upon their country's literature, which the next century will efface. Take the example of Macaulay, who husbanded every talent, who used every virtue of prudence and economy, and who—great as his abilities certainly were—has a thousand fold greater chance of living as a British classic than men of almost infinitely higher powers.

The next paper was on Leigh Hunt:

In the obituary of September, brought us by the Malta, is the name of Leigh Hunt. He died at Putney on the 28th August, in the 75th year of his age. Forty years ago Shelley addressed him from Rome in the dedication of "The Cenci." "One more gentle, honourable, innocent, and brave—one of more exalted toleration for all who do and think evil, and yet himself more free from evil; one who knows better how to receive and how to confer a benefit, though he must ever confer far more than he can receive; one of simpler, and, in the highest sense of the word, of purer life and manners, I never knew: and I had already been fortunate in friendships, when your name was added to the list." Loftier tribute of respect has rarely been paid, or sincerer—for the man was never born that Shelly would have flattered. How precious this truth of character in a world where our friends tell as many lies to please, as our enemies to pain us!

Leigh Hunt's nature was of the most graceful and beautiful kind,—fresh, resilient, and flowering to the last. Like the Shepherd Boy in Sir Philip Sidney's "Arcadia," he piped as if he never would grow old. His mission seemed, as Spenser said of the presence of Una, to make sunshine in the shady places of the earth. There was too much boyish goodness and sweetness in him, to sympathise very heartily with the fiercer struggles of men. At his heart was for ever the whispering consciousness that things might be better brought about by the Power of Gentleness he has sung with a grace more delicate than the grace of the Sicilian muse he so loved. He was right, if men would only look upon the thing as the loving poet did. But meanwhile, Leigh Hunt had Philosophy as well as Pleasure on his side. "Nothing," says Goethe, "is an illusion that makes us happy."

No truer heart than Hunt's and no more courageous intellect in the cause of Right, and what he held to be Truth, will you find in the history of modern literature. His faith in good, his unquenchable hope, his charity, tender and boundless, made his writings a fountain and an oasis in an era when Sahara under the breath of "the most lone Simoom," was thought a type of the higher ideal; and this will make them lovely and a solace for ever. He had his own sorrows and his struggles; and his circumstances in life were always dim and sorry enough,—now, a poor man tossing with his family in Italy, trying to throw up a *gunyah* under the somewhat bleak and gloomy ranges of Lord Byron's friendship,—now in late age, flying into such raptures as saw in Royalty, after its decided liking for the "Legend of Florence" at the theatre, something like an embodiment of all human virtues conceivable. We allude to this, because we see, or think we see in it, the pathos of an overflow of gratitude from one who had grown old in comparative neglect. It

> Flattered to tears that aged man and poor.

Yet no moodiness of hate, or shade of uncharity, in his poetry the while. There, the precious elements of his genius—its sweet airs, its sunbeams, and its dews—the bloom and the fragrance of a nature more like Chaucer's or Boccaccio's than any in modern times, were gathered as his contribution in aid of that cause of Human Happiness which he looked upon literature as altogether created to serve.

He was the Stothard of poetry. The region of Grace deepening ever and anon into Beauty, was the haunt and vantage ground of his genius. His poems were sensuous, but with a spontaneous organic growth out of his own nature, which neither the sensuousness of the great living poet Tennyson, nor Mr. Dobell's, nor that of any of the laureate's other disciples, possesses. Art is with *them* often conscious, and has to seek. The thing was in Leigh Hunt part of his temperament; the weakling tendril as much as the rich bough grew out of and belonged to mother Earth. He was deficient in passion; and this disqualified him not only for dramatic Art, but, combined with the sunny hilarity of his nature, made the depths of tragic strife and tragic woe distasteful to him. He shows in his preface to the "Stories from the Italian Poets,"— one of those charming critical prefaces which Leigh Hunt alone could write, alike fitted for schoolboy and sage, from the transparency of expression and simple directness of thought—the superiority in Shakspere to Dante, because of the large element of human gladness. We suspect, that even if Shakspere had been inferior to the "sad Florentine" in essential poetic power, Leigh Hunt, on the one ground that the former had admitted more of the light of human gaiety and cheerfulness into his world, would have preferred him. The grim images of the Dolorous City, we conceive, were not a whit less in unison with his natural tastes than "the dark sorrows of the line of Thebes." But this scarcely ever impaired his fine critical instinct. He devotes pages to an attack on the sort of taste and feeling exhibited in the mediæval theology of the "Inferno," for reasons which would make the "Paradise Lost" only a degree or two less objectionable. But Carlyle himself, with all his worship of Power, has said nothing finer of the intensity of Dante. A single passage will give one who has never read the "Divina Commedia," either in Italian or English, a livelier, more concrete idea of the general characteristics of the poet than a volume of tolerably good criticism. "The invisible is at the back of the visible; darkness becomes palpable; silence describes a character, nay, forms the most striking part of a story; a word acts as a flash of lightning, which displays some gloomy neighbourhood where a tower is standing, with dreadful faces at the window; or *where, at your feet, full of eternal voices, one abyss is beheld dropping out of another, in the lurid light of torment.*" And the ineffable majesty and beauty of Dante's angels, and the Elysian interspaces of repose in the poem, are described with almost equal felicity.

He was the kindest and most genial, as well as one of the best of critics. He came disposed to find merit, high or humble, much or little, in the book before him. He had a word of praise—so wise and so gentle it was! for the poor daisy that grew beside the field-style, as well as for the most gorgeous blooms. Search through the wide range of his miscellaneous writings, from the days of the *Indicator* upward, and you will find no one harsh, much less arbitrary, phrase of criticism. A blow at Cant he aimed whenever he could, but his nature always overflowing with ruth, in nine cases out of ten, when the blow fell, the Canter was dead and gone. A collection of Leigh Hunt's criticisms, inclusive as well of his special essays on books and of the notices scattered throughout his numerous publications, as of such comparatively brief observations as occur in his notes and prefaces, would make one of the most fascinating books in the language.

The "Legend of Florence" was his dramatic effort. It is very graceful; full of purity, gentleness, tenderness, pity. The husband is a wretch; the lover much to be sympathised with; the lady a sweet and noble creature to love and to be sad for. But it is not a great drama. To compose one, there was, as we have just said, too little sympathy or self-identification in Leigh Hunt with the grandeur of passion—the magnificent warfare of the daring spirit with circumstance. He thought—far overmuch—this world too beautiful and good, ever to be a great dramatic poet in any sense, much less a tragic poet. The "burthen and the mystery" pressed on him too lightly : his spiritual being had struck no root deep enough in the Unseen, where the solutions wait. It is perfectly impossible, under any circumstances, to conceive Leigh Hunt creating such grand types of the struggle as Robert Browning's Djabal, or Luria, or King Victor, or Richard Horne's Cosmo de Medici, or his magnificent Marlowe,—

> Bright is the day, the air with glory teems,
> And eagles wanton in the smiles of Jove.
> Can these things be, and Marlowe live no more?

Circumstances long prevented Leigh Hunt's recognition as a poet, which shows how much tact might have done in the world of letters as it does in lower and coarser regions. He was saluted by the scribblers of the day as the Coryphœus of the Cockney School. Keats, as his *protegé*, of course belonged to it ; Hazlitt was sometimes ranked on the forms, (as by Maginn in his parody on "Yarrow Unvisited,") and so was John Hamilton Reynolds, whose promise never gave fruition. So might have been Hood. Now if there was any internal weakness in the school—any affectations at all—Barry Cornwall, in his earlier and longer efforts, exhibited them in common with Hunt and his friends. But he had never written sonnets about Hampstead and the other pleasant environs of London. "He sang of Africa and golden joys"—he took himself in fact to Sicily, and

> The shores of old romance.

And if Hunt had consented to burn a great many occasional verses, written under suburban inspirations, he might have saved himself much annoyance. His beautiful story of "Rimini," in its own history affords a proof of how little ground, as regarded Hunt's poems, there was either in philosophy or fact for the cry of cockneyism—how little a man of genius requires the culture of "travel" to enable him to write fine poetry of which the scene happens to be laid in foreign lands. "Rimini" with its landscapes—the wood of Ravenna included, was published before Leigh Hunt visited Italy, and the beauty of scenic description sank into the soul of every reader of sensibility, to remain there for ever. After the poet had beheld the actual places, he altered the scenery—treated the thing photographically, but with so deep and pursuing a sequence of failure that, late in life, in the last editions of his poems, the original landscapes were restored as the "environments" of Francesca and her lover. How the beautiful episodes of "Rimini" live in the memory—the Nuptials, the Journey through the Pine Forest, the Garden, and the Funeral of the Lovers, at close of autumn, with the last few leaves flying over the chill and darkening road, and the crowd awaiting till the sad *cortege* made its appearance, when

> Turn'd aside both young and old,
> And in their hands the gushing sorrow roll'd.

But the poem of the "Nymphs," so full of "the warm South," and the sonnets in the volume called "Foliage," long out of print—appear to us most to exhibit the *specialite* as a poet of Leigh Hunt. Of his prose writings, his romances of real life, his charming revivals of classic story, copies as it were by Fiamingo and Canova of the women and children on a Greek frieze, and his exquisite essays, forming, in themselves, the freshest and merriest work in the great literature of the day which saw them produced, we have no time to speak. They will never be read by a man fitted to appreciate the grace and affection for all good that inspire them, without a love for the author, simultaneous with admiration for his work.

In that grave of Leigh Hunt sleeps as true a Friend of Human-kind as ever drew the breath of life. An earnest, we trust, of the living admiration which awaits his memory, wherever the language and the literature of the land is known, is the poor offering we have tried to hang up, as it were in funeral honour,—the tribute of one born and bred in a community which had scarcely existence at all in the days when Leigh Hunt began the noble labour of his life long years ago.

The fourth paper, on Mrs. Jamieson, affords some further evidence of the writer's familiarity with Fine Art topics :—

One of the first female critics in Literature, and the only female writer deserving the title of a critic in Art—Anne Jamieson—is, we regret to find by the latest European obituary, no more. Thick as the autumnal leaves of Milton's Vallombrosa, the maturer celebrities of English Literature are, week by week, falling to earth. Each mail-steamer brings us tidings that the place of some illustrious writer, whose nobler part has passed into the "life of life" of millions, knows him no more. Leigh Hunt, De Quincey, Washington Irving, Macaulay ; the fact that these men departed, one after another, some months ago—recent ships bringing successive obituaries—how it seems to loosen a link, beautiful as some golden clasp covered with the historical chasings of a Cellini, that bound the palmiest days of modern English genius with present time. Leigh Hunt, his tribulations, trials, and cheerfulness—for him, enchanted Hope ever smiling and waving her golden hair,—were of the days of "Lord Byron and his Cotemporaries," and far back therein. Shelley wrote to him, a lad at Oxford, fire even then at the root of his spirit ; "Zastrozzi" and "The Rosicrucian" all he could do—" Prometheus Unbound" and "The Cenci " among the things that were not. De Quincey's Opium Confessions are incidentally mentioned in "Don Juan." With Washington Irving—how far back it *must* be —dates belief in England that a Yankee could write readable English prose. But the other day, as it were, an American who handles English as only three or four writers have ever done, Emerson, painted British society a portrait of itself which made British society open its eyes. A philosopher abroad on his travels was for the first time a fact ; and something new realised in that most impertinent department of literature—voyages and travels—namely, persons and places, landscape and character, depicted from a philosophic point of view. Macaulay's youthful essay, "Milton," with its solid richness of diction and its æsthetics as shallow as Burke on the Sublime, carries us on to the time of Robert Hall. The account of Dante made the fascinated preacher think of learning Italian at an age as advanced, or more so, than Alfieri's, when the poet tackled the Greek conjugations. What a success, in the broadest and most emphatic sense, the career of the man from the publication in the "Edinburgh" of his early papers, to the hour, almost, when Baron Macaulay of Bothwell was laid at the foot of Addison's statue in the august glooms of Westminster, to rest him in honour for all time.

Though Mrs. Jamieson's *specialite* was the criticism of Art, yet her rank as a critic of literature is very high. Her distinction was won, too, in the loftiest field—the Shaksperian drama. Wilson made her "Female Characters of Shakspere" the basis of a series of papers in "Blackwood." The eloquence is Wilsonian—that is saying a good deal—but for real criticism—for fine analysis—the lady's book has stuff in it that you nowhere find in the writings of the great critical authority. Judging from her books, no more exquisite womanly instincts could have existed than those of Mrs. Jamieson; and then, with the finest sense of the ideal and of poetic art, she proceeds, from the woman's point of view, to examine and report on Shakspere's women. And she does it with consummate truth and grace and beauty. Neither Margaret Fuller, nor George Sand, nor Rahel, nor any of the great women, could have done it as well. Their really vast intellects—particularly in the case of Margaret Fuller and Rahel, both endowed with a high analytic faculty, left them scarcely *woman* enough for the task. Talk as we will, extraordinary intellect, which means extraordinary strength in one specific direction, has a tendency to subtract from the *morale* of womanly nature —and to lessen somehow what Chaucer and the Ettrick Shepherd call "*feminitie.*" Pallas, with the broad, lofty, and serene forehead, the gaze that, as Winckelmann said of the Belvidere Apollo, looks forward as it were steadfastly into the Infinite, and the straightly pure, calm Greek profile is very good in marble; but Pallas in charge of a baby in long clothes would be a bright idea! Vittoria Colonna must have been an august impersonation of womanly intellect and womanly character, and those noble Platonic attentions of Michael Angelo's did him quite as much credit as they did her. But then the Signora Colonna was hardly the person that, restored to one's *Lares* after a long journey, one could suddenly throw one's arms about with a view to osculatory proceedings. Those stately and pensive lips could hardly be expected to utter any Italian synonym for "duck of diamonds." The style of the work is as pure, as fresh, and as sweet as a flower. The man who owns a refined and high-bred woman "yestreen a blushing bride," could, in the form of wedding-gift, pay his wife no more delicate, no truer compliment, than the donative of Mrs. Jamieson's "Female Characters of Shakspere."

This beautiful womanly element is the charm of Mrs. Jamieson's writings. Beautiful it is, reader, when you bear in mind that this gifted lady was neither a poetess nor a novelist—with prerogative for all sorts of overflowing love for everything in the first instance, and unlimited right to put any amount of fine things into the mouths of her *dramatis personæ* in the second. She was a critic ; as true and as thorough when she looked at historical fresco or at portrait, as William Hazlitt. The result, as seen by woman's eye, and the effect on the feminine soul, she gave you clearly, steadily—with the science of a connoisseur, with the gentleness and the mild truth of a woman. England had patronised Angelica Kaufmann, and has seen Horace Walpole's friend, Mrs. Damer, ("*Non me Praxiteles fecit sed Anna Damer*") and Mrs. Thornycroft cutting marble ; but no female critic in art—and a critic in high art is not quite so easily made as a critic in literature, because of certain peculiar elements which are absolute conditions of existence—till Mrs. Jamieson appeared. The literature of France and Germany has no equivalent ; and though George Sand has talked grandly and profoundly of music—for the highest type of female opinion upon pictorial art every inquirer, either artistic or purely psychologic, must consult English literature and the writings of Anne Jamieson.

The following article, written on the death of Mr. Whitty, may be taken as another specimen of his critical appreciation. It possesses a deeper interest than that, however,—for the early death of the writer suggests to us reflections painfully similar to those with which he mourned the death of Whitty : while the sympathy he so tenderly expressed for another was felt far and wide in these colonies when his own death became known :—

"Alas, for poor Whitty ! He died last night in Boroondara," was the telegraphic message from a dear and honoured mutual friend* of Edward Whitty's and our own, put into our hand on Thursday morning. The author of "Friends of Bohemia" and "The Governing Classes," had passed away in the very spring-tide of his youth—having given the world early indication of his extraordinary powers. For years few things have more shocked and saddened us than this. Mingled with our intense admiration of his genius, was a deep sympathy with grief which made his case signal and salient in the annals of domestic sorrow. We had never had the pleasure of seeing Mr. Whitty, but kindly letters had been exchanged—mutual friends had created mutual interest—and he once wrote of his intention to visit Sydney. Some weeks since, however, we met in this city the amiable physician who had

---

* R. H. Horne.

attended Mr. Whitty with fraternal care, and his notification at once quenched a hope we had very dearly cherished. In the opinion of the medical man, Mr. Whitty's health would not even sustain the slight fatigue of the voyage up from Melbourne. But still we had not thought the dark hour was so near.

Only a few months since, he arrived at Melbourne. In England, his wife and his two children had been carried off within the space of a fortnight by typhus fever. Far advanced in consumption, he was driven abroad to seek, in change of scene, some little relief from the terrible weight of his anguish—some little solace, too, for his own poor withering frame. And with the darkness of these things about him, in a strange land—though well we know he had beside his pillow, in the last hours, friends as true and tender and loyal as ever man had—Edward Whitty died on the night of the 21st instant, in his thirty-fifth year or thereabouts.

There is, to our mind, no story in the whole melancholy chronicle of the misfortunes of men of genius so sad as this of Edward Whitty. That he was something more and something higher than a man of genius—that his nature was moulded of the profoundest sensibilities, and that he altogether lived upon deep and passionate affections, is evinced by the utter shattering and subversion of health, hopes, and interests in the world, which followed the loss of his dear ones. Others, and men of fine mind and fine feeling, too, would, perhaps, have come out of the typhoon, dismasted and with broken timbers, but eventually to regain and to ride quietly for years on the world's waters. So young, too—so gifted—so abounding and ebullient with the life-blood of intellectual power, not the mere faculty of writing graceful verses or beautiful trifles of any kind, but with that power—disciplined by learned experiences of the ways of life—to deal with men and things—hard and cold and clear, and bright, warm, and joyous, just as they are. He knew life. He knew Men and Women, as it is only given to those destined in time to become Masters in Literature to know them. And in indications of this lies the value of "Friends of Bohemia," as an implement for guaging the author's genius. The book, it is true, is a mere bundle of sketches, with no connecting thread of story, and a very shadowy and undefined plot. It was obviously no intention of the author's to make it specifically a story. He only cared to present sketches of life and character of a peculiar kind. But there are scattered through it gleams of insight into human nature—worn and haggard and wilful as it is under the *régime de Bohême*, such as are seldom found beyond the pages of Thackeray or Balzac. Any writer with adequate "experience" can write of Bohemia; but to know and tell how the poor, jaded, wild heart beats in Bohemia: to see and depict clearly and keenly,—without cloud or impediment of any kind—the story of a human life flowing forward, all heartless and reckless through the systematic vice of communities with an intensified civilization, only Edward Whitty could do. His creation of Nea, in "Friends of Bohemia"—the poor girl-wife that her father, a selfish peer deeply in debt to an old commercial speculator, had given to the latter's

Bohemian son, though but a sketch, is a creation of the very highest beauty, and positively a contribution of the imaginative literature of England.

Saddest of all, now that Edward Whitty has passed away, is the fact that his genius has developed itself in no adequate degree, and in no work commensurate with its power. "The Governing Classes" is a collection of the most brilliant, and, as a hostile reviewer admitted, the "justest" political sketches of modern times. But they are the mere *croquis* of an artist who could paint, if he chose to work, like Hogarth. "Friends of Bohemia" was thrown off so hastily, and with such little purpose of matching his abilities with the task, that we are told Mr. Whitty never even corrected his proofs. But we have no heart to write criticism of his genius and his writings *now*. Some other time, perhaps. Enough to pay this tribute to his memory. And to think, too, with a sad, sad heart all that might have been, and all that never will be—to shape sorrowfully for ourselves some image of the face and presence of the man we admired so deeply, and hoped once to know personally, and to learn to love.

His last letter to us was as cheerful as if written by a healthy and prosperous man in the sunshine of a happy home. He spoke of several projects, and said he was engaged in writing "a Frenchy little book." How that gay little expression haunts us! Poor Whitty! it is to us somewhat like the little watch and the trifles taken by the friends out of Jack Wortley's pocket—"things that women who had loved him had given him"—when the poor youth fell with Diego's bullet in his heart. Alas! alas! poor Edward Whitty! many of the vastest and dearest projects that employ those foolish hearts of ours must yet lie away in that dim, melancholy region where the "Frenchy little book," which the wasted hand with a sad wistful purpose of amusement was writing when the cloud descended, must stop for ever!

Another series of brief critical remarks appeared in the *Southern Cross*, under the title *Horæ Otiosores:*

What a royal movement there is in Bossuet's sentences! Only a hand clothed with an episcopal glove, flashing with embroidery of jewels, could give gesture in keeping with the stately sweep and the aulic magnificence of his periods. He seemed born to preach only to Congresses of Princes. With the elegiac grandeur of the funeral oration of Henrietta Maria of England still flashing dimly about one's mind, as the echoes of the dying organ-notes of some vesper *Miserere* wander through the aisles of a darkening cathedral, how like the finger of Mephistopheles is History's, as she points to a picture (hung in an obscure corner of the gallery) of the widow of King Charles the Martyr beaten by her degraded paramour, Jermyn. She suffers, and History (with almost the fiend's chuckle) whispers "*avec quelle grace vous le savez, Messieurs,*" from that sentence of Bossuet's sermon, engraved upon every educated Frenchman's memory, as one of the most exquisite in his country's language.

De Stendhal's (Henri Beyle) book "*De l'Amour*" is intended to be an exhaustive treatise on Love. The diagnosis of the passion in its earlier stages, though elaborate, is—perhaps of necessity—incomplete. One undescribed symptom of a nascent *tendre* occurs to me which many will, possibly, out of the fullness of their own experience, recognize as worthy of tabulation in the schedules of Beyle's *gaie science*. When a glance, a tone, a gesture, or any little peculiarity of gait or bearing in a woman for whom you have no special regard, or perhaps casually meet, pleases *because* it recalls something not dissimilar in *another*, depend upon it that *other* is already on the marches of what is in old English termed your "fancy."

I think Heinrich Heine, of whom you speak so unkindly, Olga, had not only wit, humour, and intellectual power of rare order, but far more of the poetic faculty than all the later German Poets—Uhland, Freilgath, Schwab, *et tous ces garçons là* put together. Can you, a woman and an accomplished Teutonic scholar, forget all the love-lays, fresh and delicate as the pearls fashioned on the leaves of that myrtle by the shower which has just passed away into the dim purple depths stretching within the arch of yonder rainbow—brief, but wild and sweet as the call of a bird in summer from the green vestibule of the woods—to be found in the "*Buch der Lieder*," particularly in the "*Lyrische Intermezzo*"—"*Du bliebst mir treu am langsten*," *Wenn ich in deine Augen seh*; "*Die lotosblume anstigt*"—and scores of others? His satire had the subtle edge and nimble strength of flame. There was somewhat of Thackeray's man of the world sense and judgment about him, but it flowed through an artist-temperament as fantastic as the scenery of a Midsummer Night's Dream. Then, Olga, his criticism; "into the sap of his subject," in a few sentences. I met these critical passages only yesterday: the translation is not mine, but that of a Mr. John Stores Smith, an accomplished man, who took it into his head, some time ago, to write a book in Carlylese, called, "Mirabeau, a Life History":—" The rose tint in the poems of Novalis is not the line of health, but the hectic of consumption; and the purple glow of Hoffmann's phantasies is not the flame of genius but of fever." And here is Heine, piercing into the central idea of Cervantes, in Don Quixote, with the same subtlety and the same result as Coleridge:—" Has he not in his tall lean knight represented Ideal Spirituality, and in the squat squire parodied Common Sense? Everywhere the latter cuts the more sorry figure! for Common Sense, with all its hoard of thrifty proverbs, after all jogs along on its steady-going donkey in the rear of Spirituality; in spite of its clearer sight, must it and the ass share all the mishaps that so often repel the noble knight? Yes: Ideal Spirituality is of such a potent dynamic nature, that Common Sense, with all its asses, must ever follow in its wake." And the "*Riesebilder*," the finest, perhaps, of his prose writings, is full of profound observation and beauty, the style everywhere of as finished grace as the group of a Roman cameo. It is often alive with a humour that has that terrible *motif* of cynical pathos about it, which trickles through Hamlet's talk to the skull of Yorick.

What a tract of imaginative grandeur, lying away dim, sublime, and gloomy, —like the isle Hy-Brasil of popular legend—Irish writers of poetry have left untouched in portions of the early religious history of Ireland ! Lough Dearg, with so much of what is mightiest and most lasting in relation to the heart and soul floating dimly about it, is an instance. Calderon, the Catholic, soars into this region for the poetic ; but the *Purgatorio del San Patricio*—though Shelley dug the finest image in the " Cenci " from it—is only a scratch on the surface of an auriferous soil.

Some of the best prose descriptions of forest scenery in our literature are from Charles Reece Pemberton's sketches of Sherwood. Ladies draw woodland effects beautifully. There are delicious glimpses of landscape in the " Francesca Carrara " of poor Letitia Landon,—(L. E. L.'s prose had a hundred times over finer imaginative beauty than her poems),—in Mrs. Howitt's prose fictions, and, if I recollect rightly, in Lady Fullerton's "Grantly Manor." But, irrespective of the results of exquisite observation, there is, in Pemberton's vigorous descriptions, the moral element. You have the wild abounding sense of freedom and of joy of a great athletic spirit, who loved Nature as the child its mother (always kind when everything else is cold) let loose in the woods among the silvery lady-birches, and the cool brown onyx lustre of the shadowed streams, and the aroma of the heather. Once in among the patriarchal trees— to quote his own words—" in twenty steps the world is quite shut out; you are in a strange, solemn, and old universe." Whately and Gilpin and Sir Uvedale Price work you in the effects of a landscape elaborately. They describe, with the minuteness of Van Huysum painting a bouquet. The poor way-worn wanderer—gigantic of soul—without neglecting essential detail, dashes you off his sketches with the *sprezzatura*, careless but consummate, of the master's hand. The *genius loci* is caught and bound for you in the *croquis*, while he remains unknown in the highly finished and gem-like miniature. "Walk down that sweep of undulation " says Charles, "like the mighty magnificent curve of a vast and green Atlantic billow, which, by some omnipotent, some invisible hand, has been suspended in its rolling, and fixed thus, as we see it." What a grand and free—what an honest, robust—nature, poor Pemberton's was. With its gigantic strength, the sad yearning character of the man had a mighty shaft of tenderness—loving tenderness surpassing the tenderness of woman, pouring always through its recesses, like some shy, lonely waterfall of the hills, nourished by thunderstorms, and through gates of savage shattered pines throwing its columns of irridescent glory and its music into the gloom of the ravines, unheard and unseen for ever. He loved children with a feminine love, and the man never lived that he feared. A thorough *man* he was, like Burns, and my own

P

friend Harpur.   Here are some verses of his, more like the carol of a bird than anything since the snatches of song in Shakspeare :

APRIL: SMILES AND TEARS.

Her cheek is pale, her eyes are wet ;
   Her voice in murmurings
Grieves lowly to the morn, that yet
   No sunshine brings.
Why linger ye, O laughing hours?
Uncurl, ye buds! unfold, ye flowers!
   Sad April sings.

The paleness fleets, the tears are dry,
   Her voice with gladness rings ;
The sunshine over earth and sky
   It's brightness flings.
Come revel through my laughing hours,
Ye warbling birds, ye buds, ye flowers.
   Glad April sings.

Notwithstanding the wilderness of verse on Eastern subjects, in English and the languages of continental Europe, I know of only two instances where the patriarchal grandeur—simple but massive—and the wild pathos of the finer Oriental poems, have been rendered. In Matthew Arnold's noble "Sohrab and Rustum" you have the first of the two qualities. In "Les Orientales" of Victor Hugo, the lonesome primitive poetry of Desert Life alternately wrestles and weeps, like the imprisoned night wind in the melancholy palm.

Political verse is seldom likely to yield essentially poetic results. What can, for the most part, alone be expected from it, is terse, vigorous, and memorable expression of passing opinion—felicitous condensation of the dogma and argument of the day in *one* point of view. Only where a broad lurid colouring is furnished by historical struggles, or the bitterness of the passion which clothes lyrical denunciations of national wrong, will political rhymes ever ascend into any region of the poetic. Then they appeal to feelings and imaginative sympathies common to all mankind. Herein lay and will live for centuries the *verve* and power of the Irish songs and ballads of the *Nation*—the best political poetry in the language. And from kindred, though not strictly identical sources, Beranger drew that fusion so fascinating of patriot wrath and passion (the *sæva indignatio* of Swift's epitaph), with his own ineffable graces of lyric *vogue la galère* gaiety. The party politics of the hour can scarcely ever ascend above the temperature of a "squib." There is everywhere a narrowness as well as a practical hardness—a character of business warfare and business tactics—about actual politics, which keep them within the domain of the understanding. When not attacked by argument, they are only assailable by ridicule, clothed as that ridicule may be with the sparkling opulence of a fancy like Winthrop Praed's, or Moore's in "The Twopenny Post Bag."

The amount in literature, as well as life, of respectable learned lying—lying with "a position," as the social phrase of the day goes,—is positively frightful. You first get an idea of it when Lingard opens English history for you; or Dr. Maitland gives you, across whole mountain ranges and gullies of erudite falsehood, a glimpse of the actual state of the mediæval religion; when De Maistre calmly walks down and unlocks for the historical student the portals of the Spanish Inquisition, or Mr. Addison takes one into the torture chamber of the hapless Templars—"the poor fellow-soldiers of Jesus Christ and of the Temple of Solomon."

Milton, you will perhaps recollect, in the "Eikonoclastes," sarcastically quotes from the "Eikon Basilike" the words, "as the mice and rats overtook a German bishop." I am astonished to find so great a scholar as Mr. J. A. St. John remark of this in a foot-note: "I have been unable to discover the story here alluded to, which no doubt would have proved of a laughable character." And, as a parallel, he cites from Herodotus the Egyptian account of the destruction of Sennacherib's army by field mice. The story alluded to is no laughing matter at all. The tradition is that Hatto, Archbishop of Mentz, was devoured by rats at the beginning of the tenth century. According to some accounts the catastrophe was brought about by mice. The legend sets forth that, at a time of great famine, Hatto shut up in a barn a number of poor people who had come to buy grain, and then set fire to the building, burning to death all within. His Grace of Mentz was pleased to remark, of this intrepid experiment in political economy, "that poor people of the soil were like rats—good for nothing but to eat corn." "But God, the just avenger of the poor," says the legend piously, "did not long let this iniquity go unpunished." Rats were sent, which at all times and in all places attended the Most Reverend Prelate, with a pertinacity as dread and as dogged as that with which the same members of the domestic *fauna* favoured the Flemings of Hamelin in Robert Browning's ballad. The Archbishop at length retired to a tower on an island in the Rhine, as an asylum; but the rats followed him thither, swimming the river, and, scaling and entering his tower of refuge, eventually devoured him piecemeal. Southey has a ballad on the subject.

De Quincey's style is, I think, the most organically, the most essentially metaphorical, in any literature. I mean metaphorical in a deep and broad sense, reaching to the innermost machinery by which all thinking processes are carried on, and to every verbal revelation made of the results. Metaphor, not always immediately perceptible—delicately defined at times, as the serrations in the moonlight shadow of a leaf—pervades the opium eater's style with the ubiquity of an electric principle. De Quincey not only thinks, but expresses himself in and by things. To use a word he himself once applied to Burke, he is the most *schematising* of prose-writers.

A course of Lectures on Modern Literature in the year 1853—when he was 25 years old—was the first public manifestation of Mr. Deniehy's talents. In these Lectures he discussed the most eminent English, French, and Italian authors of modern times, and gave convincing proof of his powers as a critical analyst. The following passage, taken from one of these lectures, will show the manner in which his subject was handled :

> Among the distinguished writers of recent times, generally regarded as representatives of the female intellect in its higher phase, there is none comparable to this extraordinary woman. In Madame de Staël you have the very *acme* of talent, a brilliant and accomplished mind—in fact, a female Sir James Macintosh, with a dash of romantic feeling superadded. . Genius is the soul working through the organs of the intellect. Take this definition, and you see at a glance the difference between genius and talent ;—one not, as is often supposed, of *degree*, but of *kind*. The latter is the operation of bare intellect, cultivated by observation, by experience, by literary training, or by instruction in the technics of literature, or of any art or science. Madame de Staël's talent was of the highest order, but in composing such a book as "Corinne," she struck into that particular path of literature for which her defect of artistic *morale* altogether unfitted her, and the consequence was, that like Chateaubriand, she perpetually confounded highly-coloured and impassioned rhetoric with poetry—the prettinesses, the blushes, the language of over-refined sentiment with the grand simplicities of all elemental human feeling. She had a certain faculty of philosophic observation possessed by no other female writer ; analytical powers, besides, of rare subtlety and keenness, and she wrote in a style superior to that of any French contemporary *prosateur*. Rahel, the celebrated Jewess, from what is recorded of her conversations, and the letters published by her husband Varnhagen Von Ense, seems to have presented in her beautiful intellect the flower of German idealism and German æsthetical culture. In Margaret Fuller, the American, coupled with a moral nature of serene statuesque grandeur, you have, to my thinking, the archetype of a female scholar. Her learning, though genuine and extensive, seems to have been built up (and this evidently without a shade of consciousness of the fact in the scholar herself) on a principle of *eclecticism*. Everything she studied seems to have come recommended to her by some animating grace or beauty ; or as endowed with some refining influence, or as containing some spiritual truth, or some ulterior power of working good. An orbicularity or encyclopædic completeness of erudition, or the pursuit of knowledge *simply as knowledge*, or as a motive power, will never, I think, characterise female scholarship. I can hardly imagine, even with the exceptional case to the general rule of *la savante Dacier* before me, a woman devoting herself to chronological compilation, or Greek verbal criticism, or to the arid

analysis of literary hypothesis ; following at humble distance Porson's labours on the lexicon of Photius, or the Phalaris Dissertations of Dr. Bentley, or storing the memory with obsolete beauties of expression, like that worthy, Dr. Samuel Parr, who wrought in exquisitely selected cantos and orthodox combinations of classic phrase, as a mosaic-worker does in porphyries and jaspars and coloured marbles. But I can, at the same time, perfectly understand Mrs. Browning's ability to execute an excellent English version of the "Prometheus Bound" of Æschylus, or Margaret Fuller's criticising the same tragedy in a manner admirable for the philological knowledge it manifested, and a perception withal so true and so profound of the distinctively solemn and Titanic grandeur of the play, that would have affected the great Bentley with a little of that amazement with which one of Coleridge's criticisms on the Shaksperian drama would, beyond all question, have oppressed Bishop Hurd, or Mr. Mason, the poet (and Precentor of St. Peter's Cathedral at York,) or Mr. Edmund Malone, or Mr. Garrick, of Drury-lane Theatre, or that very clever man, Mr. Murphy, who "did" Tacitus into English. Entirely different from the leading female intellect of latter years, is George Sand—differing from them, most of all in that colossal individuality which is behind her books, and overshadows them. Of her errors and her accountabilities, not less than of certain unjust and erroneous opinions pretty generally entertained concerning her writings, I shall hereafter speak. Her powers as a delineator of character we shall consider when placed beside those of Balzac, which we shall presently analyse. An artist, she has an imagination—the pure creative faculty in a degree beyond any other French writer of the age. Her perception and her sense of beauty are clearer and stronger too, and invested with a passion seldom found under the precise frigid *regime* of French rhetoric. For a broad fresh sunny loveliness, and a healthy treatment of the subject, and a certain delightful pictorial character—a resemblance to what I can conceive of the brighter landscapes of Gaspar Poussin, or the Venetian site-pictures of Turner, (we Australians can, for the most part, only dream of the *chef d'œuvres* of painting) those tales of 'George Sand, written during the middle epoch of her career, are unique in literature. Perhaps, after all, her style is her most wonderful characteristic. French, that language in which it was a matter of astonishment to Walter Savage Landor, that Voltaire could have written with such ineffable grace, that most artificial of European tongues becomes, in the hands of George Sand, like a new and marvellous instrument that should emit every tone, from the roll of an organ to the dipping notes of a violin. Thackeray said in his "Paris Sketch Book," that her brief rich melancholy sentences affected him like country bells, provoking he knew not what vein of musing and meditation, and falling sweetly and sadly on the ear. It is that quality of style for which you can scarcely account on any received principle of rhetorical arrangement. There is a certain bloom and *aroma* about it, that goes far beyond all *that*, which Shelley evidently felt evaporating in the grasp of critical analysis, when saying he could only describe Plato's diction as "*something like* the language of a superior being."

Mr. Deniehy went to Melbourne in 1862 to edit the *Victorian*, a weekly newspaper established by the Roman Catholic party. He remained there for about two years, till the death of that journal, and then returned to Sydney. His mind was at that time so far affected by constitutional causes that all literary power had well-nigh vanished. Even then, however, an occasional flash served to remind the reader of the flame that had once burned so brightly—e'en in his ashes lived the wonted fire. A few articles contributed to *Punch* still remain to testify to this; and among them the following is perhaps the best. It will serve at least to illustrate another side of the writer's mind—his exquisite humour. This was shown rather in the delineation of character than in anything else. His capacity in this direction was very great—so great, indeed, as to qualify him for the highest style of fiction, that in which knowledge of life and character forms the chief merit of the writer. In the following sketch, entitled *Honi soit qui mal y pense*, he contrasts the vulgar "aristocracy" of the present day, which bases its pretensions on its wealth, with the refined society of early times—a society in which officers of the army represented the *noblesse*. The setting of the sarcasm is ingenious:

> Dear Mr. Punch,—I know, you charming old gentleman, that you are the determined foe, not only of public abuses and immoralities, but also of everything that invades the minor morals of life. Above all, that you are a knight ready to break a lance at any time with people who trifle with the weaknesses of ladies and females generally. In this colony particularly, where many of us ladies (and we are after all as good as *any* ladies, and don't lower our heads to the best at pic-nics and flower-shows) are the ladies of gentlemen who have got on (God bless 'em) and made ladies of us, and kicked your fine aristocrats out of Parliament, and sit there and are called your Honours, and have *us* with 'em at the opening of the House, with as much money's worth on our backs at once as the Governor's daughters in old times ever saw in their chests of drawers in five years. But I must be quick, for Mr. Slapup is punctually home at five to dinner, and unless I am ready in the new Mecca-and-Medina caftan-patterned dress he brings from Madame Bene's, ordered by himself, he will perhaps punish me by not taking me to the play for three successive nights. Dear duck of a lamb! He is that kind since we've got on, that I sometimes lock myself

up in my bed-room to cry over the thoughts of him. And to think that I was
hired from the ship and taken up to Campbelltown only fourteen years ago,
and that when I first knew Mr. Slapup he had only twenty-two shillings a week
and his board at Bradawl and Co.'s wholesale hardware, in George-street,
established 1828. Gracious me, old Bradawl, with all his fashionable daughters, and his branch-houses in all the colonies, was never an M.P., and had
never gentlemen like Mr. Cowper to call him "his honorable friend," as Mr.
Cowper calls Mr. Slapup right before the whole Parliament, and well knowing
the very compliment to my husband will be published all over the colony in
the next morning's papers. And I know that Mr. Cowper means what he says
and speaks the truth; for don't I remember his dear old cherubim of a father
preaching in the old church now pulled down on Church Hill, and is not his
brother a clergyman and a Dean? To be sure, a gentleman like Mr. Cowper
wouldn't disgrace his pious family by falsehood, and saying anything that he
doesn't mean? Therefore, when he not only acknowledges Mr. Slapup as his
friend, but his "honourable friend," he means it. It's all very well to say a
thing, as that spiteful little Gus. Turquoise did, who was a fellow-clerk at
higher salary than my Mr. Slapup, and married a lady wife with no money (she
certainly had a sweet, long face, like those in Lady Blessington's old Books of
Beauty Mr. Slapup brings home) and is very uncomplaining, and pretends
that she is not stuck up, though *in my heart*, without reflection at all, *I know
she is*, and couldn't be flesh and blood if she wasn't, with that calm Countess-
like face, and long, white hands, almost as transparent as the ground-glass
shade on the hall lamp I ordered yesterday. It was all very well when I used
to say jocosely to that idle, do-nothing Gus. Turquoise, that I expected an
"honourable" person home, for him to pretend to quote Shakspere and say
"we're all, all honourable men." An "honourable man," sir, if I wished to
moralise, and be what they call in some of Mr. Slapup's books "dogmatic," is
a man that gets on and makes his wife happy with plenty of money, and is
fashionable, and the envy of people who havn't got on, and does the same by
his children. As ladies, *we* of course have nothing to do with *how* he gets on;
and we know the world is censorious and spiteful, and has been since the time of
the Patriarchs and Martyrs and Roman Catholic Confessors. Enough for us
ladies to know our husbands *do* get on, and respect them accordingly. You know
there is a proverb about where the proof of a pudding lies. But I am taking up
your valuable time, and I am therefore coming to the point,—in fact, I must, for
my music-mistress comes at three. I am *a leetle* advanced in years, but my sweet
lamb, Slapup, insists even now on my taking lessons. I never try to pronounce
Italian myself; but Slapup, with his dear domestic fun, when he comes home
asks if I've mastered *Non scold there at tea* from the opera of *Throw it o'er you?* *
By the way, poor Miss Hermione Alfreton, who gives me lessons, is an officer's

---

* Does Mrs. Slapup allude to the divine *Non mi scordar di te* of Verdi; and is *Throw it
o'er you* an auricular misconception of the word *Trovatore?*

daughter, and her father was a captain in the 28th or 50th, I forget which, when the regiments were out here. Long before there was an Assembly, you know, and when, as I have heard, the highest civil honour in this country even captains in the army could get, was to sit on "a military jury," which anybody could have that liked, if they only chose to go and do something wrong; and those juries used to try a man for stealing a bundle of slops, or a female for not being particular about a couple of fowls. She is foolishly proud at the bottom, I think, that Miss Alfreton, though a good creature, and with a voice so rich and deep when she speaks—it is the only thing, that kind of voice in talking, that *we* ladies ever envy the other ladies, for it is a thing our husbands really cannot buy for us. But still she is impertinently as well as foolishly proud. When last Christmas she was receiving her quarter's fees—the only time I ever saw her really gentle face change—Mr. Slapup was paying her, he happened to add a sovereign additional in token of approval, when her pale forehead flushed crimson, and she said politely and *very* quietly, as she placed the coin before him, "There is a mistake, sir; three pounds only are due to me." But I have at last come to my story.

Over and above my eight pounds a week for house-keeping, Mr. Slapup allows me six for myself, for what he politely calls my *toilette*. Heavens! how much he has acquired of fashionable habits and language since first we met, and I used to look for him at the gateway of old Captain Trevelyan's, in Macquarie-street, of a Sunday evening, when the Captain and the ladies had gone to St. James's. I think really there have been scarcely any novelties, London or Parisian, for the last four years that I haven't had in heaps; indeed, and in fact, anxious as I am to appear distinguished for Mr. Slapup's dear sake, I really can scarcely carry all the things, this weather particularly, that fashion allows us to put on. And my husband insists on *so* much at a time, for he likes, he says (but it is his parliamentary talk), that "people should carry weight with them!" Ah! Joseph William Slapup, well may your wife be proud of you, and laugh at the notions about you of eloquent and brilliant and scheming and fast and restless people, who were all a-gog in Parliament when you were on four pounds a week, and who have come since then to nothing or to grief, or what is all the same—to that shocking, shameful place at the top of King-street, where I am told it is quite common for men to take false oaths when they are questioned about their wives' extravagances.

Well, dear Mr. Punch, I actually had exhausted all the superior places in fashionable novelties. I really was sick of going over what they had. As for the *recamier pardessus* and the *harouda*, Mr. Slapup had already bought them for me in different materials. I wore the *harouda* at Mrs. Finnigan's party. But on the morning of Monday last, as I was looking over the paper I found that some people in Hunter-street advertised a "just received" novelty called *jarretieres*. I had never heard of this affair before, though even Miss Alfreton, who was educated at Paris, does often translate the French words for me in the fashions out of the *Folly* periodical. Thought I, it must be very delightful and (from the unheard-of name) quite the newest thing out. What kind of fashionable article can it be? But, heavens! to be one of the very first in it. And then Mr. Slapup and I were going on Tuesday evening to the Kraut's Ball; they were German bakers on Brickfield-hill originally, but they are long since become distressingly rich; and their son, Mr. Karl Maria Kraut, is a magistrate; and their second, Mr. Heinrich Wolfgang Kraut, *was* studying for the Bar, but gave the thing up in disgust some three weeks ago, when he heard that a gentleman, formerly a clerk in the District Court, was admitted a barrister. "*Ja, mein sohn,*" said the German, "dere is noddink left in dis gussed kundree in de way of purvesshun for a jendilman!" I don't know myself, of course, what the first words mean; but as we all laughed at the old fogey, he seemed so much in earnest, I got Fanny Cratcher to take the sentence down that it might amuse Mr. Slapup, and there it is for *you*, Mr. Punch.

Well, I took Mrs. Trumper with me, and down we went to Hunter-street to "shop" for the newest thing out—the *jarretières*. Mrs. T.'s husband, in the oil and colour line, was born next door in London (Cock-hill, Ratcliffe-highway) to Mr. Slapup, and Mr. Trumper was in our Assembly last time. We wondered whether it was a head-dress or a basque, or anything the Empress Eugenie had invented as a substitute for hoops, or if it were anything in the point-lace collar way. I don't know why it was, but poor dear Mrs. Trumper got it into her head somehow that it was a new style of silk *corsage* to wear under "bodies" of muslin dresses in summer. Heigho! However, we got to the shop, and the shopkeeper, I trust, you will show up at the first opportunity, in justice to the ladies. Why should little hosiery and fancy dealers play tricks upon the wives of members of Parliament and the lady-public generally? I suppose, Sir, to know French—in this case, haberdasher's French—is not indispensable to a lady? How many French ladies at the Toolleries, that's the Emperor's palace, I believe, are there who can speak English? How many English gentlewomen with husbands in Parliament, and blood as old as the Normans, who, away from town ways and town vices, know no more of French than they do of Jew's Hebrew or Roman Catholic Latin?

Well, in we went, and as neither Mrs. Trumper nor myself were quite sure about the pronunciation, I took up the newspaper and laid my gloved finger on the advertisement (my gloves were silvery grey, gauntlet tops). The young man—he had lovely hair, and the parting was as smooth as bridal satin—smiled politely, and asked us to take chairs. Poor Mrs. Trumper whispered nervously to me, "I don't know; but there doesn't seem any caps, bonnets, or articles of that kind about!" The young man took down a large cardboard box, such as hosiery or ribbons might be very well kept in. "Ladies," said he "do you prefer any particular colour? there are *cendre de rose*, pearl grey, brides' white, camelia pink, hacarat, blue louis, and bishop's purple." Then, earnestly looking out of the door into Hunter-street, where a vegetable man was bargaining with an Irish servant girl about some wretched cabbage, this nice young man, Mr. Punch—this nice young man took out six pairs of different coloured—O Mr.

Q

Punch—O Mr. Slapup, M. P.—O Mrs. Trumper (and Mr. Trumper)—six pairs of

Garters!

If we compare the literary disquisitions given above with the ordinary run of critical notices in periodicals of the present day, we shall not exaggerate the merits of Mr. Deniehy in saying that his qualifications as a critic were of the highest order. It may be said, indeed, that we rarely meet with such criticisms as his in any periodical whatever. Whether we look at the 'slashing' notices in the *Saturday*, or the more elaborate productions of the quarterly Reviews, we shall not easily find any criticism that can be read with greater satisfaction. The art of 'cutting up' an unfortunate author has undoubtedly been brought to perfection some time since; and in this particular branch of analysis we can claim no praise for our countryman. He never desired it; at least we have no proof that he ever sought it. Perhaps he erred, if he erred at all, the other way. He was evidently disposed to find something to admire in every book he took up, and where the book happened to be written by a personal friend, his judgment was evidently swayed by his feelings. This was the more remarkable in him, inasmuch as a gushing benevolence of disposition formed no part of his character. Few could be more cautiously deliberate in weighing the merits of others, and few were greater adepts in the use of biting and remorseless sarcasm. Except in matters of Art, he had apparently no faculty of veneration whatever. But Art, and all that appertained to it, were sacred in his eyes. With the exception mentioned, his judgment was rarely, if ever, at fault. Let us recollect that he brought to his task a knowledge of Literature and the Fine Arts, marked as much by its accuracy as by its extent,—a knowledge gained by the intense and unremitting study of his early years. This is an indispensable 'pre-requisite,' to borrow a phrase from Coleridge, of all criticism of any value. Before a man can conscientiously pronounce judgment on a work of art, be it a book or a painting, his mind must be familiar with much, if not with everything, that has been done before in the same direction. Now, it is evident that the criticism in our periodicals is, to a large extent, written by men whose knowledge of the subject may be profound, but is rarely accompanied by a full development of the higher faculties. Hence we have either dry, colourless scholarship, or the flashy pretentiousness of the Cockney School. It was Mr. Deniehy's signal merit that he combined both the qualifications of which we speak : that he was a scholar, and at the same time a man of vivid imagination. Keen and subtle in the highest degree, he possessed a mind at once comprehensive and minute, equally capable of grasping principles and appreciating facts. Analytical power was perhaps the 'individualising' faculty of his intellect—in other words, it was the power by which his intellect could best display its strength, and through which its greatest triumphs could be gained.

Recollecting the difficulties under which every scholar must necessarily labour in this country, we shall be able to appreciate the earnestness of his labours, at the same time that we feel astonishment at their success. The want of necessary appliances is so great here, that deficient scholarship can never be without an excuse. We have only temporary substitutes for a library, while an Art Gallery has not yet been dreamt of by our legislators. The higher manifestations of artistic power must consequently remain, more or less, unknown to us. They can be known only through the medium of imagination, like the scenes of foreign lands. What credit is not due to one who, barely arrived at manhood, had yet contrived to master difficulties which were little less than insuperable ? who not only passed from one language and one literature to another, conquering as he went, but made himself familiar with Painting, Sculpture, Architecture, Music, and those minor arts in which human ingenuity is most happily displayed ? Everywhere throughout his writings we find traces of these incredible attainments ; we track the steps of one who followed Beauty wherever she led him, into her deepest and most secret recesses as well as on the open plain. We think of Chatterton in the garret, peering into 'Mr. Canynge's cofre,' and then of the fatal manuscripts which gave him both death and immortality.

That a mind so stored should have produced so little as it did, may by some be thought a strange matter; and it may be thought that this mind, rich as it was in other gifts, was devoid of creative power. As to these points, it must be borne in mind that Mr. Deniehy's early entrance on the political stage precluded, in a great measure, all hope of distinction in literature. The period at which he turned his attention to politics was a peculiar one. Responsible Government had just been introduced, and the country was anxiously watching the working of the new machinery. His powers of speaking made him at once a prominent figure, while his reputation as a man of letters served still more to arrest attention. With the enthusiasm natural to his character, he flung himself wholly into the stormy strifes of faction; but he was not 'cut out' for a working politician. That which acted as a gentle stimulant to coarser minds, was rank poison to his, and soon 'fretted the pigmy body to decay.' Then came the reaction of the long strain upon his constitutional energies during his years of study; and then too came the result of the disastrous remedy in which he sought relief He died at the age of thirty-five, but even in that short space, the last few years were little more than years of torpor. That he was not deficient in creative power will be readily believed by those who are familiar with his writings as well as his personal history, and perhaps it will not be doubted even by those who have no other means of judging than the contents of these pages. Minds of his stamp are essentially creative. They are never satisfied with absorbing the productions of others. Plastic power is part of their natural constitution. Instances are only too numerous in which the most brilliant faculties have gone down to darkness without leaving any adequate result behind them: and Mr. Deniehy, unfortunately for us, adds another to the list.

ROBERT SEALY.

ROBERT SEALY was born in Ireland in 1831, and came to this Colony in 1852. Arriving shortly before the establishment of the University, he entered himself among the students of the first year, having previously kept several terms at Trinity College, Dublin. He obtained a scholarship, and was considered among the best classical scholars in the University. He did not remain long enough to take a degree, but soon after accepted an appointment in the Government service—a clerkship of Petty Sessions at Molong, subsequently exchanged for a clerkship in the Colonial Secretary's Office. He died in 1861.

Under the title of *Scraps*, he distributed among his friends, in 1859, a small volume of miscellaneous pieces—principally in verse. Nearly all of them are humourous. In some he ridicules the prominent absurdities of the time at which he wrote; and in a few others he expresses himself seriously. Mr. Sealy never professed authorship, and seems to have written for the occasion merely. His productions appeared, from time to time, in different Sydney journals, under the signature of "Menippus:" Menippus being a character in one of Lucian's Dialogues—an author whom Mr. Sealy must have thoroughly appreciated.

The following ballad, addressed *To Miss F——*, exhibits true Irish humour :—

If I might make so free without boldness
I'd ask but two favours, at most ;
The one is for lave to address you,
Discoorsing by manes of the post ;
The next—and you can't well withhold it—
Is the pleasure of seeing your face,
When you sit in your stall at St. Patrick's,
And I'm poked by that chap with the mace—
   Hard case,
I never can get a good place.

'Tis elegant pious divarsion,
To hear the fine tunes that they play,
And to see all the quality sitting,
While I stand—as I'm told—in the way,
The sermon—least said soonest mended—
A hint by the way apropos,
If it's preaching we want sure there's plenty
At churches wherever we go—
   I know
At St. Patrick's the likes is thought slow.

'Tis yourself takes the shine of the Meeting
Though the pick of the City go there;
Why them sweet little boys in white linen
Feel bothered by features so fair,
And the martial young haroes from barracks.
Forget their own selves when you smile,
The deceivers a squinting through glasses,
And hiding their grins in their tile—
   In th' aisle,
Neglecting their duty the while.

What's the good of comparing your beauty,
The like wasn't known to the Greeks ;
Thim haythens may talk of their Helen,
Or Briseis with beautiful cheeks ;
Oh ! 'tis you set me all in a fluster,
Not one word of the service I hear,
I'm snared by your dark shining tresses,
And lured by your bright eyes, my dear—
   I fear
You'll think that I'm going it here.

When the blessing's been read by the Clergy,
And all make a rush for the street,
I linger about in the passage
A watching the stairs for your feet ;
I hate those long dresses that hide them,
With your lave—I'll just say 'tis a shame,
No chance in the world but the crossings,
I'm thankful, dear knows, for that same—
      Small blame
If I watch at a turn I won't name.

Another in the same style is entitled, *Farewell to the Seventy Seventh*. It was written on the departure of the Regiment for India, at the time of the Sepoy Mutiny.

Is it going ye are to the Indies,
  To fight with them murdering blacks,
After licking the Roosians and Proosians,
  Circassians, Sclavonians, Cossacks?
Sure it's chillies all day ye'll be eating,
  And curries as hot as—Ah! well—
Take it out of the spalpeens in beating,
  If you find that their feeding's a sell.

Troth 'tis sorry we are that you're leaving
  Australia for furriner parts,
For though short's been your stay on the Island,
  You've carried by storm many hearts.
And when, by the means of the papers,
  We hear of your glory and pluck,
We'll say to our colleens, "by jabers!"
  May the Lord never send them worse luck.

Though many a loved one we're mourning
  Who fell in that far distant land,
We'll bury our sorrow in prayer,
  For we know the Avenger's at hand.
Then farewell, gallant hearts, God be with you,
  When you fight with them Turks of Sepoys:
Here's the Seventy-seventh for ever!
  (They're devils for fighting, them boys!)

As a piece of classical humour, the following has hardly been excelled:—

CORESSUS AND CALIRRHÖE.

As Bacchus one morning beside the beach wandered
He met his pet priest looking very so so:—
    Says Bacchus, "God bless us,
    Is that you, Coressus,
Old fellow, what's up? 'Pon my life, you distress us.

"If they cut off your liquor you could not look glummer,
Perhaps you feel seedy,—you don't look the thing,
    Take a nip of my brandy,
    I have some here handy,"—
('Twas a Greek word he used meaning 'nobbler,' or 'dandy.')

Says Coressus, "I've not been queer since the last Orgies,
'Tis love, Sir, not liquor, that bothers me so;
    There's one Calirrhöe,
    I call her 'mou Zöe,'
And 'tis she'll be the death of me, I'll bet a joey.

"She has put *the come hither* upon me, entirely,
The boys and Bacchantes all laugh me to scorn,
    The devil receive her,
    I wish I could leave her,
And I would, for two pins, but I know 'twouldn't grieve her."

Says Bacchus in wrath, "I'll astonish those natives,
And bring them to reason by driving them mad—
    They shall go on the batter,
    As mad as a hatter,
Them ould Caledonians, until you get at her."

He ended:—each man in the district grew tipsy,—
Some asked of the oracle what they must do,—
    Which said, "Would you know, eh?
    Well, drunker than Chlöe
You'll be till Coressus gets Miss Calirrhöe!

"But if she runs rusty and shies at the parson,
The God has decreed there's but one thing to do,—

Cut her throat at the altar,
Cut boldly, don't falter,
You've got full permission from me to assault her."

To cut short the story: at no price she'd have him,
So up to the altar they led her to die;
When, seeing the victim
Who used to afflict him,
Coressus cried, "Kill me, and spare her!"—they nick'd him!

This may be set off by another piece in a very different style. It is entitled, *A Cabman's Philosophy*.

Tell me, Cabman—thou hast studied
 Human nature on thy stand—
Is there any truth in Woman,
 Any faith in plighted hand?

Slowly putting down his pewter,
 Thus that Cabman spoke his mind,—
"Gammon, if you trust such cattle,
 That they're bolters, you'll soon find."

Cabman mine, your words are bitter,
 Haply wrong'd in love, you speak,
You have trusted—"Not I, blow me!
 Trust a Woman? trust a Beak!"

Bitter fruit of observation,
 Sad experience sours your heart,
But thy words are words of wisdom,
 Prythee all thy love impart.

"Draw it mild," replied the Cabby,
 "And I'll tell yer wot I think,
If yer wants my conversation,
 Why, you'd better stand my drink."

Then he dipp'd his nose in porter,
 Sigh'd, and wip'd it on his cuff,
And express'd a firm conviction,
 That that 'ere was just the stuff.

"Keep gals well in hand," he added,
 "Touch 'em gently on the raw,—
Don't be gammon'd by their sawder,
 Nor be bullied by their jaw."

Another piece in the same style is entitled, *The Publican's Daughter:*

>   Than the beer which she served,
>   Her complexion was clearer;
>   Than the price which she charged
>   For that beer, she was dearer;
>   And stronger than spirits,
>   (For spirits they water)
>   Was my love for fair Ellen,
>   The Publican's Daughter.
>
>   Oh why did she add
>   To my score on the shutter,
>   And tell me to pay
>   And be—something'd or other?
>   I saw at a glance
>   She was not what I thought her,
>   For falser than fair
>   Was the Publican's Daughter.
>
>   Alas! that another
>   My pewter is filling!
>   That she charged one-and-four-pence
>   Instead of a shilling!
>   Alas, that she cheated!
>   Alas, that I caught her!
>   And alas, for my love
>   For the Publican's Daughter!

Some of Mr. Sealy's prose writings have a great deal of quiet graceful humour about them; especially those in which the quaint peculiarities of Old English are reproduced. As a specimen of the latter class, we may take the following, entitled *Some love to roam:*

Now am I bound in a vessel sore wind-baffled, wave-buffeted to a land attorneyless, where bailiffs dwell not, and beadles are unknown—*gratissima tellus* so far; yet is it a country pestilent, infested by mosquitoes that bite like terriers, and drone like bag-pipes; where creeping things disport themselves *terra omnino repentibus dedita*, such as triantilopes, falsely so called; centipees, so mis-named of the inhabitants, if inhabitants there be; yet of this solitude it may not be said *ne musca quidem*, for it is the capital and stronghold of flydom. Jupiter Hospes! aid me in these straits, going, even as he who bilked Dido, *ignotus egens*, among strange folks, strange faces, other minds. I doubt not that in a place so sun-smitten, fly-bitten, snake-beset, I shall sigh sorely for familiar faces—catchpolls, *et hoc genus omne*, not to name my familiars, friends, *sodales*, who used to wander with me through Sydney *per devia viarum*, for to us indeed George-street was no thoroughfare, and Pitt-street but a *cul de sac*. O! thrice and four times happy ye whose lot it was to stroll through the main streets, tricked out bravely; but to me and mine it was not given, *aliter dis visum*. Yet was there pleasant beer in P——street, and reeking rumbos in taverns ye wot of; nor do I envy those who spend their time and money with the Gaul, quaffing costly Badmintons,—marry, a shilling drink—cost of two goodly pints! Do ye still, F. and M. and O., at four of the clock wash down the dust of office with a cheering pint; for mark you, my masters, beer is a notable disperser of melancholy, concerning which our great Milton hath well sung—

> Tired Nature's best restorer, bitter beer.

Yet would I not decry claret, sack, and other light wines of France, which do well accord with the stomachs and purses of some ; now I am none of these. I marvel does our N——, called among his familiars, Torquatus, by reason of his collars—still care-oppressed, *aes alienum cogitans*, and morally drunk, urge the smooth balls upon the level green, despite resolves to the contrary.

The thought of leaving the Sydney beauties doth especially disquiet me, for "what is knight without ladye fair?"—concerning which I might quote at large. For my sins, I go to a land where no woman is, or hath been, save the dark daughters of the soil, of whom I may say that which was writ of Rosamond, called the Fair, *non redolent sed olent*. Methinks I see the young and fascinating S., "the darling of his crew," proudly bedight, walking with her he loves in the gardens. Is he happy? Meseemeth something disquiets him —*alea anget*—he hath lost at play. 'Tis better to have tossed and lost, than never to have tossed. Courage, *Patientiâ vincimus*.

P——, ever faithful to the South Head Road; so serious in thy gaiety, high priest of the Salii ! Still go the giddy round—*nec tu, puer, sperne choreas*.

Alack and well a-day! As the land lessens, memory fades. I go from fair faces and gay attire, perchance for ever. Even clean linen is rare "in the land I'm going to," at least among the commonalty; the gentler sort, albeit rudely clad, are easily known. A gentleman *noscitur a sociis*, is known by his socks.

And now, *valete omnes*, including him who once graced London's gayest haunt, cabbage-consumer, graceful cane-carrier, moodish maid follower: still may men say of thee, "Incedit Reg-ent Street."

The same peculiar humour is shown in the following Extract from the *Chronicle of Heraldus Matutinus*. It refers to some delay in the payment of Civil Service salaries at a time when Sir S. A. Donaldson was in office as Treasurer :

Atte thys time, one Donaldson did addresse ye people, a portly man, tricked out in all manner of braverie, and after much belauding of himself by dispraise of others and such like surquedrie, he set forth fluently, (he has a trick of words) how hee would manage the Revenue of ye country, promising prompt payment to ye poore man, and readie attention to Dives, whereby he was chosen Treasurer. Now one poore clerk, noting how poorly hys performance did tally with hys promises, wrote a pleasant ballade, showing how he suffered from a scurvy catchpoll by reason of ye Treasurer hys delay in payment."

> Now wherefore here, thou proude Bailiffe,
>   Now wherefore here, I pray ;
> What would'st thou with my poore chattels?
>   I prythee go away.
>
> Then answere made that Bailiffe proude
>   From our Sheriffe soe dear,
> "I hold a writ, and not a bit
>   Will ever I move from here."
>
> " I hold thy hosen, eke thy shoon,
>   Thy smalle hair-trunk also,
> Thy linen all is held in thralle."
>   Gramercie, Bailiffe, go !
>
> Sweet Bailiffe, 'tis our Treasurere,
>   Whom Donaldson men calle ;
> Go tell that swelle how greate a selle
>   He hath sold hys clerklings alle.
>
> "Nay, nay, now nay, thou clerkly wight
>   I will not go him to,
> With words at wille he would talk until
>   I'd be fulle fain to go.
>
> "I would rather stay by thy blucher boots,
>   And by thy shirts of blue,
> And would rather keep thy chattels cheap,
>   Than listen him unto.
>
> "O, a wordie man is the Treasurere."
>   Soe saide that Bailiffe proude,
> " He would talk off your hede," soe that Bailiffe said,
>   " Hys voice and hys dresse are loude."

"O some to a bagman liken him,
  And some to a prince of pride,
But they call him here the Treasurere,
  And a lot of names beside."

The Bailiffe sits on my small hair-trunk,
  Nor hosen nor shoon have I :
'Tis the 9th to-day, and I've got no pay,
  And I ask ye reason why.

Mr. Sealy was happy in his imitations of the old ballads. A serious effort in this style, called *Robin Hood*, is equally good :

FYTTE THE FIRST.

The noble Earl of Huntingdon
  Gaz'd through the casement drearily,
While friar Tuck, with cassock on,
  Yawn'd o'er his missal wearily ;

Maid Marian with her gosshawk toyed,
  Scathlock and Scarlett nodded near,
Pall'd were they all of bower and hall,
  And sigh'd again for woodland cheer.

"By God his death," quoth Robin Hood,
  "I'll off to Bernysdale again,
To bended bow, and Lincoln Green,
  And stout meynè of merry men.

"The licensed hunting of the deer,
  In royal livery suits not me,
Nor can I teach my English horn
  The blasts of Norman venerie.

"Of state and fee I weary all,
  I've lost the cunning of the bow ;
But yester e'en I missed the butts|
  By half a cloth-yard shaft or so.

"And all these knaves of mine grow fat
  On nut-brown ale and warden pie,
Not one can wield a quarter staff,
  Or wing an arrow to the eye.

"I mind me when yon burly priest
    Could play at buffets with our king,
Ring nine with quarter staff on pate,
    And stand best wrestler in the ring.

" And who like him could troll a stave
    Waking the forest echoes wide,
After the breaking of the deer,
    As we reclined by some brook side?

" What time the evening sun streamed down,
    Casting long shadows at our feet,
When all the dappled herd had strayed
    To uplands fair, and pastures sweet.

" At night we held a merry rouse
    On wine from some sleek Abbot ta'en,
Then slept beneath the trysting tree
    Until the east was red again.

"O merry 'twas in woodlands, then,
    To scour the woods with tough yew bow,
Bring down the wild goose on the wing,
    Or lay the antler'd booty low.

" Or watch for ambling jennet pass
    With portly churchman on its back,
Or steed of knight of high degree,
    Or merchant's mule with heavy pack.

" Or be it pedlar, prior, or knight,
    I trow he paid us toll and fee;
Nor any passed withouten pay;
    We brook'd not then scant courtesy.

" Sometimes a churlish miller passed
    With dusty sacks towards the town,
Who liked a bout at quarter staff,—
    I mind one crack'd our friar's crown.

" Sometimes the sheriff came on quest
    Of outlaw bold to forest green,
And, by the rood, we prick'd his hide
    Right shrewdly with our arrows keen.

"And once it chanced, on summer eve,
  A full tryste knight, all wan of blee,
Pac'd on his way-worn destriere
  Beside our ancient trysting tree.

"All soil'd and rent, his nightly gear,
  His last rose-noble long since spent;
We bade him welcome to our fare,
  And to our sylvan merriment.

"He told us how a prior knave
  Had robbed him both of land and fee,
While he did battle with our Lord
  King Richard against Paynimrie;

"We filled his purse with red, red gold,
  We clad his limbs in harness new,
And sware by him who died on tree
  The shaveling monk this wrong should rue.

"And so each day fresh venture brought,
  In forest glade 'twas merry then :
What belted Earl is half so free
  As outlaw 'mid his merry men ?

"Then wind a blast upon your horn,
  Will Scathlock, for my leal yeomen,
I'll doff these weeds for Lincoln suit,
  And seek green Bernysdale again."

Then up rose Tuck : "By cock and pye
  This carpet life it irks me sore : "—
He tore his cassock from his breast,
  And dashed his missal on the floor :

His Lincoln suit was all too scant,
  His baldrick lacked a span or twain,
He roundly swore he'd go in buff,
  Until his belt should meet again.

And how these yeomen fared in wood,
  With cloth yard shaft and bended bow
I trow another fytte shall tell,
  If that ye gentles care to know.

FYTTE THE SECOND.

On bush and spray the birds sang clear,
  The heron soared above the lake,
The rabbits sported in the fern,
  The deer sought cover in the brake.

When yeomen three in Lincoln green,
  Rested beneath a spreading oak,
Quoth one, "Beshrew the laggard monk,
  He bears our dinner in his poke.

"But see the knave comes toiling up,
  The sweat-drops running from his brow,
And, by the mass, the wallet's slack;.
  He did not lag for nought, I trow."

"Ho, masters mine! ye speed apace;
  I stayed but at Saint Hubert's shrine,
To breathe a passing orison "—
  Quoth Robin shortly—"Where's the wine?"

"Alack, my masters, when sore spent
  With travel, and a heavy mass,
A beggar churl upon me set
  And spilt the vintage on the grass.

"But an this staff of mine—'tis sooth—
  Tann'd not his hide, I'll ne'er fast more;
A stouter villain never crossed
  A quarter-staff with mine before."

"Ye lie, false priest," quoth Robin Hood;
  Ye drank the wine, and ate the pie."
May all the Aves I e'er said,
  Fail me," said Tuck, "if that I lie."

"Well, since it mote not better be,
  I'll beat the thickets for a deer"—
Said Robin,—"Scathlock, you can seek
  For feather'd game to mend our cheer."

The dewdrops on the fern were dry,
  A blue haze bounded all the wood,
When forth in quest of forest cheer,
  Fared Scathlock and bold Robin Hood.

Broad-back'd lay Tuck beneath the shade,
  Untruss'd, his jerkin open wide ;
While Scathlock, resting on a root,
  With cutting jests the friar plied.

At eve they shot a bout at butts,
  Will Scarlett won a silver crown ;
For buffets next the garland tried,
  The chaplain knock'd the yeoman down.

    * * * *

Footsore, bemoil'd, his arrows spent,
  At set of sun Will Scathlock came,
Without a feather at his belt,
  Or any head of sylvan game.

" A sorry larder," quoth the Priest,
  " Greets our return to gay green wood :
But mercy, God ! whom have we here ?
  By God his pine ! 'tis Robin Hood !"

With bow unstrung, and broken brand,
  Halting, with garments soil'd and torn,
Came Robin to the trysting tree
  Never was yeoman more forlorn.

When all the West was red, he said,
  He, toiling through a briary maze,
Came sudden by a brawling brook,
  Upon a hart of grace at graze.

Swifter than falcon when she stoops
  To pierce her quarry, from his bow
The grey-goose shaft unerring sped,
  And laid the antler'd monarch low.

When out there stept a Ranger proud
  Smote Robin sorely on the head ;
" Marry, come up ! I trow, here's sport,"
  Quoth he, as Robin lay for dead.

Then with yew bow across his back,
  He laid such strokes 'twas sin to see,
The stranger gone, up Robin rose ;
  " My curse," he said, " on venerie."

* * * *

Up from the marsh the grey mist curled,
  A chill wind crept beneath the wood,
Four never pray'd for dawn as these,
  Tuck, Scarlett, Scathlock, Robin Hood.

And never more, as legends tell,
  Did Robin and his freres again
Leave castle tower for leafy bower:
  God rest him and his merry men!

There is little here in the way of action to satisfy the reader, but in other respects he has not much to complain of. Nothing, it has been said, is so easy as to write a ballad, and nothing so difficult as to write a good one. Mr. Sealy hits off the peculiarities of the old ballad very happily. Here and there, perhaps, he is at fault; but unless we determine to be hypercritical, we are bound to admit that the foregoing stanzas are excellent.

We cannot take leave of this writer better than by quoting two short pieces in which he is speaking seriously. They are both addressed to ladyes fair: the first, *to W. M.;* the second, *to Minnie.* The latter is said to be the last thing which his hand attempted.

You should have lived in olden time,
The golden time of chivalry,
When knights to beauty bent the knee,
And for the guerdon of a glance,
Did battle with the sword and lance.

Methinks it would have liked you well,
Sitting among your maidens there,
To work a scarf of quaint device,
To flash in many a foughten field,
Upon the breast of that true knight
Who held you fairest of the fair.

And, had he fallen on distant plain,
Crying your name with latest breath,
You would have said " He met his death

In harness, as became a knight
Doing devoir for ladye bright."

I trow you would not shed a tear,
But sitting in your castle bower,
With steadfast, haughty face would sing
An ancient Lay of Troubadour.
Of Lancelot and Bedivere,
King Arthur and Queen Guinevere,
Of Knight and Squire, of helm and spear.

The bower maidens would wonder all,
Up-gazing from their tapestrie,
At your set lip, and tearless eye :—
But in your turret-chamber high,
For him who fell, I wis you'd sigh,
And break your heart, unseen, and die.

TO MINNIE.

I'm all unskill'd in tuning lays of love,
For I ne'er bow'd at Aphrodite's shrine,
The golden-girdled goddess of the sea,
Until my heart leap'd forth to cling to thine.

My life has been one sorrow : From my youth
Hopeless I've trod the thorny brakes of life,
Without one wild flower cull'd to cheer my path,
Or loving smile to nerve me for the strife.

And so, uncomforted, sad, motiveless,
I never join'd in issue with my peers,
To win renown, and glad a ladye-love,
But lonely stood, heedless of passing years.

And now, youth's stream of grief full fed by time,
O'erwhelming sweeps me to that precipice
Which men call death ; then turn, my love, and strain
Thy lips to mine, and speed me with a kiss !

W. B. DALLEY.

WILLIAM BEDE DALLEY was born in Sydney in 1831.* After his education was finished, he read for the Bar and was admitted in 1856. A public speech or two delivered shortly after, on political questions, furnished evidence of brilliant ability, and Mr. Dalley became at once a distinguished man. He was elected a member of the first Representative Assembly in 1857, and was appointed Solicitor-General by the then Premier, Mr. Cowper. By this time he had secured the reputation of an orator. With unusual quickness of perception he combines great command of language, irresistible humour, and all the minor essentials of oratorical success. As an impromptu humourist he has never been excelled in this country. His humour is an instinct, and not a result of study. In fact, he possesses no faculty for study or elaboration of any kind. So much is this the case that it is questionable whether any amount of elaboration would at all improve his powers. There are men of letters who, while totally devoid of all humour in their conversation, and of all power to impress a public audience by its means, can yet manufacture with pen and ink the finest and most delicate specimens of this delightful quality. But it is probable that, were Mr. Dalley to attempt this kind of manufacture, his humour would evaporate in the process, and

---

* In "Literature in New South Wales," the date of Mr. Dalley's birth is incorrectly stated to be 1833.

nothing would be left but a bare network of elegant sentences. It is a natural result of this peculiarity that his writing should be no adequate representation of his powers. We listen to an *improvisatore* with feelings of astonishment : but what should we think of him if we tied him down to a desk, and then compared the result of his labours with Balzac or Thackeray? At the same time, there is no defect in the writing itself. As a matter of style, simply, it deserves the highest commendation. It is equally clear and vigorous; the language is faultless; and there is a degree of gracefulness about the whole that is not often met with in our newspaper contributions.

A series of political sketches were contributed by Mr. Dalley to *Punch* a short time ago, entitled, *Political Biographies*, and in these he has described, with exquisite irony, the most prominent of our political characters. The following is devoted to Dr. Lang:

> We are told in the Lives of the Illustrious Fathers of the Catholic Church, that when a rather pretentious Prelate held the see of Ravenna, during the Pontificate of St. Gregory the Great, it was his custom (the archi-episcopal Brummell) to wear his pallium, not only in the services of religion, but as an ordinary decoration. Thereupon, we are informed, St. Gregory wrote him a severe reprimand (the letter is extant) telling him that no ornament shines so brightly on the shoulders of a bishop as humility. Had John Dunmore Lang occupied the see at that time, the letter never would have been written. The adorning virtue of the episcopate is the characteristic one of our subject. We cannot give an idea of his splendid career. We propose simply to sketch his character. The extreme courtesy of his nature has carried him, unstained and uninjured, through conflicts in which violence of manner and extravagance of expression would have brought down signal and deserved punishment. Continuously engaged in great public employments, he has always, with marvellous skill and admirable self-control, so conducted himself as to inspire general sympathy and avoid individual offence. With his clerical brethren of all denominations, he has been uniformly the object of the highest esteem and purest affection. The purpose of his priestly life has been the accomplishment of a perfect union of ministers of religion of all denominations. Although no one could pretend to such high qualifications as such a leadership imperatively demands—humility, forbearance, charity—he was, unhappily, not successful in achieving a result which would have immortalised him and conferred lasting benefits upon society. The glory of a heroic struggle for that cause is his—of that no one can deprive him—and the sympathies

and love of his brother ministers have been augmented by a contemplation of his unaided efforts. Like Wolsey, (of the genius and character of whom he is a fervent and outspoken admirer,) the venerable priest has been a munificent patron of public education. As the great English Pontiff founded his colleges in Oxford and Ipswich, so the great Australian clergyman established his college in this city. The princely halls of this institution were reared by a noble and devoted band of Caledonian masons, and adorned with professorial chairs filled by the leading men in their departments of scholarship of the "modern Athens." The founder undertook the great responsibilities of the office of Principal in this institution, and with the occasional exception of a long vacation for two or three years, in Europe and the United States of America, exercised a vigilant and unremitting superintendence over the course of studies and general management of the College. As the vast genius of the greatest of the Spanish Princes of the Catholic Church embraced at the same time the government of Spain and of America, the generalship of armies against the Moors, the foundation of the University of Alcala, and the publication of the polyglot Bible—so our Presbyterian Ximenes ruled his College, sat in Parliament, edited several papers, governed his Church, travelled over the whole world, and published books and pamphlets innumerable. His scrupulous avoidance of all purely controversial topics, and his exquisite discretion in treating all matters upon which difference of opinion generates a strong hostility of feeling, have saved him repeatedly from condemnation, which less prudent and more bigoted essayists would undoubtedly excite. Unfortunately, it is the peculiarity of most ecclesiastics who take a prominent position in secular affairs, to manifest an enthusiasm unqualified by deference to the opinions of others, and as loudly to condemn honest error as unreasoning opposition. Such people begin to libel when they fail to convince. Unable to demonstrate the truth of their own views, they denounce their opponent's; and in proportion to the sincerity of their own convictions is the danger of their unscrupulousness. To this class the venerable Dr. Lang does *not* belong. In his polemical difficulties the crosier has never been used to knock down his antagonists. His priestly acrimony only contains those apostolical weapons of which the greatest of Apostles has given us the catalogue. His sweet persuasive accents have been listened to with reverence by those at whom the thunders of the Vatican would have been launched without effect. St. Francis de Sales has always been his great model as a priest, and he has studied with a profound appreciation of their policy and politeness, the lives of the illustrious followers of Loyola. Scholarship without sophistry—concession to the extremest verge of principle—a Christian recognition of the merit and virtues of his opponents— these have been his characteristic qualities as an expositor of the Gospel. There have been some who have mistaken his prudence for pusillanimity—his mildness for a want of earnestness—but none have doubted his sacerdotal charity. As a politician, he is a devoted admirer of the British constitution, and on one or two remarkable occasions has testified his faith in the glory and advantages of our alliance with England. His touching and eloquent allusion to the sacred protection which the British ensign gives to the British citizen, is remembered and quoted by all who admire eloquence and love England. At his own expense, without aid of any kind, he has been the means of transporting many hundreds from the old to the new world of ours. His own limited resources, combined with his holy ambition, led to some slight inconveniences in carrying out this great object, but while a few entertained a mere shadowy doubt of his prudence, none dared to question the purity of his motives. Such a character is as far above, as many are beneath criticism. We shall not, therefore, presume to lift the veil which conceals the early history of "Cooksland." Rather let it be our grateful part to paint the statesman, the scholar, the priest, and the journalist, as he is—as he legislates, teaches, preaches, and writes in our midst. Though a minister of the Presbyterian Church, he loves the Catacombs as well as Antonelli. He can talk to you of the sculpture and the paintings of those dreary sepulchres—of their *terra cotta* lamps and glass chalices—as glibly as a Parisian would talk of the *immortelles* of *Père le Chaise*, or a Dublin carman of the tombs of *Glasnevin*— or a Newtown 'bus boy of the Camperdown cemetery. We shall not intrude further upon a learned leisure which his friends know the illustrious divine is employing in revising for a new edition the great work, *Mabillon Annal. Bened.*

Mr. Holroyd, the present Master in Equity, is the subject of the following sketch :

The adventurous spirit which so strongly characterises our race furnishes us with colonists of strange history—large acquaintance of mankind—and immense stores of information. Among these the subject of our notice is not the least remarkable. Of a grand and gloomy religious nature, his attention was in early life naturally directed to Palestine. His studies were undertaken and professions selected with the sole view of assisting him to be of service to mankind as a traveller in the Holy Land. With this object he became a barrister, and regularly attended the Middlesex sessions. The precise connexion between this occupation and his subsequent employment we cannot perceive, but at a later period of his life his recollections of his generous struggles for innocence and honesty in that tribunal furnish him with the purest sources of pleasure. He was then known in small forensic circles, formed of the youngest and most innocent members of his profession, as the '*Dragoman of the rope-walk.*' No amount of ridicule or misconception of the purity of his motives could in the least degree divert him from his lofty purpose. Having taken an affecting leave of his friends, he started in 18— from the *Old Bailey* for *Jericho*. He had procured an appointment from the Palestine Colonisation Society as *Colporteur*, and those who know him require no assurance that he discharged the duties of his office with affectionate solicitude towards those to whom he came as a missionary. Having had some slight difference of opinion with the Jews at *Saphet* (mainly about the style and dimensions of their turbans, to which he took exception,) he returned to England, and after some time became a physician. Immediately after this he left England for this country, where he remained for some time in a state of uncertainty as to which of his numerous professions he would employ as a means of ameliorating the condition of society. Having visited the offices of the Society for the Propagation of the Gospel in Foreign Parts, three apothecaries' shops, the Police Office, and the Central Criminal Court on the day of his arrival, he was led by an accidental circumstance to devote his genius and energies to the succour and support of hapless wretches wrongly charged with criminal offences. The cause of this solemn determination was briefly this:— An unhappy man, who, a few days before, had left with the highest character one of the most humanely conducted of our penal establishments, had the misfortune to meet at night, a few hours after his release, an inebriate and insolent citizen in one of the back streets of the metropolis. Through the violence of the latter, a quarrel was forced upon the accused, and the police coming up during its progress, insisted that he was in the wrong (as they always are), and basely sought a confirmation of their suspicions in the circumstance that some hundred pounds, which the citizen affirmed to be his property, was found in the breast pocket of the accused. Mr. Holroyd made an earnest and successful appeal to the Jury in his behalf, denounced the infamous conduct of the constabulary, was complimented by the Judge, and secured the acquittal of his client, who munificently rewarded the genius and devotion which had been employed in his rescue from a groundless prosecution. From this moment, the learned gentleman assiduously prosecuted his humane labours in the cause of all innocent persons charged with criminal offences. To widen the circle of his philanthropy, a place was procured for him in Parliament, and as a number of constituencies in the course of his career were ambitious of the honour of being represented by him, it became absolutely necessary that he should never be re-elected for the same place. No circumstance could be more conclusive in considering the evidence of his rare popularity. His chief characteristic, as a politician, is his extreme unselfishness. He was for years Chairman of Committees, with a large salary, which he devoted to sumptuous entertainments. He was also for some time (during a temporary absence from Parliament) District Court Judge. In the latter office, his judicial conduct, decisions, and the ordinary proceedings of his Court, were modelled upon the solemnities of Oriental tribunals. He retired from the Court amidst the most complimentary expressions of public and professional satisfaction. His opinions have not been obstinately opposed to the popular tendencies, but have been humbly and philosophically moulded to correspond with the varying phases of the views of the majority. In a word, his political faith is a safe one,—its great principle being elasticity. He is a man of remarkable intellectual activity, and extremely versatile accomplishments. He has frequently in the same day made a successful defence for a burglar of unimpeachable character—presided at the adjudication of prizes to the exhibitors at a Poultry Club—and lectured in the evening on the Well of En-rogel. His great measures have been freely criticised as of too revolutionary a character for immediate acceptance—but he has tried to smile down from the heights of legislation upon those puny critics who attacked while there was a chance of injuring, and prophesied failure when schemes too vast for their understanding had obtained the solemn protection of law. To those among our readers in whose recollection the brilliant struggles of his mature genius are still fresh, we triumphantly recall the "Amended Pawnbrokers' Act," and the "Sale by Green-grocers of Colonial Wine." The titles of these pieces of legislation are the proudest he can claim as their author—and will be the noblest epitaph we can inscribe to endear his memory to posterity.

The following sketch of Mr. Martin may be compared with the remarks on that gentleman given in a previous part of this volume :

Many superficial judges of genius and character would pronounce the subject of this memoir a wonderful example of what may be accomplished by a clear head, inflexible will, and unfailing industry. They would point him out as one of the victorious workers, the men of self-help. It is our pleasing and conscientious duty to dispel such illusions. The Honourable James Martin was born a poet, and although circumstances have interposed to deny him the privilege of being recognised as a master of song, it is a melancholy truth that we have lost, in the misdirection of his genius, a great bard. From an extremely early age he exhibited a love for verse. "Muiopotmos, or the Fate of the Butterflie," the sweetest of Spenser's minor poems, was his favourite in childhood. A dreamy, imaginative, and delicately sensitive youth, his modesty was mistaken for dullness. He grew up shy, pensive, abstracted, passionately devoted to the Muses, and having, or manifesting, no interest in the practical affairs of life. We shall pass over his boyhood hurriedly, for two reasons: firstly, because it is the period of all human life least likely to furnish matter for edifying or improving reflection ; and secondly, because in this particular case we are not fortunate enough to possess a scintilla of information on the subject. His early manhood presents to us the picture of a tall, slight, and languid figure, of a face shadowed with tearful melancholy, full of the

Glimmering incarnation
Of hopes, and fears, and twilight fantasies.

The profession of the law, to which this young and tender nature had been compelled to bend his energies, was, we need hardly say, the most distasteful of pursuits for one whose large heart was longing for the golden fields of old romance and the fountains of classic song. But do many of us walk in the paths to which our hearts would direct our feet? Does not Placidus, whose gentle spirit would have shed a mild radiance upon the life of the cloister, usually get a commission, and fall pierced with a Kaffir or a Maori bullet; whilst Iratus, whose only priestly quality is his sympathy with anathemas, takes off his boxing gloves and puts on the surplice? Thus it happens every day. Could humanity devise no other employment for our young poet, with the vision and the faculty divine, than to make him an accountant of six and eight-pences? We think of Burns and of Wordsworth, and pass from the early life of our distinguished subject with a tear for the world's misunderstanding of its great men. Having been torn away from the Muses, and compelled to exchange the divine Spenser for the *nisi prius* Selwyn, the young and accomplished practitioner felt as the great commentator of our jurisprudence, who celebrated his farewell to the Muse in those touching lines with which articled pupils of literary tastes are so familiar :—

> No room for peace, no room for you,
> Adieu, celestial Nymph, adieu.

A brief, but not inglorious career as an attorney, naturally and properly terminated in our hero's becoming Attorney-General. He had, meanwhile, by the same perverse misconception of his peculiar faculty on the part of the vulgar, been dragged into the storms and contentions of public life. Nothing could have been more alien to his poetic nature. The marriage of a skylark to a stormy petrel could scarcely furnish a stronger illustration of a *mésalliance* than the wedding of our subject, brimming o'er with "harmonious madness," to the savage discords of parliamentary life. But in his exalted, though hateful station, the world had a glorious opportunity of seeing how the man of genius can, like the man of the world, accommodate himself to circumstances. Spurning the old delusions of politics, which would fetter commerce by vain attempts to foster its expansion, our poet-politician led the van of great and beneficent Reform. That unrestrained intercourse with the noblest thoughts of the loftiest spirits of all times and ages which he had enjoyed, at once suggested to him, that the policy of nations should be based upon an unrestricted intercourse of all commodities. At Protection, its old professors, and besotted believers, he laughed with all the strength of his powerful intelligence. His advocacy of principles now universally acknowledged, anticipated the political wisdom of the old world. Firm, resolute, and uncompromising on great matters, he was reverential, submissive, and yielding on minor points, happily combining the purpose of the conscientious statesman with the student's gentleness. His victories were admired by those who were vanquished by his argument, and his loudest praises were sounded by his opponents. To the prestige of unsurpassed talent, he added those inimitable charms of manner which belong to deep sympathies and heroic natures. Abhorring that self-assertiveness which is characteristic of the despot in politics, he fascinated those who would have been repelled by his opinions, and alienated from him by his associations. Thus, in his mature age, one who should have dwelt with "the cherub contemplation," with "looks commercing with the skies," "his "rapt soul sitting in his eyes," became a leader of practical men, a pillar of the State, an example of the highest and rarest virtues. As the advocate of the causes of widows and orphans, and indeed of mankind in general before our courts, he is not less distinguished for the variety of his learning than for his diligence and attention to his duties. Miraculous as are his attainments, he is not ubiquitous, and consequently when his engagements necessitate his attendance in three courts at the same moment, and in a spirit of perfect equity he denies to each the advantages which all ought to enjoy, the unreasonable clamour at his absence, and hint at the expensiveness of his impartiality. We, who know that on these occasions he is solacing himself with the sweet recollections of his boyhood, that he is wandering in the elysian fields of imagination, and singing the songs of his early life,—we pity his detractors and respect his retirement.

Mr. Cowper, who is next treated, has been at the head of the liberal party for many years. It was under his auspices that manhood suffrage and vote by ballot were introduced into the Constitution :

Although frankness is one of the most fascinating traits of social character, it is also a dangerous virtue for the politician. No man is more charming in the domestic circle than he who, in the plenitude of his confidence, in the affection and secresy of his friends, pours out his attachments and antagonisms, his hopes, his apprehensions—lays bare his heart, so that children may read what is written there. Such revelations, however, are of a highly perilous nature when made publicly and unreservedly by politicians of the highest position. The subject of this memoir sadly illustrates the truth of these reflections. The basis of his character is undoubtedly a most confiding simplicity. Incapable of thinking meanly of mankind, he is the victim of each crafty speculator in politics who tries to deceive him. Preserving all the attractive ingenuousness of his early boyhood, Mr. Cowper has never acquired from his intercourse with mankind the knowledge which places limits to an excessive trust in human perfection. Believing that all by whom he is surrounded are as open, candid, and generous as himself, he speaks as freely to the world as to his family. His opinions on every question are consequently as widely diffused as possible ; and it is his noble, but still to be deplored ambition, that all the world may not only hear of his actions, but be informed of his motives. The most relentless of his antagonists have never accused him of concealment ; but the most devoted of his friends have frequently had the strongest cause to complain of his indiscreet disclosures. It is well that he is not a member of any religious communion which prescribes private confession. The whole world is his confessional, and he tells us his most secret thoughts as if he were under an obligation to confess, and we to absolve. It is hardly necessary to say that this lovable sincerity has frequently led him into great public errors. Associated with men who, though they admired his talents, could hardly appreciate the almost saintly innocence of his nature, he was left without that protection which colleagues of a larger acquaintance with, and a lower faith in, mankind, might have secured to him. Knowing the facility with which the least contriving might make him the dupe of artifice the most transparent, it would have been a worthy occupation for even superior talent to have stood sentinel over the treasures of his heart exposed to the thefts of every passer-by. Mr. Cowper, for a longer period than perhaps any statesman in the colonies, held the post of First Secretary in our Government. He had of course during this time the dispensation of a vast amount of patronage. The distribution of those prizes, which most public men regulate by considerations of expediency, he effected solely on the ground of his own faith in the virtues of the recipient. To reward the attachment of a friend—to disarm the virulence of an opponent—to strengthen and augment party by the inspiration of hopes in the fulness of time—to secure votes that were wanted for party triumphs, by promises—to remove those that might prove inconvenient, by holding out temptations—all these operations of craftier politicians were quite foreign to the nature and principles of Mr. Cowper. Capable of the most generous friendships, and prepared to make any sacrifices, he was only selfish in preferring the maintenance of his honour to the preservation of friendships which were inconsistent with his principles. It will not be a matter of surprise that a man of such Quixotic sensibility on all matters of public morality should have manifested a reverence, almost amounting to religion, for the administration of justice. During his long career no man was placed in any judicial position who was not remarkable for his learning and his piety. The combination was insisted on in two cases, which first directed public attention to the severity of his requirements in estimating men's fitness for the magisterial office. He refused to place in the commission of the peace a senior wrangler, who in his youth had committed some indiscretion, and a churchwarden of high character who had left an English University without graduating, alleging that the union of cultivated intelligence with unstained character was absolutely essential, and playfully observing that if he could unite the qualities of both in the single person of either the church officer or of the wrangler, he would be at once appointed. The consequence of a line of policy so pure and exalted, was the collection of a body of men engaged in administering justice in the humbler courts, whose talents and virtues would adorn the highest. In the far interior the courts of Petty Sessions are presided over by gentlemen whose scholarship would be admired in cities—whose manners are of the best school of courtiers—whose morality is unexceptionable; while in the metropolis itself the benches of our police offices are packed with the *elite* of our intelligence and virtue.

It is no detraction from the merits of Mr. Cowper to remark that in this great result of his labours as a minister, Mr. John Robertson is entitled to some share of the glory. More discriminating and reticent than Mr. Cowper, Mr. Robertson supported as high a standard as his colleague. Indeed, it was at one time asserted that in doubtful cases Mr. Robertson insisted upon all candidates submitting themselves for legal and theological examination to the Attorney-General and Dr. Lang before they were gazetted.

Within the limits of a slight but truthful sketch of this kind, it would be obviously impossible to discuss the scope and tendency of the numerous acts of Mr. Cowper's public life. We content ourselves with pointing to one or two of the triumphs of his government, and endeavouring to convey some idea of his character. The absence of all subtlety in his organization, while it has interfered with temporary advantages, has secured to him the allegiance of those who would doubt a diplomatist and despise a schemer. His candour, while it has exposed him to attacks, has naturally diminished their malignity. Nobody disbelieves in his assurances, and everybody knows what he means. Mr. Punch expresses a hope that Mr. Cowper will not be displeased with this portrait, and that a fair contemplation of it will not be without beneficial effects when Mr. Punch's friend (Mr. Cowper) returns, as he undoubtedly will, to office. When he looks back upon his public life—

> ―――― cœcosque volutat
> Eventus animo secum,

Mr. Punch believes that Mr. Cowper will find this record to be the most friendly, as well as the most truthful, of his biographies.

Mr. John Robertson, a very prominent politician, is the subject of the next sketch :

It is the pleasing duty of Mr. Punch to uncover to the world this morning the statue of the most remarkable of our modern statesmen ; and in the contemplation of that fine face the metallic indifference of Mr. Punch as a judge is somewhat softened by the warmth of his artist nature. It is really a good face ; but it is of the life and character of the possessor that Mr. Punch is called upon to speak. Well, would anybody credit that the owner of that noble countenance (with an expression of comprehensive benevolence which would suit the features of a Shaftesbury, a Peabody, or a high official of the Royal Humane Society), was first heard of as a Poisoner !!! Mr. Punch disdains sensational writing,—he abhors the white-handed murderer who lives in good society, rides in Rotten Row, and puzzles Taylor and Herapath—but, being a truthful biographer, it becomes his melancholy duty to state that Mr. John Robertson and the wholesale administration of *strychnine* to - ――― native dogs, were first heard of together. In a series of letters, as remarkable for their bitterness as their chemical knowledge, the future statesman then preached his poisonous crusade against the aboriginal hounds of his native country. In this employment of humanity he first manifested those marvellous powers with which, at the present time, we are all so familiar. It would be entirely out of place in these columns to attempt anything like a review of his splendid career as a public man. The monuments of his labours are to be found in our statute-books; and the living witnesses of his genius are upon the electoral rolls of his country. The destructive policy which he at first advocated as an extensive agriculturist was abandoned when the necessity for its adoption had disappeared. He then became what he has been consistently for many years, a member of the high conservative party in the Government. Avoiding popularity with the solemn consciousness that it is not unfrequently a pitfall for independence, he has only sought the approbation of the thoughtful and the cultivated. His oratory has been condemned by those who prefer impassioned appeals to the prejudices of the masses to the philosophical discussion which fairly considers and equitably adjusts universal interests. Though not a lawyer by profession, his acquaintance with the great principles of jurisprudence has frequently proved of inestimable value when the ordinary tribunals have unhappily mistaken the law. With regard to enactments of which he is himself the author, his opinions of their scope and tendency have been occasionally at variance with the elaborate judgments of the Supreme Court. Under such circumstances he has—with that becoming reverence for judicial authority which is the glory of British citizenship—enlightened the Bench and satisfied disappointed suitors. It was, probably, owing to his extensive acquaintance with, and high regard for, the law of England, that the crowning honour of his life was conferred upon him—without canvas or solicitation on his part. When a survey is taken of the leading men of our limited society, and their qualifications for positions requiring judicial calmness, combined with great firmness, are considered—it will be at once conceded that no man in our community could compete with Mr. Robertson in a candidature for the presidency of the Australian branch of the Irish National League. This distinguished office he has been recently called upon to occupy. That he will discharge its onerous duties satisfactorily, no one doubts—and that, under his direction, this body will become a formidable engine of agitation, those who know the character and intelligence and power of the president, feel assured. The ceremonies by which his inauguration was celebrated are described as in the highest degree solemn and impressive. Led up to the presidential chair, amidst solemn silence, a liqueur glass of pure and untaxed spirit was placed in his right hand. Elevating the vessel to his lips, he bowed to the assembled crowd, and drank to a change of Government, and a replenished Treasury. The acclamations of his hearers were deafening. The regeneration of that beautiful but unhappy island which has *expatriated* so many *patriots*, seemed on the verge of accomplishment. Who would despair, now that a peaceful revolution was about to be headed by a fearless statesman—who could hesitate in following a leader so crafty and so courageous ? It was thus that he inspired an enthusiasm for the cause, mingled with an admiration for himself, which no one else would have dared to excite. The vast amount of time and labour which he devotes to this object, with the numerous public engagements which an imminent general election necessitates, are the most undoubted evidences of his single-mindedness. Some of those unblushing detractors of all public virtue who, when the action is honourable, attempt to stigmatize the motive as infamous, have been hardy enough to hint that the League is rather an Australian Central than an Irish Branch Committee—that the attention of the illustrious President is more particularly directed to the actual Parliament in Macquarie-street, than the possible one in College Green. But it would be beneath us to do more in noticing such aspersions than to remark that history furnishes us with no career which has not been darkened by the malice of the impotent, and the jealousy of the unsuccessful. Had the sceptical hydropathist, who now fills the office lately occupied by Mr. Robertson, been invited to the higher and nobler office as President of the I.B.N.L., we should, of course, have expected to hear the most biting things whispered of his motives and his actions ;—for is he not in office ?—and is it not essential to retain it by all means, and at any sacrifice ? But when we know the high moral standard of opposition,—the reluctance of even the most unprincipled to imperil his independence by the acceptance of ministerial responsibilities ;—when we know that we have some men who could only be forced into these high offices at the point of the bayonet, as it were ;—we can admire the unselfishness, the large-hearted sympathy, the nobility of nature, of our hero.

Mr. Darvall, an eminent barrister, comes next:—

It was once humourously said of the subject of this notice that he was a kind of compromise between Coriolanus and Beau Brummell. It might be suggested as an improvement that Antoninus Pius and the younger Matthews would be more likely to convey a fair idea of his character, cast of mind, and peculiar talents. Or, if historical combinations are capable of pourtraying most faithfully modern celebrities, perhaps the union of Alcibiades and Major Pendennis would be regarded by some of our readers as more satisfactory. The Athenian should, of course, be a member of the United Service Club, and enjoy the friendship of the Marquis of Steyne. Mr. Darvall is a politician of large experience, a barrister of large practice, and a gentleman of large fortune. He has resided nearly all his life in this country, but was once tempted to transplant himself to the neighbouring colony of Victoria. The temptation presented itself in the form of the Chief Justiceship of that colony, and at a time when its society was hardly so well regulated as at present. Mr. Darvall visited the place, and having speedily ascertained that at that period the capital was mainly inhabited by the proprietors of bowie-knives and nuggets, returned at once, and immediately recommended several young surgeons of his acquaintance to start incontinently for the El Dorado of their profession. With the exception of this public service rendered to Victoria, he has been for a great number of years a settled inhabitant of this colony. His character can only be sketched with difficulty. A political epicurean, he discovers enjoyments on all sides. To him every falsehood has some truth—every truth some falsehood. His mind is so exquisitely balanced that his impartiality, in matters of public opinion, can hardly be called into action. With the sole view of possessing a thorough political independence, he has successively occupied the stand-points of all parties. The advantage of these diverse views of all questions is that he becomes familiar with all opinions and commands all arguments. His natural urbanity of disposition is fostered by his consciousness (as he would express it) "that something can be said in favour of everything, and that nearly every fellow is right on most subjects." It may be supposed by the superficial that this intellectual Dundrearyism is combined with a langour of thought and an indecision of action somewhat inconsistent with the successful and conscientious discharge of important public duties. This is a mistake. As the military dandies—the creatures of wasp waists, perfumed linen, and gazelle-like softness of manners—have been in all ages the most dashing and daring warriors—as these "curled darlings" ride boldly and with a loose rein into bloody trenches and up to belching cannon—so the political dandy is occasionally capable of courage of opinion and heroism of expression from which the ordinary parliamentary soldier would shrink. In the stormy agitation of public questions which preceded the possession of our present constitution, our readers will recollect in various public assemblies one remarkable figure—that which our artist has attempted to depict at the head of this memoir. In the midst of violence and insolence, wild assertion, and revolutionary extravagance, he sat with an awful Sphinx-like calm, and with that air of grand repose—of perfect super-sensualism which belongs to that lofty brotherhood in whose robes our artist has dressed him for this portrait. Having no particle of sympathy with the motives, the objects, the hopes or the fears of those by whom he was surrounded, he lent his name, his powers, the prestige of his position to gentlemen whose existence, except upon a public platform, he would hardly care to acknowledge. With a persuasive eloquence as sweet as the honey of the Sicilian mountain, he could second a resolution for the five points of the charter, and with the most delightful imperturbability cut the mover dead in the street in the next half hour—and both operations would be marked by a grace and appropriateness which none could hope to emulate. He has been more than once Attorney-General of this country, and of course on each occasion transferred his genius and attainments to gentlemen irreconcileably at variance with each other on all questions. This delightful eccentricity has been more than atoned for by his marvellous industry in the service of each. As a public prosecutor one almost envies the criminal against whom he is stating a case. The misfortune of the accused seems to augment the high-bred courtesy of the accuser. Appearing for the Crown, he upholds its dignity by his conduct, and sheds a lustre upon his office by his eloquence. In an assembly where the large majority are not always actuated by the loftiest motives, and where some not infrequently adopt and encourage a tone somewhat lower than that of the best society, it is gratifying that Mr. Darvall remains to correct, to improve, and to adorn our Parliament.

The following sketch of Mr. Plunkett was written at the time when that gentleman held office as Attorney-General with Mr. Cowper. It is necessary to explain that, a few years ago, when Mr. Plunkett was Chairman of the Board of Education, he was summarily dismissed from that office by Mr. Cowper: whereupon he resigned various offices held by him—such as the Presidency of the Legislative Council, the Commission of the Peace, etc.,—and declared that the 'reign of terror' had commenced. The circumstance occasioned a great sensation at the time. However, he was subsequently induced to join Mr. Cowper as Attorney-General:

The Honourable John Hubert Plunkett, the most graceful, mirthful, and genial of lawyers, is a native of a small and fertile island, which has for a long time been celebrated for abundant crops of brilliant, patriotic, and subtle advocates : Mr. Plunkett is an Irishman. In his early professional life he was the Yorick of the Bar Mess on circuit, and was always engaged to perform that delicate and Punch-like operation of laughing cases out of court. So irresistible and contagious was his humour, that men of great solemnity, engaged in business of the highest importance—his grave seniors at the Bar—were repeatedly carried away by the sparkling, rollicking, and dashing young advocate. At that period of his life, he was a kind of compromise between Mercutio and Father Prout ; or, perhaps, it would be more correct to say, Falstaff and the gifted author of the "Biglow Papers." Humour, however, like shamrocks and patriotism, being a commodity always rather in excess of the demand for home consumption in Mr. Plunkett's native country, the gay youngster—then one of the " curled darlings" of Dublin, the merriest of the *jeunesse dorée* of the Phaynix, and the most popular lawyer in the Four Courts—resolved upon emigrating. Eyes that had sparkled at his *mots* were wet with tears when his resolve was known. Men who could look upon bankruptcy without terror, and the haughty domination of the Saxon with indifference, felt a keen pang of suffering when the light, airy, and graceful wit was about to leave the capital of his country. The then Secretary for the Colonies was an inveterate punster. He accidentally met Mr. Plunkett, and the Minister was delighted with the young fellow's brilliancy. The morning following this memorable interview Mr. Plunkett was appointed Attorney-General of this country. In this remarkable way were most of the appointments to the colonies made in the good old times. There was then a chance for genius. The prizes now are only taken by the boisterous and the impudent. Having arrived in this colony, he addressed himself to the discharge of the onerous duties of his high position with commendable industry. His passion for a joke was so irrepressible that even the solemnity of his functions could not restrain the exuberance of his fancy. He kept the Court couvulsed with his good things, and even the prisoners in the dock enjoyed their trials as if these gentlemen were spectators of the comedies, in place of being actors in tragedies. They could hardly get the form of the mad-cap prosecutor out of their heads before the Judge put the black cap on *his* head, and sentence of death wound up an otherwise delightful entertainment. A solemn and melancholy advocate of those days (Mr. Broadhurst), whose constitutional gloom no mirth could altogether dissipate, was sometimes surprised into a feeble smile at the overpowering gaiety of the leader of the Bar. Victorious in his profession, Mr. Plunkett was equally conspicuous in his success as a politician. On ceasing to hold office, he attached himself to the party of Mr. Cowper and Mr. Martin. United in opinion, bound to each other by many mutual obligations, and by the tenderest ties of friendship, these gentlemen formed a powerful and popular coalition. They were reproached by the cynical (who hate all praise of virtue) for taking advantage of every opportunity to proclaim the purity of each other's motives, and the value of each other's public services. But the thoughtful and the good only saw in such conduct the devotedness of chivalrous friendship, and that noble sincerity which is now, alas! so rare. Short as is the period of our constitutional history, it is long enough to familiarise us with many examples of friendships shattered by politics, and attachments broken by the heavy hand of party. Those who were in perfect agreement a year ago, are now as hostile as the opposing military commanders in a faction fight. Of the graceful subject of this sketch nothing of this kind can be said. As Mr. Cowper was the object of Mr. Plunkett's early admiration, so has he always been; and now the two men, who know each other thoroughly (if the depth and tenderness of Mr. Cowper's heroic nature can ever be thoroughly known to any one), are once more associated in the sublime labour of governing this infant empire. If the rumour be true which assigns the Solicitor-Generalship to Mr. Martin, the three dearest friends in public life will form the most powerful Administration that this country has hitherto seen. Let those who have scoffed at the inconsistencies, the deceits, and the living lies of our rulers, for ever hold their peace. There are bonds which unite men of honour, of the strength of which the vulgar can form no opinion. When we are asked to defend our public men from charges of caprice, utter want of principle, and reckless disregard of the laws of party prevailing in civilised communities, we shall simply say the Honourable John

Hubert Plunkett has occupied office in the Government of the Honourable Charles Cowper.

Under the title of *The Autobiography of a Public Man of Four Weeks' Standing*, Mr. Dalley paints the sufferings of a mercantile gentleman who suffered himself to be put in nomination for a seat. The unavoidable brutalities of an election, as they present themselves to a sensitive and cultivated mind, are certainly not exaggerated:

Hateful as my reminiscenses of political distinction are to me, I feel compelled to give them to the world. They may serve as a warning to others of my class whom a similar conjunction of circumstances may expose to a similar temptation. Be it known, then, that I am a man of middle age, and of some means. My life, passed in strict attention to my business, was, up to a recent period, an uneventful one. My experience of public affairs was limited to an occasional glance at the reported debates of Parliament, and on two occasions to a view of the Assembly from behind the Speaker's chair. This privilege was enjoyed at an extremely late hour at night on each occasion, and had been the consequence of two dinners, of which, for many days subsequent to each banquet, I had an extremely painful recollection. The entertainments form an era in my domestic history, and are invariably referred to by my wife when she is engaged in unfavourably reviewing our married life, as chronological finger-posts pointing to my moral deterioration and ultimate ruin.

On the morning upon which the melancholy intelligence was announced that the country was without a Parliament, I felt, in common with the rest of my fellow-citizens, that proper degree of sorrow which so mournful an event ought to inspire. The expression of grief which I saw upon the countenances of many estimable men who had formerly occupied seats in Parliament moved me to pity; and I thought of the bitterness of their suffering with a sympathy which, I trust, was honourable to my nature. I am, I may confess at once, a man easily affected by the spectacle of misery in all its multifarious forms; and I know of no sight so calculated to inspire a deep and respectful sorrow as that of a brave man stripped of the honours of a public station, and in a state of extreme uncertainty as to whether he will again be clothed with those distinctions, or allowed, by the tyrannical caprice of the multitude, to remain in a state of political nudity for ever. One or two gloomy faces passed me in the streets, the faces of men who were only a few days before pillars of the State, and I marked with painful surprise the humbled expression of those haughty countenances. Can it be, I thought, that this meekness of aspect—this submissiveness —this gentleness born of affliction—is all brought about by a damp sheet of the

Government Gazette? Can an official notification in this by no means exciting journal inflict deeper wounds than the stings and arrows of outrageous leaders in the daily press? On the morning of the eventful day of which I write, there were, however, many faces which spoke of hope, of joy, of coming pleasures. Entirely unaccustomed to the uncertainty of political contests, I was then unaware of the employment of the people whose insolent happiness seemed to be an outrage upon the public mourning. Since that period I have ascertained that these people were mainly journalists, canvassers, poll-clerks, printers of placards, and licensed victuallers. The unseemly merriment of these persons pained my sensitive nature. Their loud voices broke discordantly upon my ears. I felt as a man might feel who, seated in a chamber of death near the coffin of some loved object, with his heart breaking, and his eyes wet with tears, is suddenly disturbed by the strains of a German band pouring out the music of waltzes and galops beneath the windows of the house of sorrow. This crew of mercenary hirelings offended me. It was like a banquet of the undertaker's men after the funeral, the grave hardly filled up, the pall just folded and put by, and the wretched mimes of the funeral pageant laughing and joking over their day's work and their beer. Full of this sadness I reached my place of business, and read the epitaphs upon the defunct Parliament contained in the leaders of the daily press. I was disturbed in this distressing employment by the entry of some four or five gentlemen, who immediately affected the ordinarily scentless atmosphere of my counting-house with a decided *aroma* of spirits which are not generally known as "perfumed." The leader of this body, all the members of which are personally unknown to me, then proceeded to inform me (in a voice of great depth, and marked with a huskiness from which I at once inferred that the owner was a public speaker, and had been engaged in the exercise of his profession uninterruptedly for a number of years,) that I saw before me a "deppytashun." My visitors were a small number of free and independent electors, who were desirous of securing my services at this important juncture. My trepidation at this moment was, I candidly confess, considerably in excess of my sense of the proposed distinction, and my nervousness would certainly have discouraged any less indulgent friends, and inspired strong doubts as to my capacity to explain precisely what I meant to convey to any audience. I attempted to decline the candidature, and endeavoured to temper a resolution so offensive to my audience with a courtesy of expression which I thought they might appreciate. But I found that their earnestness in my behalf was exactly proportioned to my timidity. It is a strange sensation, that of finding for the first time that a number of your fellow-citizens discover you to be the possessor of genius of which you have been yourself conscious for a long period. The leader and spokesman of the deputation particularly impressed upon me the fact that society was immensely interested in my resolve, and frankly intimated to me that the general public expectation was decidedly in favour of the view that I would accept the nomination of my friends. To find oneself the centre of popular interest, the cause of public anxiety, the dispenser of bliss or suffering to one's fellow-creatures, according to one's simple resolve, is indeed a painful discovery. I pictured the thousands of men and women who at that moment were awaiting with feverish impatience the dread *fiat* of my determination. I thought, too, of the sweetnesses of obscurity, of the delightful immunities of a merely social life, of the awful publicity which I was courting by a consent, and I hesitated for a moment. My friends were loud in entreaty, and in that moment I was lost. I have a vague recollection of the deputation pressing round me—of my hands being seized in those of the individual members of the body—of my being vaguely but affectionately directed to "go in and win," and I was sensible for the first time of the excitement of a contest. I was more composed after this. Tranquilised by the great effort I had made, I surveyed with the calmness of an indifferent spectator the faces of my friends. A strict regard for truth compels me to declare that a collection of more forbidding countenances was, perhaps, never presented to the view of a critical, though benevolent, observer of his species. I have a distinct recollection of the thought flashing through my mind upon the instant, why all the repulsive men should have resolved upon inviting me to be their representative in Parliament? To this fleeting interrogatory I was unable to furnish myself anything like a satisfactory reply.

CHAPTER II.

The suddenness with which intimate friendships spring up in public life is a phenomenon worthy of philosophical attention. My principal supporters were continually hanging about my business premises, tendering me valuable suggestions with regard to my course of action, and highly commending certain popular opinions for my adoption in the forthcoming contest. These gentlemen were never weary of pledging my political success,—a ceremony which was repeated so frequently, that in a short space of time a number of sample bottles of delicate wines and superior spirits, which in my days of private life adorned my counting-house, were speedily emptied of their precious contents. I am not a hater of the soothing weed; indeed, no man more highly appreciates a cigar of superior quality when the fatigues of the day are over; but I had a commercial prejudice against transforming my office into a smoking divan. This, however, I now discovered, was a matter of absolute necessity in order to ensure my return to Parliament. The chairman of my committee invariably waited upon me at an early hour of the morning, and uniformly commenced our intercourse by filling and lighting a short black pipe. Though possessed of a respectable knowledge of figures, I should hesitate to furnish any precise information of the number of times during the day on which he availed himself of this means of enjoyment. He would sit sometimes for a long period, noticing my movements through a dense cloud of by no means fragrant smoke. My natural timidity—my inexperience of public affairs—the horror which I still foolishly entertained of the violences and excesses of public contests, seemed to inspire him with mingled feelings of pity and surprise. He would sit there, looking at me with an expression of boozy sympathy—with an aspect of maudlin compassion which I could hardly regard as complimentary. As far as I was enabled to ascertain from an intercourse of the most open character which subsisted between us during my candidature, the literature of my friend was limited to a familiar acquaintance with the Electoral Roll, in which we were both so much interested. This document he constantly carried about with him, and seemed never weary of perusing it with all the devotion of a scholar poring over a precious M.S. of the Vatican. The filthy appearance presented by this entertaining and engrossing document probably prejudiced me against its interest and value as a means of literary enjoyment. It was always produced from the coat-pocket of my friend in a state of increased dilapidation. I remember that on one occasion nearly the whole of the Smiths had been reduced to ashes, by the pipe of the Chairman having been incautiously dropped into the pages of this document, before the fire was extinguished. On another, the Browns were found to be entirely undecipherable, and their political qualifications could not be in any way discovered, from the circumstance that the leaves devoted to the political *status* of this family were saturated with some thick fluid (which looked uncommonly like inferior treacle) and coated over with bread-crumbs and ashes. The delight of my friend at these two incidents at first almost inclined me to believe that the obscuration was premeditated. He laughingly gave me to understand that among these two families of voters my supporters were not to be found. "They're agin yer," he observed with a roar, and I was silent, though somewhat astonished that two such powerful and respectable sections of the community should at once, and apparently by instinct, have resolved upon meeting me with the bitterest opposition.

I now determined to prepare and publish my address to my constituents, and having gone home somewhat earlier than usual, and immediately locked myself into a small apartment—in which the most prominent and serviceable articles are a hip-bath, two chairs and a small table, a wash-hand stand, and two or three cases of bottled beer—I began to think about the first publication of which I was so soon to be the author. The privacy of my chamber and the occupation of my intellect were rudely disturbed by a violent knocking at the door, accompanied with the most piteous and tender entreaties on the part of my devoted wife to open the door at once. With a heart pierced by the apprehension of some domestic misfortune (I am the father of twins of three years old, whose aquatic predilections invariably lead them to the banks of a neighbouring pond, and in imagination I saw at once the drowned bodies of those lovely babes), I sprang to the door, and, on opening it, the mother of my children rushed into my arms, exclaiming, "Thank Heaven!" Thinking that this expression of religious gratitude could have no reference to the calamity which I had anticipated, I asked for an explanation. It is not my intention to lift the veil which hangs between my hearth and public curiosity, but I may be permitted to say that my unusually early return home, my paleness and distraction, and the secrecy of my movements, had alarmed one who truly loves me; and, suspecting I had sustained some heavy commercial losses, she feared I was resolved upon suicide. I kissed away her anxiety, but guiltily concealed the cause of my disquiet. I thought, one day she will glory in my strength of mind. When she takes up the daily paper at the morning meal, and reads column after column of her husband's eloquence—notes the approving " hear, hears" which close each rounded sentence, and the cheers amidst which her soul's idol resumes his seat—she will think, amidst her pride in his genius, of his tenderness in hiding from her the anguish of his early struggles, and her tears of joy and love will fall upon the glowing page. But I must go on with the history of my first published composition—or perhaps it will be better if I furnish it now to my readers. It never was published before (having been immediately and unanimously condemned by my committee, to whose critical inspection it was submitted the morning after it was written) : and the address which really appeared in the newspapers was the production of those gentlemen, with some of the peculiarities of expression dispensed with, and the grammatical eccentricities restrained by myself. This is the original work :—

" To the Electors of ——.

"Gentlemen,—To my great surprise, although the intelligence has occasioned me a feeling of sincere gratification, I am informed by some of your body that you have resolved upon nominating me as a candidate for your representation in Parliament.

" Having never taken any part, however humble, in public affairs, but contented myself with, I trust, the conscientious discharge of my duties to my family and my fellow-creatures, I fear you will find in me few of those qualities which ought to adorn the man to whom so great a trust is committed as that with which you purpose to invest me. I can offer you nothing but very ordinary intelligence, zeal in your service, and, I devoutly hope, a conscientious consideration of all matters submitted to me ; and, should these humble qualifications appear to you insufficient, I shall accept your refusal to support me as a proof that, while you respect my character as a citizen, you are indisposed to permit my imprudence to imperil it in a public station.

"I shall take an early opportunity of presenting myself before you at a public meeting, for the holding of which I am now engaged in making arrangements.

"I have, &c."

I have said that this address was never submitted to my political constituency. It now goes before a far larger, nobler, and wiser constituency, and I humbly but confidently ask you, electors of the vast electorate of Punch, whether great and successful and honoured men have not put forth manifestoes more impudent, less truthful ?—if containing more, only an excess of that which degraded the writer and insulted the readers ?

I do not say that mine is eloquent, profound, or even taking ; but it is the composition of a sober man. (I have read some very intoxicated addresses since, which, if literature had a police office, might and ought to have been taken up, charged with being "drunk and disorderly.") I do affirm that my address is not that of a snob writing to snobs, but it is the sincere statement of a man to his fellow-men of his desire to serve them, and his consciousness of his defects.

CHAPTER III.

It was the night of my first meeting, and if, instead of the assumption of an extremely wide-awake air, I had, with all the confiding simplicity and candour of childhood, bravely and honestly confessed that I had made a terrible mistake in consenting to become a candidate at all, I should to-day be very much more satisfied with the truthfulness of my nature than, I am grieved to say, I am. As I entered one of a series of public apartments in various parts of my electorate, which had been (as I was then informed, and subsequently in an unpleasant way reminded) expressly retained for the convenience of myself and friends during the election, I was received with one of the feeblest and dreariest attempts at what the reporters style acclamation that I had ever witnessed. A long table was admirably provided with business appliances for a full meeting of my committee. My experience of election meetings has placed me in possession of the articles necessary for the conduct of committee business. Spirits of all kinds are indispensable; hot water also plays a conspicuous part, and it is regarded as a matter of the last importance that every one should speak at once, and in tones of voice in no way subdued. The intelligence of such a gathering, with the marvellous mode of conducting its deliberations, struck me as being one of the most noticeable features of my canvass. As everybody talked and nobody listened, the result was, no doubt, if we could have ascertained it, a delightful unanimity of sentiment. At least, no man, unless he had an uncontrollable spirit of contradiction, could commit himself to opposing statements and opinions which he refused to hear. Somewhat bewildered by the tumult, I was actually thinking about an escape from the apartment, when I heard my name shouted from a hundred voices in the streets, and, rapidly and incautiously advancing to the front windows I was saluted with some applause, and boisterously exhorted by some, and sarcastically implored by others, to "go it, and not keep the public waiting." Looking down upon the sea of upturned faces, in none of which I could discover any kindly feeling but that of pity, which shone in one or two intellectual countenances, I confess my first resolve was to "go it" in the direction of my home, and to be guilty of the discourtesy of keeping the public waiting for the rest of the public's life. The scene was so new, so terrible—my feebleness in the presence of such an awful and irresponsible power as that before me oppressed me so heavily—the undisguised contempt for, the loud insolence of these people towards, me—excited an aversion mingled with terror. I should have, I say, recoiled; but providentially for the existence of a still subsisting but delusive faith in my pluck, I became aware of the presence of a couple of pale-faced, slight, and gentlemenly-looking men, whose sobriety and intelligence were strikingly at variance with the intemperance and brutality of most of those about them. The two were reporters; and when I saw with what placid patience they sat there, with their little slips before them and pencil in hand—with what calm indifference they glanced over that raging sea beneath—with what inoffensive and furtive curiosity they occasionally glanced at me, I was ashamed of my cowardice, and bowed to the crowd. I shall not weary my readers with my own report of my speech. Indeed, the work would be one of some difficulty, as I have no distinct recollection of a single sentence of it. My memory is only full of unpleasing incidents—the cries from the crowd, the prominent and pertinacious interest taken by one gentleman in a man bearing my name, and of whose life he expected me to give some particulars of thrilling interest, and did not attempt to conceal his bitter disappointment at my reticence. As it accidentally transpired that the object of this engrossing anxiety had been hanged some years since, and as this was the only information concerning the individual of which I was ever possessed, I was of course unable to gratify the curiosity of my interrogator; but he had possessed the assemblage with a sense of the appropriateness and importance of his examination; many were apparently of opinion that the unfortunate deceased was an immediate relative of mine, and one gentleman ventured to affirm that it was I myself, upon whose lips the audience were hanging, who had been legally suspended; and a large majority were manifestly of opinion that my suspension ought to have taken place long since. Hoarse, trembling, perspiring, humiliated and almost in tears, I thought of the sweet faces at my own fireside—of the loving tenderness of my household—of the round, warm arm of my wife encircling that neck about which the people below me would be quite resigned to see a hempen collar, and I invoked upon the heads of all my fellow-citizens a fearful curse—an imprecation which dishonoured freedom and degraded society, an anathema so terrible that, but for the necessity of procuring that absolution which can alone be given to full confession, I should blush to acknowledge. I d——d the Constitution!

CHAPTER IV.

The melancholy narrative of my experiences is drawing to a close. I could have hardly believed that so much distress of mind, so much remorse for indiscretion, could be compressed into so short a space of time. The expense of the agony also struck me as something fearful. The luxury of public grief is beyond the means of a man of ordinary fortune. To lose the comforts of home, to gain the intense hostility of men who were your friends yesterday, and to become the subject of the compassion or contempt of those who are your friends to-day—all the pleasures of public life cost immense sums. The accidental omission on the part of my committee to bury a copy of my address in the columns of an obscure newspaper, was doubtless the cause of the appearance in that journal of a biographical notice of me, which was certainly not of a flattering character. The gratification of reading one's own life is usually reserved only for that limited class whose acts and speeches are the materials of national history. But in my case, obscurity even did not protect me. In this veracious publication I became acquainted for the first time with many important circumstances in my life, and ascertained that in a humble and quiet way I had industriously earned a rascally reputation. I was surprised at the discovery. I learnt with horror that I was untruthful, and with terror that I was a trimmer. When I thought upon the practical falsehood of addressing my committee as "gentlemen" (of which I had been repeatedly guilty), I was compelled to acknowledge the truth of the first charge ; when I reflected upon my abhorrence, both of my supporters and antagonists, I was obliged to admit that the second was not entirely without foundation. Still I lamented that the world believed me to be an impostor, and I grieved that I should have been instrumental in obtaining a public expression of the world's opinion.

The circulation of my biography was very much enlarged by the admiration for it, as a purely literary work, entertained and proclaimed by the friends of my opponent. A large number of copies of the journal in which it appeared were immediately procured, and promptly disseminated through the electorate. The life appeared to excite very great attention and interest, but little astonishment. I discovered that the public presumed me to be a rogue or a fool, and that the indication of popular opinion was decidedly in favour of the adoption of the first view of my character. I have only incidentally alluded to my opponent. I shall not, I trust, in describing him wound charity, cause pain, or stain these pages so generously given up to my confessions. My opponent was a gentleman whose commercial career had not been a success, and I was astonished to learn that his creditors were not among the most prominent of his supporters. His opinions appeared to me somewhat revolutionary, and his oratory of an extremely boisterous character. His voice was eminently suited to the requirements of a monster meeting held during a gale of wind. But perhaps the most remarkable thing about him was the intense malignity which he invariably displayed towards myself. Anything like the bitterness of this animosity I had never witnessed before, and being a creature fond of inspiring love and attachment, I deplored this unreasonable malevolence almost with tears. His frequently and forcibly expressed contempt for my opinions, expressive of my incompetency, and denunciation of my baseness, were universally greeted with loud demonstrations of approval. I was informed of the vigour of his eloquence, and I resolved to hear him. I attended one of his meetings, concealed myself in a convenient corner, and heard him. He was so utterly unscrupulous, so unnecessarily violent, so cool and confident in misrepresentation, so courageous in slander, that I felt a virtuous craven in the presence of such heroism. I bowed in spirit before his superiority for public life. I felt (and perhaps I thanked heaven for the feeling) that I was not, and could not be, the equal of this man. I repented of my presumption, and commenced my atonement. The first fruits of my repentance were seen in my immediate abandonment of the canvass; the last are now submitted to you—*Peccavi!* Father Punch, *Peccavi!* Absolve, and let me go!

Some of the minor characters in our political drama are described in the following papers, entitled *Political Snobs, by One of Themselves:*

When the great historian of Snobs resolved upon the re-publication of his noble work, he purposely omitted the precious papers on Political Snobs. His reasons will be found in a foot-note, and are sufficiently strong to inspire a reasonable apprehension of failure in the endeavour to imitate so illustrious a master. But it may be urged in our favour that we are in this country essentially political. We have no "Noble Snobs," no "Military Snobs," and very few "Party-giving Snobs;" but we do possess a host of political Snobs, and the present serene season of politics seems specially suited to the portraiture of some of them by one of themselves. Now that Parliament is closed, that our indolent snobs have no occupation of a more improving character than perusing these pages, we shall not be charged with political hostility. We shall escape the perils of privilege, and avoid the ignominy of being quoted in the House. The most prominent of our political snobs—the one deserving most censure—is the man who is perpetually on the watch for flagrant offences among the subordinates of the Government. He is fond of a continual search in each of the Government offices,—would have porters detective policemen,—and office-keepers spies. To gratify his passion for information, the contents of the waste-paper should be preserved, indexed, and bound; blotting paper pads should be seized each evening, and kept under lock and key till impressions were read. His notion of the contract between the State and its servants is that the latter sell not only their service, but their privacy of life, their sensibilities, their secrets, to the former. He has no difficulty in asking the House to consent to the production of returns shewing, in a tabular form, the number of times in each day on which various officers have left their desks, or writing tables, with the causes or pretences of their absence—whether they are in the habit of looking about more than is absolutely necessary—and whether they are ever thirsty between 9 and 4, with some account of the preparations used to quench thirst. This important information is published for the snob's gratification, and to the terror of the unhappy wretches who may have snatched a moment to write to a sick wife, or a boy at school—or who may have gone out for a glass of beer, or profaned the majesty of a public department by procuring from an adjoining public a couple of glasses of sherry and a biscuit. Oh, think, my dear snob,—for these letters are written for your edification and improvement—not to expose and chastise, but to counsel and instruct you—think, I say, what a melancholy fate were yours if heaven had determined that you should be a gentleman and a public officer! Reflect upon the strange dispensation of Providence, which has made you a much higher—a far more powerful creature—a snob and a member of Parliament. You might have had the training, and the consequent necessities of a poor swell, with the responsibilities of a large and young family. You might have experienced the bitter trials of supporting and educating these children upon a sum barely sufficient to humbly feed, and not extravagantly clothe them and yourself. You might have felt the double misery of an increasing family and a decreasing income. Oh, snob, if you thought sometimes of these things, you would not dare to cry so loudly in divisions on the estimates against that little increase of £25 or £30 to Brown's or Jones's salary. That little increase on the paper tells perhaps of a large increase in poor Brown's or Jones's family. The last baby, snob, is to be carried through all his infantile ailments by that little sum. Nurse and accoucheur have to be paid,—little comforts to be bought for poor Mrs. B. or Mrs. J., and the coral, and the electro-plated mug— all look for payment to the increase. How much more merciful, tender-hearted, and nobler you would become, did you think for awhile over these matters. Don't be too exacting; throw down that duster which you are eternally flipping about desks and tables. Disregard the advice of Ovid (if you know what it was), "*si nullus erit pulvis, tamen excute nullum.*" Go down to J. or B. and humbly and affectionately ask them to translate it for you, and resolve not to do it again. When you feel tempted to be too patriotic, let the angelic image of the infant J. or B. rise before your mind's eye, and vote the child his baby-linen and his go-cart. Contrast that helpless dependent upon your political conduct with the independent little Parliamentary snobs who enliven your leisure and noisily gladden your private life. Reflect upon the possible calamity of their little shoes appearing upon a "Supplementary Estimate," and a heartless majority being against the procurement of those necessary articles of costume. And when the dread possibility softens your heart, and disposes you to clemency, thank the snob who has suggested the means of your regeneration.

A second paper treats *The Omniscient Snob:*

One of the most conclusive proofs of the genius and wisdom of our Constitution is the high degree of cultivation which characterises our public men. Yesterday Brown may have been a deficient arithmetician, struggling with educational and pecuniary difficulties—to-day he is a member of the Assembly, fitted to discuss the most complicated questions, and to control the expenditure of a nation. Last week his intelligence was severely taxed in the negotiation of an insignificant piece of paper at which bank clerks smiled, and which directors peevishly put aside—not anticipating the possible historic value of the autograph with which it was adorned. Last night, from his place in the House, he voted for the issue of debentures to the extent of half a million, and spoke familiarly of the money markets of Europe. You perceive that Brown must have undergone a marvellous change. In the instant of his return to Parliament he who

knew no more of figures than you or I became not merely an accountant, but a
financier. How is this transformation effected ? Brown's friends are astounded
—his enemies endeavour to conceal their surprise beneath a mask of incredulity
—and the only person who seems to preserve his self-possession and manifest
no astonishment is, Brown himself. We must confess that we are ourselves
believers in the inspiration of the representative system, if we may be permitted
so to describe the intellectual change which takes place in an elected senator.
The reader will perceive that this confession of faith is limited to the elected—
the chosen of the populace ; for in the case of the nominated senators no such
transition is noticeable. These gentlemen remain precisely as they were—men
of genius or the reverse—of academical training or mere commercial education.
They cannot graduate in the Political University which showers its learning and
honour upon the friends of the people—instructs them *de omni scibili*. Let us
take an illustration of this surprising faculty to deal with the most difficult
matters in the most masterly manner.. Civil engineering is generally looked
upon as a profession requiring the possession of average intelligence—considerable
mathematical education—a large space of a student's life—with varied experience and opportunities for experimental study. Jones, we know, did not
employ his early years in bewildering studies of Archimedes or Euclid, nor
waste his riper manhood under Brunel and Stephenson. Indeed, we are pretty
well aware (living in a small community where biographical dictionaries of our
remarkable men could be written by almost anybody) that Jones was permitted
the fullest natural development without the restraints of any kind of scholastic
discipline, and in his mature age knew no more of these matters than he might
have attained in the deviation of water-courses to his various claims on the
diggings. But Jones becomes a senator, and the construction of some mighty
viaduct is proposed for his consideration, involving the most intricate calcula-
tions, and enormous outlay. Convinced of its usefulness and importance, Jones
sanctions the expenditure ; but, in the progress of the work, doubts the scientific
accuracy of the estimate, disapproves of the design, and proposes important
alterations. The engineer is brought to the bar of the House and is examined
by Jones—cross-examined by Brown—and again examined by Jones: The
position of the engineer is a pitiable one. Fancy Porson, on Greek particles,
under the terrifying cross-examination of a body of sixth-form boys, with the
most absolute power to torture him at any length. Realise the late Duke of
Wellington on the movements of an army in the field similarly placed before a
tribunal of volunteer subalterns with commissions a fortnight old. And yet
these will give you a very faint idea of the position of the engineer, for the boys
know something of Greek, and the citizen soldiery a little of drill, but Jones
knows nothing—absolutely nothing—of engineering. And yet the officer—
an accomplished and able man, it may be—a conscientious public servant
perhaps (there are such phenomena, though Jones will not believe it)—leaves
the bar with the conviction that both Jones and Brown are extremely dissatisfied.
They are. They propose a select committee (with power to send for persons

and papers) to enquire into the plans, specifications, and progress of the work. The motion is carried, and the awful tribunal is created. Jones is, of course, the president; and, from day to day, short-hand writers are employed chronicling the interminable examinations of contractors, engineers, and all kinds of officers of Government. The reporter does more (he puts the interrogatories into English), and months afterwards a report is published condemning everybody engaged in 'the work—and glorifying Jones and his friends. Now what does this all mean? Well, it means in the first place a partial suspension of the efficient performance of important public duties; it means the disorganization of departments—the encouragement of popular suspicion of all intelligence in the public service; and it lastly means a most shameful extravagance of public money in printing the memorials of Jones's audacious ignorance and intolerable self-sufficiency. A fellow like this would examine Ericsson on his caloric engine before a select committee, and report a condemnation of his slide valves, his cylinders, and his pistons. As of engineering so of any other question submitted to the House. This kind of man may be described as the omniscient snob. And, oh! my brothers and sisters of snobbery, when we think how great men have devoted their precious lives to profound study, and how diffidently, how humbly, they have spoken of themselves—how generously of others—in the end, shall we not do well to remonstrate with the senatorial snob of whom this paper treats. Is it not an insult to education, and an outrage of our sensibilities, to tolerate his dictatorship? Why should we suppose that men of high position, superior training, and large responsibilities, are necessarily asses or rogues when they take the pay of the Government. And yet this is the fundamental principle upon which the reputation of the omniscient snob is built. Let us denounce it and chastise him, and we shall become economists of the public money, guardians of our own reputation, and priceless patriots.

It deserves to be pointed out that these sketches—and everything else from the same pen—were written 'at the spur of the moment,' and never subjected to revision. Most men who write well do so at the expense of some labour, and their 'copy' is ornamented with many erasures. De Quincey's manuscript, we are told, exhibits a degree of elaboration that would scarcely be credited. Whatever may be the worth of Mr. Dalley's compositions, they are certainly not the result of laborious efforts. A bitter satirist once said of him that he possessed 'a mind of so much instinctive grace and brilliancy, so much tact, as to manifest genius, and genius of a charming nature.' He who wrote this had certainly no intention to exaggerate. But Mr. Dalley's genius does not tend to literature so much as to oratory. In the one, impromptu manifestations of power go for little : in the other, they go for a great deal. Now Mr. Dalley's qualifications as a speaker are of a rare order. He has evidently a full command of language. Let the reader examine the foregoing sketches carefully, both as to the construction of sentences and the selection of language. To what exceptions are they open? The strongest impression they convey is that of eloquence—eloquence combined with graceful humour and refined feeling. But we do not detect any evidence of literary art in their composition. They do not present the brilliant finish of what may be called magazine-writing—a species of writing which is as much the result of art as any mechanical process whatever. In conversation and in public speaking, Mr. Dalley's powers of humour are irresistible; no gravity can be proof against them ; and this humour is invariably clothed in faultless diction. This indeed is the peculiarity of it. The conversation of wits and humourists generally derives its charm from the idea rather than the expression. In Mr. Dalley's case the one is as exquisite as the other. Recollecting that he owes absolutely nothing to the '*limæ labor*,' and yet that, whether writing or speaking, he displays an elegance of style that would please the most fastidious critic, we may fairly conclude that the gifts which nature has bestowed upon him are not often met with even in much wider circles than our own.

HENRY KENDALL.

HENRY KENDALL was born at Ulladulla, near Shoalhaven, in 1842. His father was an officer in the Navy, and had served under the celebrated Lord Dundonald. His death, which took place soon after his son Henry was born, left his family in straitened circumstances; and his children consequently suffered in their education. At the age of fourteen Henry Kendall went to sea, and spent two years among the South Sea Islands. It is strange that the poetry he has since written bears no traces of that period of his life.

On his return to Sydney, Kendall made some attempt to study law in the office of an attorney, but soon abandoned it. At this time, he appears to have endured much suffering, and this, combined with a natural despondency, has served to colour his subsequent writings with a shade of morbid melancholy. None of them are wholly free from it, and this peculiarity has done much to affect their reception by the public. In 1862, he collected various pieces, and published a volume. Considering the circumstances under which this volume was produced—the author's youth, his privations, his want of sufficient education—it is entitled to the very highest praise. Its merit is so great as to justify us in pronouncing it a work of genius. Let us compare it with the "first volumes" of men renowned in letters, and see how far it suffers in the comparison. To mention an unknown writer in the same breath with the demigods of literature would provoke ridicule ; but there can be no absurdity in examining the earliest efforts of the demigods in question with a view to a correct judgment of the work before us. In most cases we shall find that, so far from this comparison being a damaging one to Kendall, it is quite the reverse. If his fame be compelled to rest upon the productions he has already published, then there is certainly little chance of that fame being a very extensive one. The value of his book lies principally in the promise it affords of future excellence. It may be that Mr. Kendall is incapable of higher efforts, and that he has already exhausted the powers bestowed upon him. In that case, we can look for nothing but repetitions of what he has already written—repetitions marked rather by mannerism than by thought. That remains to be seen. But, on the other hand, it is equally possible that Mr. Kendall is capable of infinitely higher things: and if so, it will be no small credit to this colony that it should, at so early a period of its history, have produced a man of great poetic genius.

One striking merit in Mr. Kendall's poetry is, that its colouring is strictly local, and that he has endeavoured to give voice to the majestic scenery of his native land. Whatever opinion may be formed of his poetry, it cannot be denied that it is distinctly Australian poetry. This is a hopeful sign ; inasmuch as it speaks of a mind naturally original, and averse to imitation. He has not commenced the practice of his Art by studying Tennyson, but by studying the wild and splendid scenery that surrounded him at his birth. His capacity in descriptive poetry is very great; in fact, it appears to be the distinctive mark of his genius. He has an artist's eye for a landscape, and if his shading is rather too dark, his outlines are none the less true. No local writer has reproduced the scenes familiar to us with so much effect. And again, he has sought inspiration in the characters and events of this country—endeavouring to paint the wild society of the interior as well as its peculiar scenery. He has chanted the savage melodies of the aboriginals—painted the sufferings of the explorers—and given a poetic interest even to the life of stockmen. These are facts which mark him out as an Australian poet, and an original poet: for there is no writer in this field whom he could imitate. This portion at least of his writings may be pronounced perfect.

The agonizing catastrophe of Burke's Expedition to the Gulf of Carpentaria is thus rendered by Mr. Kendall, under the title of *The Fate of the Explorers—a Fragment*:

> Set your face toward the darkness—tell of Deserts weird and wide,
> Where unshaken woods are huddled, and low languid waters glide;
> Turn and tell of deserts lonely; lying pathless, deep, and vast,
> Where in utter silence ever Time seems slowly breathing past;
> Silence only broken when the sun is flecked with cloudy bars,
> Or when tropic squalls come hurtling underneath the sultry stars!
> Deserts thorny, hot, and thirsty, where the feet of men are strange,
> And Eternal Nature sleeps in solitudes which know no change.
> Weakened with their lengthened labours, past long plains of stone and sand,
> Down those trackless wilds they wandered, travellers from a far-off land;
> Seeking now to join their brothers; struggling on with faltering feet,
> For a glorious work was finished, and a noble task complete.
> And they dreamt of welcome faces—dreamt that soon unto their ears
> Friendly greetings would be thronging with a nation's well-earned cheers;
> Since their courage never failed them, but with high unflinching soul,
> Each was pressing forward hoping, trusting all should reach the goal.
>
> * * * * * *
>
> Though he rallied in the morning, long before the close of day
> He had sunk, the worn-out hero, fainting, dying, by the way!
> But with Death he wrestled hardly: three times rising from the sod,
> Yet a little further onward o'er the weary waste he trod;
> Facing Fate with heart undaunted, still the chief would totter on,
> Till the evening closed about him,—till the strength to move was gone.
>
> Then he penned his latest writing, and, before the life was spent,
> Gave the records to his comrade; gave the watch he said was lent;
> Gave them with his last commandments, charging him that night to stay,
> And to let him lie unburied when the soul had passed away.
>
> Through that night he uttered little, rambling were the words he spoke;
> And he turned and died in silence, when the tardy morning broke.
> Many memories come together, whilst in sight of death we dwell,

Much of sweet and sad reflection through the weary mind must well ;
As those long hours glided past him, till the east with light was fraught,
Who may know the mournful secret—who can tell us what he thought ?

Very lone and very wretched was the brave man left behind,
Wandering over leagues of waste land, seeking, hoping help to find ;
Sleeping in deserted wurleys ; fearful, many nightfalls through,
Lest unfriendly hands should rob him of his hoard of wild nardoo.

* * * * * *

'Ere he reached their old encampment—'ere the well-known spot he gained,
Something nerved him—something whispered, that his other chief remained.
So he searched for food to give him, trusting they might both survive
Till the aid so long expected from the cities should arrive ;
So he searched for food, and took it to the gunyah, where he found
Silence broken by his footfalls—death and darkness on the ground.

Weak and wearied with his journey, there the lone survivor stooped ;
And the disappointment bowed him, and his heart with sadness drooped.
But he rose and raked a hollow with his wasted feeble hands,
Where he took and hid the hero, in the rushes and the sands ;
But he like a brother laid him out of reach of wind and rain,
And for many days he sojourned near him on that wild-faced plain.
Whilst he stayed beside the ruin—whilst he lingered with the Dead,
Oh ! he must have sat in shadow, gloomy as the tears he shed.

* * * * * *

Where our noble Burke was lying—where his sad companion stood,
Came the natives of the Forest—came the wild men of the Wood ;
Down they looked and saw the stranger—he who there in quiet slept—
Down they knelt, and o'er the chieftain bitterly they moaned and wept :
Bitterly they mourned to see him all uncovered to the blast—
All uncovered to the tempest as it wailed and whistled past.
And they shrouded him with bushes, so in death that he might lie
Like a warrior of their nation, sheltered from the stormy sky.

* * * * * *

Ye must rise and sing their praises, O ye bards with souls of fire !
For the People's voice shall echo through the wailings of your lyre ;
And we'll welcome back their comrade, though our eyes with tears be blind
At the thoughts of promise perished, and the shadow left behind.
Now the leaves are bleaching round them—now the gales above them glide,
But the end was all accomplished, and their fame is far and wide ;
Though this fadeless glory cannot hide a grateful nation's grief,
And their laurels have been blended with a gloomy cypress wreath.

Let them rest where they have laboured ! but, my country, mourn and moan ;
We must build with human sorrow grander monuments than stone.
Let them rest, for oh ! remember, that in long hereafter time,
Sons of Science oft shall wander o'er that solitary clime ;
Cities bright shall rise about it : Age and Beauty there shall stray,
And the Fathers of the People pointing to the graves shall say,
"Here they fell, the glorious martyrs ! when these plains were woodlands deep;
Here a friend—a brother laid them ; here the wild men came to weep."

Here is music in a livelier key, in the shape of a *Song of the Cattle-hunters*. Those who are familiar with station life can hardly fail to relish verse of this kind, where we have exquisite melody combined with perfectly accurate description :

While the morning light beams on the fern-matted streams,
   And the water-pools flash in its glow,
Down the ridges we fly, with a loud ringing cry—
   Down the ridges and gullies we go !
And the cattle we hunt, they are racing in front,
   With a roar like the thunder of waves ;
As the beat and the beat of our swift horses' feet
   Start the echoes away from their caves !
     As the beat and the beat
     Of our swift horses' feet
   Start the echoes away from their caves !

Like a wintry shore that the waters ride o'er,
   All the lowlands are filling with sound,
For swiftly we gain where the herds on the plain,
   Like a tempest, are tearing the ground !
And we'll follow them hard to the rails of the yard,
   O'er the gulches and mountain-tops gray,
Where the beat and the beat of our swift horses' feet
   Will die with the echoes away !
     Where the beat and the beat
     Of our swift horses' feet
   Will die with the echoes away !

Another piece of the same kind, and equally good, is entitled *The Barcoo*:

From the runs of the Narran, wide-dotted with sheep,
And loud with the lowing of cattle,
We speed for a Land where the strange Forests sleep,
And the hidden creeks bubble and brattle!
Now call on the horses, and leave the blind courses
And sources of rivers that all of us know;
For, crossing the ridges and passing the ledges,
And running up gorges, we'll come to the verges
Of gullies were waters eternally flow!
Oh! the herds they will rush down the spurs of the hill
To feed on the grasses so cool and so sweet;
And I think that my life with delight will stand still
When we halt with the pleasant Barcoo at our feet.

Good-bye to the Barwan and brigalow scrubs;
Adieu to the Culgoä ranges!
But look for the malga, and salt-bitten shrubs,
Though the face of the forest-land changes.
The leagues we may travel down beds of hot gravel,
And clay-crusted reaches where moisture hath been,
While searching for waters, may vex us and thwart us,
Yet who would be quailing, or fainting, or failing?
Not you, who are men of the Narran, I ween!
When we leave the dry channels away to the South,
And reach the far plains we are journeying to,
We will cry, though our lips may be glued with the drouth,
" Hip, hip, and hurrah for the pleasant Barcoo!"

In the following verses, entitled *Kooroora*—a dirge on the death of an aboriginal chief—we feel that true poetry may be drawn from a source which is too often regarded as a degraded one:

> The gums in the gully stand gloomy and stark;
>   A torrent beneath them is leaping;
> And the wind goes about like a ghost in the dark,
>   Where a chief of Wahibbi lies sleeping!
> He dreams of a battle—of foes of the past,
> But he hears not the whooping abroad on the blast,
> Nor the fall of the feet that are travelling fast.
>   Oh! why dost thou slumber, Kooroora?
>
> They come o'er the hills in their terrible ire,
>   And speed by the woodlands and water;

They look down the hills at the flickering fire,
  All eager and thirsty for slaughter.
Lo! the stormy moon glares like a torch from the vale,
And a voice in the beela grows wild in its wail,
As the cries of the Wanneroos swell with the gale—
  Oh! rouse thee, and meet them, Kooroora.

He starts from his sleep and he clutches his spear,
  And the echoes roll backward in wonder,
For a shouting strikes into the hollow woods near,
  Like the sound of a gathering thunder.
He clambers the ridge, with his face to the light,
The foes of Wahibbi come full in his sight—
The waters of Mooki will redden to-night.
  Go! and glory awaits thee, Kooroora.

Lo! yeelamans splinter, and boomerangs clash,
  And a spear in the darkness is driven;
It whizzes along like a wandering flash
  From the heart of a hurricane riven.
They turn to the mountains, that gloomy-browed band,
The rain droppeth down with a moan to the land,
And the face of a chieftain lies buried in sand—
  Oh! the light that was quenched in Kooroora.

To-morrow the Wanneroo dogs will rejoice,
  And feast in this desolate valley;
But where are his brothers—the friends of his choice?
  And why art thou absent, Ewalli?
Now silence draws back to the forest again,
And the wind, like a wayfarer, sleeps on the plain,
But the cheeks of a warrior bleach in the rain.
  Oh! where are thy mourners, Kooroora?

Mr. Kendall does not seem to have occupied himself much with love affairs: yet there are two or three lyrics from his hand which show his capacity to deal with the master passion of our nature. Even they, however, are dark and gloomy, and speak of disappointed hopes instead of lovers' joys. Here are some graceful stanzas under the title of *Clari*:

Too cold, O my brother, too cold for my wife,
  Is the Beauty you showed me this morning:

Nor yet have I found the sweet dream of my life,
  And good-bye to the sneering and scorning.
Would you have me cast down in the dark of her frown,
  Like others who bend at her shrine ;
And would barter their souls for a statue-like face
  And a heart that can never be mine?
    That can never be theirs nor mine.

Go after her, look at her, kneel at her feet,
  And mimic the lover romantic ;
I have hated deceit, and she misses the treat
  Of driving me hopelessly frantic !
Now watch her, as deep in her carriage she lies,
  And love her, my friend, if you dare !
She would wither your life with her beautiful eyes,
  And strangle your soul with her hair !
    With a mesh of her splendid hair !

The following, entitled *The River and the Hill*, has been quoted in the *Athenæum*:

And they shook their sweetness out in their sleep,
  On the brink of that beautiful stream,
But it wandered along with a wearisome song
  Like a lover that walks in a dream:
    So the roses blew
    When the winds went through,
In the moonlight so white and so still;
    But the river it beat
    All night at the feet
  Of a cold and flinty hill—
  Of a hard and senseless hill !

I said, "We have often showered our loves
  Upon something as dry as the dust ;
And the faith that is crost, and the hearts that are lost—
  Oh! how can we wittingly trust:
    Like the stream which flows,
    And wails as it goes,
Through the moonlight so white and so still,
    To beat and to beat
    All night at the feet
  Of a cold and flinty hill—
  Of a hard and senseless hill !

"River, I stay where the sweet roses blow,
  And drink of their pleasant perfumes!
Oh! why do you moan, in this wide world alone,
  When so much affection here blooms?
      The winds wax faint,
      And the Moon like a Saint
Glides over the waters so white and so still;
      But you hear me and beat
      All night at the feet
    Of that cold and flinty hill—
    Of that hard and senseless hill!"

The following is entitled *Etheline*:

The heart that once was rich with light,
  And happy in your grace,
Now lieth cold beneath the scorn
  That gathers on your face;
And every joy it knew before,
  And every templed dream,
Is paler than the dying flash
  On yonder mountain stream.
The soul, regretting foundered bliss,
  Amid the wreck of years,
Hath mourned it with intensity
  Too deep for human tears.

The floweret fadeth underneath
  The blast that rushes by—
The forest leaves are white with death,
  But Love will never die!
We both have seen the starry moss,
  That clings where Ruin reigns,
And *one* must know *his* lonely breast
  Affection still retains;
Though all the budding hopes of life
  That clustered round and round,
Are lying now, like withered blooms,
  Forsaken—on the ground.

'Tis hard to think of what we were,
  And what we might have been,

Had not an evil spirit crept
    Across the tranquil scene :
Had fervent feelings in your soul
    Not failed nor ceased to shine
As pure as those existing on,
    And burning still in mine :
Had every treasure at your feet
    That I was wont to pour,
Been never thrown like worthless weeds
    Upon a barren shore.

The bitter edge of grief has passed,
    I would not now upbraid ;
Or count to you the broken vows
    So often idly made.
I would not cross your path to chase
    The falsehood from your brow,—
I *know*, with all that borrowed light,
    You are not happy now :
Since those that once have trampled down
    Affection's early claim,
Have lost a peace they need not hope
    To find on earth again.

In a different style we have the following stanzas, entitled *Campaspe*:

Turn from the ways of this woman ! Campaspe we call her by name—
She is fairer than flowers of the fire—she is brighter than brightness of flame.
As a song that strikes swift to the heart with the beat of the blood of the South,
And a light and a leap and a smart, is the play of her perilous mouth.
Her eyes are as splendours that break in the rain at the set of the sun,
But turn from the steps of Campaspe—a woman to look at and shun.

Dost thou know of the cunning of Beauty ? Take heed to thyself and beware
Of the trap in the droop of the raiment—the snare in the folds of the hair !
She is fulgent in flashes of pearl, the breeze with her breathing is sweet,
But fly from the face of the girl—there is death in the fall of her feet !
Is she maiden or marvel of marble ?—O rather a tigress at wait
To pounce on thy soul for her pastime—a leopard for love and for hate.

Woman of shadow and furnace ! She biteth her lips to restrain
Speech that springs out when she sleepeth by the stirs and the starts of her pain.

As music half-shapen of sorrow, with its wants and its infinite wail
Is the voice of Campaspe—the beauty at bay with her passion dead-pale.
Go out from the courts of her loving, nor tempt the fierce dance of desire
Where thy life would be shrivelled like stubble in the stress and the fervour of fire.

I know of one, gentle as moonlight—she is sad as the shine of the moon
But touching the ways of her eyes are : she comes to my soul like a tune,
Like a tune that is filled with faint voices of the loved and the lost and the lone,
Doth this stranger abide with my silence : like a tune with a tremulous tone.
The leopard, we call her Campaspe ! I pluck at a rose and I stir
To think of the sweet-hearted maiden—what name is too tender for her !

Under the title of *Fainting by the way*, Mr. Kendall gives us a 'Psalm of Life' that some readers may prefer to Longfellow's :

Swarthy wastelands, wide and woodless, glittering miles and miles away,
Where the south wind seldom wanders, and the winters will not stay;
Lurid wastelands, pent in silence thick with hot and thirsty sighs,
Where the scanty thorn leaves twinkle with their haggard hopeless eyes;
Furnaced wastelands, hunched with hillocks like to stony billows rolled
Where the naked flats lie swirling, like a sea of darkened gold;
Burning wastelands, glancing upward with a weird and vacant stare,
Where the languid heavens quiver o'er red depths of stirless air!

" O my brother, I am weary of this wildering waste of sand ;
In the noontide we can never travel to the promised land !
Lo, the desert broadens round us, glaring wildly in my face,
With long leagues of sunflame on it—O, the barren, barren place !
See, behind us gleams a green plot : shall we thither turn and rest
Till a cool wind flutters over, till the day is down the west ?
I would follow but I cannot ! Brother, let me here remain,
For the heart is dead within me, and I may not rise again !"

" Wherefore stay to talk of fainting ? rouse thee for awhile, my friend,
Evening hurries on our footsteps, and this journey soon will end.
Wherefore stay to talk of fainting when the sun, with sinking fire,
Smites the blocks of broken thunder blackening yonder craggy spire.
Even now the far-off landscape broods and fills with coming change,
And the wither'd moon grows brighter bending o'er that shadowed range ;
At the feet of grassy summits sleeps a water calm and clear,
There is surely rest beyond it ! comrade, wherefore falter here?

" Yet a little longer struggle ; we have walked a wilder plain,
And have met more troubles, trust me, than we e'er shall meet again !
Can you think of all the dangers you and I are living through,
With a soul so weak and fearful, with the doubts *I* never knew ?
Dost thou not remember that the thorns are clustered with the rose,
And that every Zinlike border may a pleasant land enclose ?
Oh ! across these sultry deserts, many a fruitful scene we'll find,
And the blooms we gather shall be worth the wounds they leave behind."

" Ah, my brother, it is useless ! see, o'erburdened with their load,
All the friends who went before us fall or falter by the road ;
We have come a weary distance seeking what we may not get,
And I think we are but children chasing rainbows through the wet !
Tell me not of vernal valleys ! Is it well to hold a reed
Out for drowning men to clutch at in the moments of their need ?
Go thy journey on without me, it is better I should stay,
Since my life is like an evening fading, swooning fast away !

" Where are all the springs you talked of ? Have I not with pleading mouth
Looked to Heaven through a silence stifled in the crimson drouth ?
Have I not, with lips unsated, watched to see the fountains burst,
Where I searched the rocks for cisterns, and they only mocked my thirst ?
Oh ! I dreamt of countries fertile, bright with lakes and flashing rills
Leaping from their shady caverns, streaming round a thousand hills !
Leave me, brother, all is fruitless, barren, measureless, and dry,
And my God will *never* help me, tho' I pray, and faint, and die."

" Up ! I tell thee this is idle ! O thou man of little faith !
Doubting on the verge of Aidenn, turning now to covet death !
By the fervent hopes within me, by the strength which nerves my soul,
By the heart that yearns to help thee, we shall live and reach the goal !
Rise and lean thy weight upon me. Life is fair, and God is just,
And He yet will show us fountains if we only look and trust !
O ! I know it, and He leads us to the glens of stream and shade,
Where the low sweet waters gurgle round the banks which cannot fade."

Thus he spake, my friend and brother ! and he took me by the hand,
And I think we walked the desert till the night was on the land ;
Then we came to flowery hollows, where we heard a far-off stream
Singing in the moony twilight like the rivers of my dream.
And the balmy winds came tripping softly through the pleasant trees,
And I thought they bore a murmur like a voice from sleeping seas.
So we travelled, so we reached it, and I never more will part
With the peace, as calm as sunset, folded round my weary heart.

Here is an old Australian legend, entitled *Ghost Glen*, pronounced by the *Athenæum* to be a poem which, 'once read, must linger on the memory in its weird horror':

"Shut your ears, stranger, or turn from Ghost Glen now
For the paths are grown over; untrodden by men now—
Shut your ears, stranger!" saith the grey mother, crooning
Her sorcery Runic, when sets the half-moon in!

To-night the North-Easter goes travelling slowly,
But it never stoops down to that Hollow unholy—
To-night it rolls loud on the ridges red-litten,
But it *cannot* abide in that Forest sin-smitten!

For over the pitfall the moon-dew is thawing,
And with never a body, two shadows stand sawing!
The wraiths of two sawyers (*step under and under*),
Who did a foul murder, and were blackened with thunder!

Whenever the storm-wind comes driven and driving,
Through the blood-spattered timber you may see the saw striving—
You may see the saw heaving, and falling, and heaving,
Whenever the sea-creek is chafing and grieving!

And across a burnt body, as black as an adder,
Sits the sprite of a sheep-dog?—was ever sight sadder!
For as the dry thunder splits louder and faster,
The sprite of a sheep-dog howls for his master!

"Oh! count your beads deftly," saith the grey mother, crooning
Her sorcery Runic, when sets the half-moon in!
And well may she mutter, for the dark hollow laughter
You will hear in the sawpits and the bloody logs after!

Ay, count your beads deftly, and keep your ways wary,
For the sake of the Saviour and sweet Mother Mary!
Pray for your peace in these perilous places,
And pray for the laying of horrible faces!

One starts, with a forehead wrinkled and livid,
Aghast at the lightnings, sudden and vivid!
One telleth with curses the gold that they drew there
(Ah! cross your breast humbly) from him who they slew there!

The stranger who came from the loved—the romantic—
Island that sleeps on the moaning Atlantic;
Leaving behind him patient homes yearning
For the steps in the distance, never returning;—

Who was left in the Forest, shrunken, and starkly
Burnt by his slayers (so men have said darkly);
With the half-crazy sheep-dog, who cowered beside there,
And yelled at the silence, and marvelled, and died there!

Yea, cross your breast humbly, and hold your breath tightly,
Or fly for your life from those shadows unsightly;
From the set staring features (cold, and so young too!)
And the death on the lips that a mother hath clung too.

I tell you, the Bushman is braver than most men,
Who even in daylight doth go through the Ghost Glen!
Although in that Hollow, unholy and lonely,
He sees the dark sawpits and bloody logs only!

There is a degree of originality and power about these productions which is not often met with. No author can be pointed out as the obvious model on which they were framed. The writer's style, as regards both thought and expression, is peculiarly a style of his own. If, for instance, we compare the various descriptive poets in the language, we shall not find one whose mode of treatment bears much resemblance to Mr. Kendall's. This may arise from the difference between English and Australian scenery; but if we take in the American poets also, we shall yet fail to find one who has painted scenery in similar colours. It is this originality of style which no doubt gives rise to the charge of obscurity so often brought against Mr. Kendall's poems. He uses language of his own. To some extent, this amounts to mannerism: but, on the whole, he deserves commendation for his taste and judgment in selecting words. So far as thought is concerned, he does occasionally become obscure—that is he fails to bring out his meaning distinctly, and leaves upon the reader's mind only some vague impresssion of solemnity. This, however, does not occur so frequently as to justify the charge. As Coleridge says, "A poem is not necessarily obscure because it does not aim to be popular. It is enough if a work be perspicuous to those for whom it is written, and 'fit audience find, though few.'" There are not many readers of a cultivated class who can experience much difficulty in comprehending Mr. Kendall's writings, if they choose.

Judging from what he has already written, his genius lies wholly in a lyrical direction. He has manifested power in no other form of poetry: but in so young a writer, it is impossible to decide the limits of his power. The lyrics he has written are by far the finest that have yet been written in Australia. They are distinguished by perfect harmony of versification, as well as by force of conception; and altogether they form a nearer approach to what we conceive to be genius, as opposed to talent, than any other poetry we have yet produced. Should he live to realise the anticipations that have been formed of him, his name will reflect a lasting honour on his native country.

MISCELLANEOUS EXTRACTS.

ONE of the latest contributions from Mr. Deniehy's pen was the following critique of his friend Mr. HALLORAN's writings. It will therefore be read with a double interest :—

For upwards of twenty years the poems of Henry Halloran, scattered through newspapers and magazines, have been before the public. A scholar as well as a poet, as Mr. Halloran is, they are remarkable for classic grace. Not, reader, as that phrase is too generally misunderstood, since the "Augustan Age" of English literature—colourless studies from Greek and Roman originals. They are inspirations, almost always overflowing with tenderness, often of very great beauty, but always confined within strict boundaries, such as the ancient poets accepted. Everywhere exhibiting what modern writers, with the single exception of Matthew Arnold, seem bent on ignoring—a sense of *poetic form*. A poem published many years ago,—" The Descent of Orpheus,"—is for classic "feeling," (as sculptors and painters phrase it, and we know no better word for the thing indicated) remarkable even in this age, when poets grow every where, plentifully as "geebungs" and "five-corners" were wont in the woods of our boyhood.

Mr. Halloran's domestic verses, as we believe it is the fashion to style a certain class of poetry since the "Delta" of "Blackwood" so named a collection of his poems, have always been favourites of ours. For manly gentleness, for tenderness, for grace, for an imagery with classic delicacy of its own, like the bas-reliefs on an antique vase, they will always endear themselves to lovers of the muse in her gentler moods. Some of his translations from the Greek of Anacreon are perfectly charming ; and we only wish we had at hand some copies of defunct colonial periodicals to present our readers with specimens.

How graceful, how thoroughly Greek in feeling, is the following, published many years ago. The "*stem of* roses" would have pleased Anacreon himself ; not, mind you, a rose solely, but a luxurious spray overbending with its wealth of rich blooms, mayhap wet with the dews of the reddening dawn. The verses might have come from the "Anthology."

> I wish thou wert a stem of roses,
> And I a golden bee to sip
> The honey-dew that now reposes
> In balmy kisses on thy lip.

> I wish thine eyes were violets blue,
>   And I a wand'ring western breeze,
> To press them with my wings of dew,
>   And melt them into ecstacies!
>
> I wish thou wert a golden curl,
>   And I the myrtle-wreath that bound it;
> I wish thou wert a peerless pearl,
>   And I the casket to surround it.
>
> I wish thou wert a lucid star,
>   And I the atmosphere about thee;
> But if we must be as we are,
>   Dearest, I cannot live without thee.

Some of his love-verses have the tenderness of the elder ballads; and lines from them often float upon our memory:

> Had not false Fortune barred the way,
> Had we but met in happier day!
> Perhaps these hearts had then been gay,
>   My Early Love.
>
> * * * * *
>
> Thy damask rose is changed for white,
> Thine eyes are filled with *mournful light*
> And I have known the Spirit's blight,
>   My Early Love.

But it is Mr. Halloran's verses connected with home affections that in our opinion give him the truest title to the rank of poet. Before giving the reader a specimen of these, (and to use Sir Philip Sydney's image, he must not think a bunch of grapes fully sets out the character of the whole vineyard,) we must notice Mr. Halloran's lines on the death of George James M'Donald, as one of the most beautiful elegies produced anywhere for many years. Mr. M'Donald, formerly a Commissioner of Crown Lands, a man of eccentric habits, was not only a remarkable scholar and a musician of exquisite endowment, but a poet, as evinced by his "Lake of Swans," and his verses "To a Lady on Playing a Movement of Beethoven's." The following are stanzas on "The Death of a Child:"

> Little Eddy! little Eddy! through the watches of the night
> Does my tortured heart turn to thee in its anguish and affright,—
> And I see thee starkly lying with the foam upon thy lips,—
> And thy beauty fading, fading, in Death's terrible eclipse.

Little Eddy ! little Eddy ! yet upon thy brow there lies
Such a look of quiet transport as is worn beyond the skiés :
Dids't thou in that fatal moment look the veil's dim mystery through—
Winning to that angel forehead something of the blissful view ?

Something that to aching bosoms should this consolation give,
Where the Shepherd leads his loved ones, does our little lamb still live.
In the sweet green pastures resting, where the living waters flow,
Does he live whom we so wildly, vainly, weep for here below ?

But that little chair is empty—doth the cot the sleeper lack ?
On the wall a cap hangs idly—will the wearer not come back ?
Will the jocund voice that greeted fondly every eve and morn
Never speak again to make our lonely bosoms less forlorn ?

When the spring-birds wake the morning with their sweet and tender cries,
Shall we hear that voice of music echoing from beyond the skies ?
When the buds and flowers sweeten all our sadden'd home around,
Sweeter thoughts of him shall gather,—him, our darling lost and found.

O'er the rugged hill-side toiling, to the valley faint and dim,
Will our wearied steps still bear us, drawing nearer still to him,—
Near to him, our ravished treasure, whom we vainly thought to hold,
Hoping, fearing—fearing, hoping, e'en as misers with their gold.

Mr. Halloran does not often write humourously. In the following verses, which furnish a fair specimen of his style of thought, he gives his ideas on the subject of the Poet's mission. The Three Poets are Harpur, Kendall, and the writer ;—referred to as *Pipe No.* 1, *Pipe No.* 2, and the *Queen's Cigar:* the title of the piece being *The Bards' Colloquy.*

>Three Poets meeting in the public way,
>   Not men of much repute for wit or learning,
>But somewhat cleaner than the common clay,
>   And each his bread by honest labour earning,
>Walked on together, as plain people may,
>   Until they came unto a sudden turning,
>Which led them out from the wild city's shocks
>Into the coolness of the trees and rocks.

Over the pleasant grass they slowly went,
   And to the margin of a gleaming bay,
Where the slant sunshine of the Occident
   Its crimson glories in a wild display
Thro' every loophole in profusion sent ;
   While the sweet influence of declining day,
In mystic softness o'er their spirits stole,
Awakening the great power within,—the Soul.

Two of the men old Time already numbered
   With those who stand among the "sere and yellow"—
Altho' they were not by their years encumbered—
   But active, prompt, and not much more than mellow ;
The third was younger far, and might have slumbered
   Some years, at least, and still been a "young fellow."
They threw them down upon a grassy bar,
Two lit their pipes, the third a "*Queen's Cigar.*"

Awhile they talked of things of small concern,
   Of one man's blunders—of another's spleen,
And what strange things come up at every turn,
   And how bold knaves can often find a screen,
What pitiful betrayers secrets learn,
   And then disclose them with some purpose mean ;
They talked too of the lecturers and critics,
Of punsters, parodists, and analytics.

"Well," said the *Queen's Cigar*, who was the oldest,
   "These coxcombs prate of what they little know,
Awarding praise with impudence the boldest
   To vulgar thought and language bald and low ;
As if that Art, which might inflame the coldest,
   Or win the saddest bosom from its woe,
Were to be measured like a silk or muslin
By every criticising puppy's puzzling."

Pipe No. 1, blowing a fragrant cloud,
   Which curled among the fragrant leaves awhile,
Yawn'd a long yawn, and said, "I mark the crowd
   Of little gentlemen whose pride, or bile,
Induces them to prate it—rather loud—
   Almost enough to make a blind horse smile.
Like cats they *mar* the sweetness of the wind,
Offend the sense, but do not reach the mind."

Pipe No. 2,—A bard with thinner skin,
　　As being younger, did not quite agree—
" I think," said he, " 'tis little less than sin
　　To scoff at what should never scoffed at be ;—
Divinest Art we follow, and to win
　　The crown of poesy were joy to me ;
And if the thing I seek be worth the task
Why should they scoff at such pursuit, I ask ?"

"But have we," said the *Queen's,* "before us set
　　Fairly and truly what the high pursuit
Should be,—'as on a mount of diamond set ?'
　　Or are we following still with weary foot
A shadow, wandering only to regret
　　That we at last can pluck but bitter fruit ?
What is it, my friends, that you and I pursue ?
I say, the Unseen—the Beautiful—the True.

" On me, if I may speak, the thought is driven,
　　In the deep night when those I love repose,—
That this high art of ours to us is given,—
　　Whether our life be one of joys or woes—
That the material darkness may be riven
　　Which still around us seems to grow and close ;
That we should pierce the Veil with glad surprise,
And read God's glories with enraptured eyes.

" All is not as it seems, full well we know,—
　　And what we know is narrowed to a mite,—
The star that to our eyes a point may shew,
　　Approached—becomes a glorious world of light,—
With flaming mountains, torrents in wild flow,
　　And splendours nameless, and yet infinite ;
What if our eyes, God's infinite splendour reach,
And we to men the revelation preach,

" How may we lead them, toiling as they do,
　　Into an atmosphere of wondering bliss,
We, seers of the unseen ; preachers too
　　Of the beheld ; travellers through the abyss
Of infinite creation, Heaven to view,
　　If we through baseness should the way not miss,—
May it *not* be, my friends ! and, if it be,
How great the mission, both of you and me ?

"How dread, if we by lust of fame beguiled,
 Turn from the path, infatuate or vain,—
Or swoll'n with pride—or by low vice defiled,
 Think only of ourselves,—and selfish gain ;
I'd rather walk through life, even as a child
 Wandering beside the ' much-resounding main,'
Seeking from wreathed shell for sounds from God,
Than 'midst Golconda's jewels darkly plod.

" It cannot be, nor will I e'er believe,
 That, what so stirs me in my better mind,
Is given me to bewilder and deceive ;
 And leave me drifting down the desolate wind,
Down to the shadows which Despair can weave
 For those who still are obstinately blind :—
I see *now* darkly,—but I pray for light,
Under the Sun, as in the darkest night.

" And Light *will* come, if not to me, alas !
 To others, when the grass for centuries
Has grown and withered on my grave ; and as
 The brighter Heaven shall shine on other eyes
The great Millennium will upon them pass,
 And they the Mystery of Mysteries
Will gaze upon, which now I *strive* to reach,
And would prefigure in my verse and speech.

" Torrents of light from yonder setting sun,
 For ever fall throughout infinitude—
Ceaseless, unbounded ;—from the Eternal One
 Another light in greater plenitude
Floods all the spiritual world, but vapours dun,
 Material darkness, blind ingratitude
Amerce us of that light—oh, brothers true !
May we, the seers, pierce the darkness through !

" The flow, and light, and splendour of all verse,
 Tho' instinct with the music of the spheres,
Is discord dire, or even it is worse,
 Without the *purpose* that itself inspheres
Within that luminous breathing—and a curse
 It may be to the sensual ear that hears ;—
What were the Universe if God was not ?
Such were the Art divine its aim forgot.

"I know the pleasaunce of the faëry lay ;—
I know how Love its radiant eyes will turn
And, gazing on the *Past* and *Future*, say
    All that the *Present* feels, in words that burn ;
I know the verse in which rapt Hope can pray,
    And how mute sorrow silently will yearn :
Nor I the jocund Earth's bright scenes despise,
But these are not our one great aim and prize.

" Friends ! I believe ye have the power, to aid
    In this high work,—to open to the view
Of those who sojourn with us in the shade,
    The glimpses of the great Unseen ; the True
Hid in the shifting False ;—not as a trade,
    Not with the vulgar hope that we should strew
Fame on our graves, or magnify our dust,
But to fulfil our Heaven-committed trust."

Pipe No. 1, arousing with a start,
    Said, "Transcendentalism to the core !
This, as I think, my friend ! is *not* our part :
    Did Homer write for this? Did Milton soar?
Did Shakspere bare for this the human heart,
    And all his wisdom, all his sweetness pour?
They painted Man and Nature as they are,—
Your aim and purpose stretch, I think, too far.

" Life as it is, and its sweet charities,—
    The beauty and the splendour of this earth,—
Shapen in wisdom by the Great All-Wise ;
    The pastoral life—its innocent joy and mirth—
The storm of battle blotting the pure skies—
    The suffering virtue—or the crowned worth :—
The voice of Freedom,—all that lives and breathes
Are for the glorious verse the poet wreathes.

"The slanting woods, on which the setting sun
    Pours down his splendours for a slope of miles
Into the hushed vale, where the rivulets run
    Like tender tears amidst Joy's sober smiles,
The mighty Ocean, the Eternal One
    Flashing and thundering amidst countless isles:
These are the themes the poet should employ—
These are *my* glory,—these my utmost joy."

Pipe No. 2, upstarting to his feet,
  Lifted his pale hands towards the rising moon,
Which shewed the glory of her orb complete,
  And said, "My friends, I'm rather out of tune,
But thank you for your converse, wild and sweet.
  I grieve that we must part this eve so soon,
But as we homeward go I will disclose
What is to *me* as perfume to the rose.

"*Fame* is the sweetness of the poet's thought,
  Whate'er my theme, my hope—my life is fame;
The hope of fame within my heart is wrought,
  And clings around it like that garb of flame
That Hercules once wore,—could it be bought
  By death, it should be mine. The poet's name
In after time be mine! I've prayed for it,
With sinful heart, o'er all that I have writ!

"In mossy caverns, by untrodden ways,
  Have I conceived it my Egeria,—
The unseen Goddess of my happiest days!
  A Voice *has* whispered,—can that voice e'er err?
But the vile scorn of men now almost slays
  That hope within me, and I fear to stir
Lest the base ribald, in his spleen, should mar
The beauty of my thought—the lustre of my star.

"I care not for the theme—the single aim,
  Stirring this weak heart, is that mine should be,
Among my countrymen, a household name,
  When I am buried in some sunny lea,
Where the bright flowers start up, like jets of flame;
  And maidens as they con my page should see
The eyes that beamed with the fond hope that they
Should name my name, when I have passed away."

And the young poet clasped his hands on high,
  Breathing perchance a prayer. The soberer two
Gazed on in pity, and forbore reply:
  That that wild hope would pass full well they knew,
And he with higher purpose learn to sigh;
  They bade each other "friends—a kind adieu"
Then to their several homes they straightway sped,
And as they went, their separate fancies fed.

Mr. Halloran was born in Cape Town in 1811, and after spending ten years in England, came out to this colony, where he has since resided. He is now Under-Secretary in the Colonial Secretary's office.

Sir Thomas L. Mitchell's Journals abound with passages of interest. The following extract refers to the melancholy fate of Mr. Richard Cunningham, a botanist attached to his Expedition. He had wandered from the main party, and lost his way in the bush. The search for him is thus narrated:

April 25.—Early this morning I despatched Mr. Larmer and the Doctor (who was one of the two who had found the track) with Muirhead and Whiting, and taking four days' provisions and water, this party was directed to look well round the scrub, and on discovering the track to follow it wherever it led, until they found Mr. Cunningham or his remains; for in such a country I began to despair of finding him alive, after such long absence. This party did not return until the evening of the 28th, when all they brought of Mr. Cunningham was his saddle and bridle, whip, one glove, two straps, and a piece of paper folded like a letter, inside of which were cut (as with a pen-knife) the letters N. E. Mr. Larmer reported that, having easily found the track of the horse again beyond the scrub, they had followed it until they came to where the horse lay dead, having still the saddle on and the bridle in its mouth; the whip and straps had been previously found, and from these circumstances, the tortuous track of the horse, and the absence of Mr. Cunningham's own footsteps for some way back from where the horse was found, it was considered that he had either left the horse in despair, or that it had got away from him. At all events, it had evidently died for want of water: but the fate of its unfortunate rider was still a mystery.

It appeared from Mr. Larmer's map of Mr. Cunningham's track that he had deviated from our line after crossing Bullock Creek, and had proceeded about fourteen miles to the north-west, where marks of his having tied up his horse and lain down, induced the party to believe that he had there passed the first dreary night of his wandering.

From that point he appeared to have intended to return, and by the zig-zag course he took he had either been travelling in the dark, or looking for his own track that he might retrace it. In this manner his steps actually approached within a mile of our route, in such a manner that he appeared to have been going south while we had been travelling north (on the 18th). Thus he had continued to travel southward, or south-south-west, full 14 miles, crossing his own track not far from where he first left our route. On his left he had the dry channel (Bullock Creek), with the water-gum trees,* full in view, without ever looking into it for water; had he observed this, and followed it downwards, he must have found the route; and had he traced it upwards, he must have come upon the water-holes, where I had an interview with the two natives, and thus, perhaps, have fallen in with me. From the marks of his horse having been tied to four different trees at the extreme southern point which he reached, it appeared that he had halted there some time, or there passed the second night:—that point was not much more than half a mile from my track out on the 21st, being to the westward of it. From this point he had returned, keeping still more to the westward, so that he actually fell in with my track of the 19th, and appeared to have followed it backwards for upwards of a mile, when he struck off at a right angle to the north-west.

It was impossible to account for this fatal deviation, even had night, as most of the party supposed, overtaken him there. It seemed that he had found my paper directing him to trace my steps backwards, and that he had been doing this where the paper marked "N. E." had been found, and which I therefore considered a sort of reply to my paper. If we were right as to the nights, this must have taken place on the very day on which I had passed that way, my eye eagerly catching at every dark-coloured distant object in hopes of finding him! After the deviation to the north-west, it appears that Mr. Cunningham had made some detours about a clear plain, at one side of which his horse had been tied for a considerable time, and where it is probable he had passed his third night, as there were marks where he had lain down in the long dry grass. From this point only his horse's tracks had been traced, not his own steps, which had hitherto accompanied them; and from the twisting and twining of the horse's tracks to where it lay dead, we supposed he had not been with the horse after it left this place. The whip and straps seemed to have been trod off by the horse, from the bridle-reins to which Mr. Cunningham was in the habit of tying his whip, and to which also the straps had probably been attached, to afford the animal more room to feed when fastened to trees.

To the place, therefore, where Mr. Cunningham's own steps had last been seen, I hastened on the morning of the 29th April with the same men, Muirhead and Whiting, who had so ably and humanely traced all the tracks of the horse through a distance of 70 miles.

The spot seemed well chosen as a halting-place, being at a few trees which advanced beyond the rest of the wood into a rather extensive plain; a horse,

---

* These trees being remarkable for their white shining trunks, resembling those of beech trees.

tied there, could have been seen from almost any part around, and it is not improbable that Mr. Cunningham left him there tied, and that he had afterwards got loose, and had finally perished for want of water.

We soon found the print of Mr. Cunningham's footsteps in two places; in one, coming towards the trees where the horse had been tied from a thick scrub east of them; in the other, leading from these trees in a straight direction northward. Pursuing these steps leading northward, we found them continuous in that direction, and, indeed, remarkably long and firm, the direction being preserved even through thick brushes.

This was making direct for the Bogan; and it was evident that, urged by intense thirst, he had at length set off with desperate speed for the river, having parted from his horse where the party had supposed. That he had killed and eaten the dog in the scrub, from whence his steps had been seen to emerge, was probable, as no trace of the animal could be seen beside his own footsteps from thence, and as it was difficult, otherwise, to account for his vigorous step, after an abstinence of three days and three nights. I regretted that I had not at the time examined the scrub, but when we were at his last camp (the trees on the plain) we were most interested in Mr. Cunningham's further course.

This we traced more than two miles, during which he had never stopped even to look behind towards the spot where, had he left his horse, he might still have seen him. Having at length lost the track on some very hard ground, we exhausted the day in a vain search for it. On returning to the camp, I found that Mr. Larmer, whom I had sent with two armed men down the Bogan, had nearly been surrounded, at only three miles distance from our camp, by a tribe of natives carrying spears. Amongst these were two who had been with us on the previous day, and who called to the others to keep back. These men told Mr. Larmer that they had seen Mr. Cunningham's track in several parts of the bed of the Bogan; that he had not been killed, but had gone to the westward (pointing down the Bogan) with the "Myall (*i. e.* wild) wild blackfellows." Thus we had reason to hope that Mr. Cunningham had at least escaped the fate of his unfortunate horse by reaching the Bogan. This was what we wished; but no one could have supposed that he would have followed it downwards into the jaws of the wild natives rather than upwards. His movements show that he believed that he had deviated to the eastward of our route rather than to the westward; and this accounts for his having gone down the Bogan.

Had he not pursued that fatal course, or had he killed the horse rather than the dog, and remained stationary, his life had been saved. The result of our twelve days' delay and search was only the discovery that had we pursued our journey down the Bogan, Mr. Cunningham would have fallen in with our track and rejoined us; and that, while we halted for him, he had gone ahead of us, and out of reach.

It was afterwards discovered that Cunningham had fallen in

z

with some blacks, who treated him kindly. His sufferings however were so great that he lost his reason, and the blacks not understanding his misfortune, became frightened and killed him.

Mr. Michael has written a vast quantity of verse. The following passage from *John Cumberland*, in which he describes the growth of a poetical mind, will give the reader a fair specimen of his style :

" Write me a song," said Ada : "here we sit,
  Featherless bipeds of all sorts and kinds,
Poets, philosophers, and men of wit,
  Schoolmen who have, and fops who should have, minds :
(No offence, any one) I'm mistress here ;
  I'll have my fancy for this time : I long
To play the critic. Won't I be severe ?—
  Which of you now can write me the best song ?"
The whimsey must be humour'd. Forth they brought
  Pens, ink, and paper. Down we sat to spin,
Each one in rhyme, his little thread of thought ;
  And some one ask'd " What is the prize to win ?"
A dozen answer'd him. " A kiss," said they ;—
  " All the world over, she who hires must pay."
" A kiss," thought I—" a dainty prize for spinning.
I'll try my chance ; at least 'tis worth the winning."
Miss Ada laugh'd—" Well, if I like the man"—
  She got no farther ; such a chorus rose
Of laughter and clapp'd hands ; and we began.
  Lady Cassandra hemm'd and blew her nose,
Preparing a remonstrance ; but we shouted
And talk'd her down, and I think Ada pouted,
  Not choosing to be cheated of her whim,
Nor much afraid of kisses. As for me,
A nervous tremor shook in every limb ;
  I fear'd the ordeal : round me I could see
Men with great names : what could I hope to do ?
Yet something I must write, and quickly too :
I crush'd the tremors rising in my breast,
And sat to write my ballad with the rest.

They brought a great old bowl of Indian China,
   Dreadfully ugly ; worth a mighty sum ;
One of those things than which there's " nothing finer,"
   The critics say,—past, present, or to come ;
Cover'd with nightmare-figures queer and squat ;
One of the ugliest things that could be got.
This was to hold our verses so that none
Might know the authors till the prize was won.
The wither'd rose-leaves that it held gave out
   A subtle fragrance, over all the room :
Like some delicious essence, flung about
   To stir the spirit with its still perfume :
So, as I felt the gentle odour float,
My soul took in its sweetness, and I wrote.

     I drop my song into the roses ;
       I write it, dear, that thou may'st see :
     Their sweetness o'er my spirit closes—
       They have no sweetness like to thee.

     These, when their beauty fades and dies,
       Still fling their fragrance on the wind :
     I claim, when death shall close mine eyes,
       The immortality of mind.

     I see thee in the dead of night,
       When sleep lies heavy on my brow,
     And dreams come robed in rosy light ;—
       Thou comest to me, sweet one, thou ;

     Not then as now, when hardly daring
       To lift my glances to thy face ;
     But, in thy tender beauty, sharing
       The passion of my warm embrace.

     I start and wake ; the vivid spark
       Not yet extinguish'd in my breast ;
     I stretch my arms into the dark—
       Why wilt thou come to break my rest ?

     Oh ! let my dreams prophetic be !
       Let day the midnight's kindness keep !
     Let me for once in daylight see
       The smile thou wearest to my sleep !

     Love to the loving ! life and light
       Wile the long hours of night away.
     Oh ! let my day-dreams be as bright
       As those that change my night to day !

This precious ditty, none too good, I'm sure,
  Lady Cassandra chose to call "divine;"
(Most of the rest, 'tis true, were very poor)—
  But how they stared when I declar'd it mine!
  They never fancied I could write a line,
I was so silent, bashful, and demure.
However, good or bad, 'twas voted best,
(No compliment, I fancy, to the rest.)
So, blushing scarlet to the very eyes,
Shyly and awkwardly I took my prize.
Miss Ada gave it as a thing of course,
  Unruffled. Not so I. I felt my blood
Rush through its channels with redoubled force,
  And my heart beat and labour'd with its flood:
The lights grew misty in a strange eclipse:
  'Twas the first kiss I breath'd on woman's lips,
So I stood lost and panting: and I heard
  Nothing except the beating of my heart,
That shook and flutter'd like a wounded bird;
  Till I threw off my passion with a start
And wrapped my pride about me, and sat down,
Like a young king that newly wears his crown.
There came a change upon me from that hour:
Ada look'd on as one who knew her power;
But now we had changed attitudes: for I
Sat, with the flush of passion in my eye
Dilating, glorious; she beheld me burn,
And blush'd up to the temples in her turn,
And shunn'd my gaze, half timid, and there fell
Something between us: what, I could not tell!
Attraction and repulsion: never more
Our eyes could meet, as they had met before,
Indifferent: we knew that something came
  Over us both,—that we should never be
Free from a presence that we could not name,
  Free from a presence that we could not see,
Not the less real;—how the evening past
  I know not. Quickly flew the hours away:
I linger'd, warm and happy, till the last;
  Flung by my silence; chatter'd, and was gay;
And when at last the time came to depart,
I said "good bye" with triumph in my heart
That rose into my face; and Ada's cheek
Flush'd again crimson—but she did not speak.

The most humourous writer here is Mr. G. R. MORTON, a grandson of the author of "Speed the Plough," "Cure for the Heart-ache," and other popular plays. His uncle has written some of the most successful farces of the present day. " Box and Cox" and " Slasher and Crasher" are among his productions. Mr. Morton's father is also a well-known writer. It is not easy to select from Mr. Morton's contributions to the press any piece that does justice to his ability. His best jokes are scattered about in short paragraphs. The following burlesque sensational novel, entitled *Maurora*, was contributed to *Punch*:

CHAPTER I.

It was on one fine morning in the month of December 1868, towards the end of the reign of King Elizabeth, that a young child might have been seen, by anybody looking that way, crossing the fertile slopes of the Bay of Biscay, which separate the smiling landscapes of Salisbury Plain from the barren moors of Kent. Apparently but two years old, there was yet an air of fixed determination in one of her verdant eyes, which contrasted strangely with the mild and gentle aspect of the other. The wind blew, the frost frew, and the snow snew, but this seemed only to add fresh fire to the little wanderer, who drew her *cul de sac* closer around her, and continued on her way, whistling "Pop goes the weasel," in the bright moonlight. On the top of her head was her *chevelure*, on the top of her *chevelure* was her *portefeuille*, and, waving proudly above both was an old gingham umbrella, which had been in the house since the Deluge, and with which she vainly attempted to ward off the summer's heat and winter's snow which were simultaneously pouring on her with the utmost confusion. Her beautiful hair, rivalling in colour the most brilliant carrot, fell in straight festoons over her delicate shoulders, while her *nez retroussé* and curly teeth would have afforded a sublime study to the most enthusiastic artist of a comic periodical.

The clock struck seventeen. The child threw an indignant glance which knocked an old horse off a tree where he was feeding his feathered progeny in a mare's nest, and the next moment the beast lay writhing on the ground in the last agonies of *cacoëthes scribendi*. To spurn him with her little tiny foot, raise him in her arms, and hurl him into the middle of the following week was the work of a moment, and then resuming her overland route, her finely chiselled features relapsed into a pleasant and gorilla-like smile with the sweet consciousness of having done a good action.

The clock struck seventeen and a half. She started and instinctively shuddered.

Footsteps were heard approaching on horseback.

Ah!
Will
He
Ever
Go
Home?

A voice was heard singing the national air of "We won't go home till morning!"

'Twas that of her first husband! He was trying to light his cigar at the pump.

He must have been eating salmon, which is known to be an intoxicating fish.

How to avoid him? Ah! there was but one way. She put her head in a bag to conceal herself, and pulled a blunderbuss from her bosom.

The voice approached nearer and nearer.

He was not alone!

Then there must be somebody with him!

What must be done?

They must. Both of them. The reflection made her sneeze.

They had seen the sneeze, and she would be discovered——Never!

Another moment would be their next.

She slowly raised the blunderbuss—when—oh horror!

(To be continued when the author can make out the plot of the novel.)

CHAPTER I. (CONTINUED).

—she found she had no gunpowder in her deadly tube.

'Tis ever thus! Life is a great mistake!

We draw a veil over what followed; but—she had the papers! Oh, how she gloated over them!

This was a redeeming trait in her character; she believed in the papers, objected to the penny tax upon them, and read them every morning on credit.

How few, and yet how many are like her!

But this woman, bold and reckless as she was, subscribed to *Punch*—

Yes, 'twas so—

And the *Herald*—

Ah! that was wrong. But who is perfect?

As we said before, she subscribed to *Punch*, and no yellow envelope stained her connection with that downright upright journal.

But why pursue this theme?

Aye, why?

Echo answers—Don't!

And we won't!

But what was to be done with the corpse?

Yet why should she trouble herself about it?

He had brought it on himself.
And yet she had not the heart to leave it there.
Besides, the police—And yet he was her husband.
She would burn the body:
She was a woman still; but how?
Aye, that's the rub.
The *rub?* Yes, that's the idea!
She remembered being told, at the last Court Ball, that two pieces of wood, if rubbed together for a considerable time, would instantaneously ignite.
She rubbed, and in one hour three minutes and half a second arrived at a spark.
She applied it to the inflammable tip of the corpse's nose.
A blare, a glare, a flare, and there—all was over. She was safe. She dropped a tear of gratitude, but, fearing it might betray her, picked it up again, and put it into her *chevaux de frize*.
She left the spot, feeling sure no human eye had seen her.
Oh, hadn't they, though, rather!
Upwards on the giddy cliff, seven hundred feet above her head, peering through the murky moonlight, was the clear, grey eye of the body-snatcher.
He knew all about it. Ha! ha! ha!
" Walk blindfold on, behind thee stalks the hangman!"
All was still except the shrill whistle of the buffalo, and the lowing of the distant owls in the ruined moat.
But the dead man lay there,
> Like a warrior taking his rest,
> To point a moral, and adorn a tail.
> With a bow-wow, &c.

Seventy-seven years have elapsed—Napoleon has triumphed at Agincourt—Freedom shrieked when Kosciusko fell—the Menangle Bridge and the Stamp Act have both been discovered by Captain Cook—and Ireland is discontented, but still we find no change in our heroine.
No, not even coppers. But why?
Because she has never slept.
And why has she never slept?
Because
She
Was
Too
Wide awake!
Wherefore too wide awake?
Because *he* was there—the red man in the black hat.
Was it for this she murdered her father, poisoned her mother, drowned her sister, strangled her brother, garotted three of her grandmothers, stabbed her first husband, shot her second, and told the milkman to call again?

Oh, Conscience! Conscience! What was she to do?

She remembered who was her hatter: his loss wouldn't be felt.

Sir Marmaduke de Pompadour might still be hers.

But, in despair at her rejection of his suit (purchased on credit at the huge monster Cohen's) he had become reckless, and resolved to have his hair brushed by machinery.

She must prevent that.

But how?

"Aye, that's the rub!" (for the second time.)

"Shakspere," she murmured, ".and Lucifer—how art thou fallen! one half-penny a box."

She seized a box of Congreves. Was she about to burn her fingers?

Perhaps.

They were damp—the Congreves, not the fingers.

A haughty smile played on her turnip-coloured turn-up nose. Congreves—pah! Brimstone—faugh! yah! gah! agh!

She waxed wroth, and pulled out a vesta from her *locum tenens*.

She thought of the time when she burnt *him* with the same humble "flaming minister."

She breathed a sigh in memory of the happy days of youth, and then, with a sneer of defiance, as she sat *in* her velvet *vade mecum*, she ignited the luciferous medium on her *priedieu*, and whispered through her teeth, in a loud voice, husky with emotion and eau-de-cologne—

"Go to Blazes!"

And so the ingenuous Sir Marmaduke did.

☞ The translation of this tale is reserved by the author.

Mr. Morton was born in India in 1829, and came to this colony in 1855.